DIGITAL HEALTH

The rise of digital health technologies is, for some, a panacea to many of the medical and public health challenges we face today. This is the first book to articulate a critical response to the techno-utopian and entrepreneurial vision of the digital health phenomenon. Deborah Lupton, internationally renowned for her scholarship on the sociocultural and political aspects of medicine and health as well as digital technologies, addresses a range of compelling issues about the interests digital health represents, and its unintended effects on patients, doctors and how we conceive of public health and healthcare delivery.

Bringing together social and cultural theory with empirical research, the book challenges apolitical approaches to examine the impact new technologies have on social justice, and the implication for social and economic inequalities. Lupton considers how self-tracking devices change the patient–doctor relationship, and how the digitisation and gamification of healthcare through apps and other software affect the way we perceive and respond to our bodies. She asks which commercial interests enable different groups to communicate more widely, and how the personal data generated from digital encounters are exploited. Considering the lived experience of digital health technologies, including their emotional and sensory dimensions, the book also assesses their broader impact on medical and public health knowledges, power relations and work practices.

Relevant to students and researchers interested in medicine and public health across sociology, psychology, anthropology, new media and cultural studies, as well as policy makers and professionals in the field, this is a timely contribution on an important issue.

Deborah Lupton is Centenary Research Professor in the News and Media Research Centre, Faculty of Arts and Design, University of Canberra, Australia. Author of 15 previous books, she is an internationally renowned scholar whose research spans sociology, media, communication and cultural studies.

Critical Approaches to Health

Series editors: Kerry Chamberlain and Antonia Lyons

The Routledge *Critical Approaches to Health* series aims to present critical, interdisciplinary books around psychological, social and cultural issues related to health. Each volume in the series provides a critical approach to a particular issue or important topic, and is of interest and relevance to students and practitioners across the social sciences. The series is produced in association with the International Society of Critical Health Psychology (ISCHP).

Titles in the series:

Constructing Pain
Historical, Psychological and Critical Perspectives
Robert Kugelmann

Digital Health
Critical and Cross-Disciplinary Perspectives
Deborah Lupton

A Critical Approach to Surrogacy
Reproductive Desires and Demands
Damien W. Riggs and Clemence Due

DIGITAL HEALTH

Critical and Cross-Disciplinary Perspectives

Deborah Lupton

Routledge
Taylor & Francis Group

LONDON AND NEW YORK

First published 2018
by Routledge
2 Park Square, Milton Park, Abingdon, Oxon OX14 4RN

and by Routledge
711 Third Avenue, New York, NY 10017

Routledge is an imprint of the Taylor & Francis Group, an informa business

© 2018 Deborah Lupton

British Library Cataloguing-in-Publication Data
A catalogue record for this book is available from the British Library

Library of Congress Cataloging-in-Publication Data
Names: Lupton, Deborah, author.
Title: Digital health : critical and cross-disciplinary perspectives / Deborah Lupton.
Description: Milton Park, Abingdon, Oxon ; New York, NY: Routledge, 2018. |
Includes bibliographical references and index.
Identifiers: LCCN 2017010635| ISBN 9781138123441 (hb : alk. paper) |
ISBN 9781138123458 (pb : alk. paper) | ISBN 9781315648835 (ebook)
Subjects: | MESH: Health Information Management—methods | Medical Informatics |
Biomedical Technology | Telemedicine | Socioeconomic Factors
Classification: LCC R119.95 | NLM W 26.5 | DDC 610.285—dc23
LC record available at https://lccn.loc.gov/2017010635

ISBN: 978-1-138-12344-1 (hbk)
ISBN: 978-1-138-12345-8 (pbk)
ISBN: 978-1-315-64883-5 (ebk)

Typeset in Bembo
by Out of House Publishing

CONTENTS

Acknowledgements   *vi*
Series editors' preface   *vii*

Introduction   1

1 Theoretical concepts   8

2 The digitised healthy citizen   27

3 Digitised embodiment   44

4 Big digital health data   60

5 The social structuring of digital health use   80

6 The lived experience of digital health   94

7 Digitised medical and health work   108

Concluding comments   127

References   *134*
Index   *166*

ACKNOWLEDGEMENTS

Many thanks to the editors of the special series of which this book is a part, Kerry Chamberlain and Antonia Lyons, for inviting me to contribute to the series and providing feedback on the penultimate draft.

This book includes some sections from a number of previously published journal articles, all of which have been updated, revised and reassembled to form part of the book's content. Details of these articles are as follows:

Lupton, D. (2012) M-health and health promotion: the digital cyborg and surveillance society. *Social Theory & Health*, 10 (3), 229–244.

Lupton, D. (2013) The digitally engaged patient: self-monitoring and self-care in the digital health era. *Social Theory & Health*, 11 (3), 256–270.

Lupton, D. (2013) Quantifying the body: monitoring and measuring health in the age of mHealth technologies. *Critical Public Health*, 23 (4), 393–403.

Lupton, D. (2014) Critical perspectives on digital health technologies. *Sociology Compass*, 8 (12), 1344–1359.

Lupton, D. (2014) The commodification of patient opinion: the digital patient experience economy in the age of big data. *Sociology of Health & Illness*, 36 (6), 856–869.

Lupton, D. (2015) Fabricated data bodies: reflections on 3D printed digital body objects in medical and health domains. *Social Theory & Health*, 13 (2), 99–115.

Lupton, D. (2015) Health promotion in the digital era: a critical commentary. *Health Promotion International*, 30 (1), 174–183.

Lupton, D. (2016) Towards critical digital health studies: reflections on two decades of research in *Health* and the way forward. *Health:*, 20 (1), 49–61.

SERIES EDITORS' PREFACE
Critical Approaches to Health

Introduction

Health is a major issue for people all around the world, and is fundamental to individual wellbeing, personal achievements and satisfaction, as well as to families, communities and societies. It is also embedded in social notions of participation and citizenship. Much has been written about health, from a variety of perspectives and disciplines, but a lot of this writing takes a biomedical and causally positivist approach to heath matters, neglecting the historical, social and cultural contexts and environments within which health is experienced, understood and practised. It is an appropriate time to introduce a new series of books that offer critical, social science perspectives on important health topics.

The Critical Approaches to Health series aims to provide new critical writing on health by presenting critical, interdisciplinary and theoretical writing about health, where matters of health are framed quite broadly. The series will include books that range across important health matters, including general health-related issues (such as gender and media), major social issues for health (such as medicalisation, obesity and palliative care), particular health concerns (such as pain, doctor–patient interaction, health services and health technologies), particular health problems (such as diabetes, autoimmune disease and medically unexplained illness) or health for specific groups of people (such as the health of migrants, the homeless and the aged), or combinations of these.

The series seeks above all to promote critical thought about health matters. By critical, we mean going beyond the critique of the topic and work in the field, to more general considerations of power and benefit, and in particular, to addressing concerns about whose understandings and interests are upheld and whose are marginalised by the approaches, findings and practices in these various domains of health. Such critical agendas involve reflections on what constitutes knowledge, how it is created and how it is used. Accordingly, critical approaches consider episte-mological and theoretical positioning, as well as issues of methodology and practice, and seek to examine how health is enmeshed within broader social relations and structures. Books within this series take up this challenge and seek to provide new insights and understandings by applying a critical agenda to their topics.

In the current book, *Digital Health: Critical and Cross-Disciplinary Perspectives*, Deborah Lupton brings a timely and critical perspective to current scholarship on digital health technologies. The book ranges across important contemporary health-focused issues that are being shaped by digital technologies and digitisation, showing how these have implications for identities and citizenship, as well as for the everyday practices of individuals, communities and healthcare systems. Lupton demonstrates how the meanings and uses of digital health technologies depend upon taken-for-granted views about technology, the body, health, illness, medicine and behaviour. She also considers the technologies themselves, documenting how they are designed and produced by humans within particular sociopolitical and historical contexts, who bring their own understandings and meanings to health, bodies and healthcare practices. The affordances offered by these technologies shape what users can do, how they work and what is possible. In taking a critical per-spective, Lupton highlights the consequences of these new technologies and the 'big data' they provide (including unintended and unforeseen consequences) and considers how they can function to sustain existing structures of disadvantage and marginalisation. This enables us to see power in operation, including how the tech-nologies (and data) frequently serve the interests of some groups within society, while ignoring and even undermining the interests of others (particularly those who are vulnerable due to different forms of disadvantage). Lupton's overview of this exciting field is as timely as it is thought provoking, particularly in terms of the implications that digital health technologies have for the politics and practices of health and medicine as well as for individual identities and everyday practices.

We welcome this important and comprehensive coverage of a multidisciplinary field which is changing the face of health and healthcare.

Kerry Chamberlain and Antonia Lyons

INTRODUCTION

Many aspects of human health and medicine are now experienced and documented with the use of digital technologies. The term 'digital health' refers to a wide range of technologies directed at delivering healthcare, providing information to lay people and helping them share their experiences of health and illness, training and educating healthcare professionals, helping people with chronic illnesses to engage in self-care and encouraging others to engage in activities to promote their health and wellbeing and avoid illness. Frequent statements are now made in the mass media and the medical and public health literature about the beginning of a transformation in healthcare, preventive medicine and public health driven by the use of new digital health technologies.

Digital health technologies are often described in a laudatory fashion in these media. Such reports focus on what digital technologies can offer both lay people and professionals and how they might operate as 'solutions' to the problems of healthcare delivery, growing medical costs, improving people's health and wellbeing and preventing illness and disease. For the most part, contributors to the medical and public health literature on digital health are concerned with instrumental issues such as how to engage patients better with digital health technologies, how medical practitioners or health promoters can use them to provide healthcare or communicate health promotion messages to targeted publics, the accuracy or validity of the data created and disseminated on digital media such as websites, online discussion forums and apps and the economic or policy implications of digital health technologies.

One such example is a commentary penned in 2013 for the prestigious and influential *Journal of the American Medical Association* by a trio of US medical practitioners, entitled 'Can mobile health technologies transform health care?'. The authors answer in the affirmative, contending that these technologies offer much potential. They outline three converging 'powerful forces' they see as contributing to the development of mobile health: (1) 'the unsustainability of current health care spending and the recognition of the need for disruptive solutions'; (2) the rapid growth in wireless and mobile devices worldwide; and (3) 'the need for more precise and individualized medicine' (Steinhubl *et al.* 2013).

In this book, I offer a different perspective and set of research interests. The book is a contribution to the development of a field of study I entitle 'critical digital health studies', which sets out to research and theorise digital health technologies, their meanings and their impact on concepts of human embodiment, subjectivity, social relations and social institutions. It is important to acknowledge the many benefits and possibilities offered by digital health technologies. However, I contend that, rather than simply accepting the often-breathless claims made by technology developers or overenthusiastic champions of the 'disruption' to health and medicine that digital technologies offer, it is paramount to investigate and identify the social, cultural and political underpinnings of digital health. This is an approach that I have adopted in many previous publications on the sociocultural dimensions of medicine and public health (see, for example, my previous books: Lupton 1994, 1995a, 2012; Petersen and Lupton 1996; Tulloch and Lupton 1997). I have also published books on other aspects of embodiment (Lupton 1996, 1998, 2013a, 2013b), risk and everyday life (Lupton 2013c; Tulloch and Lupton 2003) and the sociocultural aspects of digital technologies (Lupton 2015a, 2016a). Critical digital health studies, as it is explored in the present book, brings all of these foci together in what I hope are important and interesting ways.

A body of scholarship on digital health is beginning to emerge from a number of disciplines and interdisciplinary fields, including sociology, anthropology, geography, psychology, media studies, cultural studies, internet studies and science and technology studies. Contributors to this literature provide important insights into the complexities of how lay people, as well as healthcare and public health professionals, engage with digital technologies and the implications for how they conceptualise bodies, selves, health, illness, medical care and health promotion. In this book, I draw upon some of this literature and highlight its implications for the newer forms of practices, identities and politics of health and medicine that are emerging alongside and in response to digital technologies.

The overarching perspective I adopt recognises that digital health technologies are sociocultural artefacts: that is, their meanings and uses are underpinned by tacit assumptions, norms, meanings and values. Digital technologies are the products of human decision making across a range of actors, carried out in specific social, cultural, political and historical contexts. Digital health technologies are invested with their makers' established ideas and beliefs about the human body, health, medicine and human behaviour (Lupton 2014, 2015b, 2015c). People who encounter these technologies may accept the meanings and intentions with which they are initially imbued. Alternatively, users may reject, resist or ignore them, or seek to transform or reimagine them. The range of choices offered to users, however, is delimited by the affordances of the technologies: or how the technologies work, what they can or cannot do.

A critical perspective on digital health involves challenging the often techno-utopian portrayals of the 'revolutionary' potential of new technologies. It seeks to identify digital technologies' unintended consequences and potential to entrench existing sociocultural disadvantage or social marginalisation. It involves addressing the power relations and differentials that are inherent in digital health and identifying how the interests of some social groups, organisations and agencies are served, while others are ignored or, in some cases, undermined. This includes consideration of the ramifications for social groups who are already socioeconomically disadvantaged or people who are living with disabilities or chronic illnesses.

A perspective informed by sociocultural theory is also able to uncover the elements that may be lost when healthcare and body care are digitised. This approach may include examining the implications for patients engaging in self-diagnosis using digital tools; of doctors using digital media to interact remotely with their patients; of people relying on quantified data derived from self-monitoring devices when they conceptualise and interpret their bodies' health and wellbeing status; or of medical students learning about human anatomy and training in surgical techniques using virtual reality images rather than real human flesh.

Many stakeholders now jostle for lay people's attention in the world of digital health, including healthcare providers, health insurance companies, pharmaceutical and medical technology companies, hospitals, patient support associations, government agencies and digital device and software developers. Many of these have developed partnerships with each other, so that the boundaries between government, employer and corporate enterprise, for example, have blurred. The digital technologies that are currently available for health and medical purposes include the following:

- Email, online audiovisual communication, apps and messaging services for contact between patients and healthcare providers, provider to provider or used by health promoters with target groups.
- Health and medical-related websites, online discussion forums, wikis, apps and social media sites providing information, support, advice and products to lay people and opportunities for professional-to-professional communication.
- Search engines used to find health and medical information online.
- Digitised devices for delivering pharmaceuticals or regulating/enhancing bodily functions (cochlear implants, cardiac monitors, insulin pumps, digital pills and so on).
- Self-monitoring and patient self-care devices, smartphone apps and attachments and 'smart' objects embedded with digital biosensors that collect detailed information on human bodies.
- Personal emergency response systems used to alert caregivers or healthcare professionals if the user has a medical emergency at home.
- Digital imaging systems for medical diagnosis, including such technologies as genomic analysis tools, ultrasound, computed tomography imaging and magnetic resonance imaging.

- Health informatics for healthcare institutions: electronic patient records, triage and booking systems, diagnostic, risk assessment and decision-making software, online payment and personnel systems.
- Digital disease surveillance systems.
- Biomedical research software.
- Gaming console technologies and apps for fitness and health-promoting activities.
- Virtual reality and augmented reality technologies for patient education, diagnosis, therapies for mental health and mobility conditions, surgery simulation and health professional training.
- Robotic surgery.
- Robotic elder caregiving.
- Three-dimensional (3D) printing technologies for surgery, prosthetics and patient education.
- Sensor-based environmental monitoring, community development and citizen science initiatives.

The types of digital health technologies now available and their capacities are associated with wider developments in the internet and World Wide Web. The internet first became readily accessible to the public's use around 1994, via commercial web browser providers able to offer access to the World Wide Web. During this first iteration of the web, most websites involved the static delivery of information, although users were able to create and share content to some extent using blogs, online discussion and message boards or listservs. They used desktop or laptop computers to access the internet, plugging modems into telephone lines to connect.

The emergence of the 'social web' (also often referred to as Web 2.0) is usually dated from around 2004 onwards. Social web technologies are far more interactive and mobile, including social media platforms, wikis and geo-locational applications. Wireless computing technologies (wi-fi) and mobile devices such as smartphones and tablet computers can provide an almost constant internet connection. The term 'prosumption' (a neologism combining consumption and production) has been employed to describe the new ways in which digital technology users are now able to create the content of online materials and share this content with many others as part of participatory web cultures (Beer and Burrows 2010; Ritzer 2014). Some commentators are beginning to remark upon the emergence of the third iteration of the World Wide Web (the 'semantic' or 'intelligent web': Web 3.0), involving the Internet of Things, in which sensor-embedded and other 'smart' technologies are increasingly interlinked and able to exchange information with each other (Greengard 2015).

Another digital phenomenon to have emerged in recent years is that of the massive data sets that are generated by digital technologies, often referred to as 'big data'. Big data are generated from routine online interactions and transactions online, the sensors that are embedded in devices and physical environments and the creation of digital content by users when they upload information to the internet. Cloud computing technologies now facilitate the production, storage and exchange of these big data. A growing digital economy has emerged in which personal data have taken on immense commercial value (Andrejevic 2013; Kitchin 2014a).

Digital technologies have been used in various ways in medicine and public health since the advent of computing in the mid twentieth century, gaining impetus with the release of personal computers in the mid-1980s and then the development of the internet and the World Wide Web. Key early uses of digital technologies for health and medicine included the computerisation of healthcare services' information, financial and communication systems and telemedicine. As I use the term here, telemedicine involves the use of digital technologies by healthcare providers to communicate with patients and other providers, effect clinical diagnoses and deliver healthcare in remote locations. It also includes patient self-care and self-monitoring systems using digital technologies (these are also sometimes referred to as 'telehealth' or 'telecare' technologies) and online medical education programs.

Health and medical-related websites were another major development in early digital health. Once the World Wide Web offered ready access to the internet, the production of dedicated websites enabled health and medical workers and authorities to develop websites to convey information to the lay public. Patients began writing their own blogs and developing interactive forums (listservs, discussion groups and message boards) to connect with each other and share information. These were largely closed groups and networks ('intrasocial' networks), not available to outsiders for access or comment. Since the turn of the twenty-first century, a host of novel digital media and devices in addition to these technologies have emerged and have been taken up in health and medical domains. These developments have brought with them even more opportunities for lay people and healthcare professionals both to seek information across an ever-growing array of news sites, websites and blogs directed at health and medical issues and engage more actively in creating, sharing, tagging and curating content.

The entry of a growing range of digital technologies into healthcare and public health domains has wrought some significant changes. Especially in countries in the Global North and the wealthier parts of Asia, many aspects of quotidian living and social institutions have been changed by digital technologies, facilitated by mobile devices and the expansion of wi-fi access to the internet. Personal relationships, families and other social groups, leisure activities, education, the workplace, policing and security and the economy have all been influenced in important ways by digital media and devices (Lupton 2015a). The realm of health and medicine is simply one of these digitised domains, but it is having a growing impact on other domains of social life. Digital technologies for health or medical purposes have been incorporated into family, working and educational lives and social relationships.

While I am not able to cover in this book all of the technologies I described earlier, I focus on several important features of digital health. One feature is that users of digital health technologies are not simply passive recipients of health and medical information delivered to them by others. As in other areas of digital media use, they are active participants in the creation of this information as well as commenting on it, sharing it, tagging it and curating it. As well as blogging about their illness and medical experiences, lay people can write or edit Wikipedia entries, set up or contribute to condition-specific Facebook groups or pages, make and upload videos and images and update their social media profiles constantly with comments and data about their own health or fitness activities. A host of patient information exchange platforms has been established that allow people with specific conditions to share information about their symptoms and treatments and to rank and rate the services of healthcare institutions and professionals. Patients can even resort to crowd-funding websites to seek contributions towards their medical expenses.

Healthcare and public health professionals and institutions can also generate far more material and establish bigger social networks on the internet than in previous times. Professionals are interacting with each other and with lay people and sharing medical knowledge on social media sites. LinkedIn offers healthcare professionals opportunities to connect with each other and join interest groups. Healthcare organisations and medical businesses are turning to social media to engage with current and potential clients and boost their 'brand' and reputation. They realise that their status may be undermined as well as promoted by the tenor of the discussions that patients may have about their services online. Hundreds of YouTube channels, Facebook pages and Twitter accounts have been set up by hospitals and healthcare organisations as part of public relations strategies.

Given that new digital technologies allow for the ready and often instantaneous transfer of data, the kinds of information that are generated by one 'smart' device can now be exchanged with another object/user. The new content can be spread across numerous platforms, often simultaneously. Many digital technologies provide features that include a range of media genres and cross-platform features that enable the distribution of content across different platforms. Some websites and social media platforms offer their own apps. Wearable devices also often have their own apps and social media platforms but may offer access to other social media sites as well. These interoperable functions embedded in the software allow users to share or combine their data readily between devices, apps and sites. More and more often, users are encouraged to move between apps, platforms and websites, sharing and re-sharing their personal details across a number of sites and using different entry points to access the sites. Thus, for example, an image that may be shared on Facebook to one group of followers can also be shared on Instagram, Snapchat or Pinterest to other followers. Smartphones and smartwatches receive notifications from email servers and apps. Videos can be uploaded to YouTube and the link then embedded in a blog post or shared on Twitter or LinkedIn.

Importantly, this content has become increasingly valuable to a wide range of actors and agencies beyond the individual content creator: used for commercial, research, managerial, policy and security and government purposes. As this suggests, another characteristic of contemporary digital health technologies is that they bring together digital media and devices with medical and consumer cultures in unprecedented ways. This type of knowledge has been commodified and commercialised in new ways, as well as reaching novel markets and uses. The mobility of personal digital data across devices and platforms is related to this feature of convergence of domains. This feature raises important questions concerning the privacy and security of people's personal health and medical data and the extent to which it is exploited by others.

The following chapters take up these topics and much more. I begin in Chapter 1 with an overview of the major theoretical perspectives I consider important to undertaking a critical analysis of digital health: the political economy approach, sociomaterialism, Foucauldian theory, the phenomenology of embodiment and surveillance and privacy theories. In Chapter 2 I move on to describing the kinds of digital technologies in use for remote patient consultation, online patient support and communication and for self-care and self-monitoring. I reflect on the prevailing ideas about human behaviour and self-responsibility articulated in discourses that promote these practices. Chapters 3 and 4 focus on the ways in which the data generated by digital health technologies portray human bodies, health and illness. In Chapter 3 I look at the data materialisations of bodies that are generated by medical imaging technologies, social media, digital self-tracking strategies and 3D printing technologies. Chapter 4 reviews the ways in which big data sets about bodies, health and illness states are generated and exploited by a diverse range of actors and agencies, and the significant data privacy and security issues at stake.

Chapters 5 and 6 address the ways in which lay people use digital health technologies. In Chapter 5 I take a broad perspective, focusing on the social determinants of digital health use. Here I rely mainly on survey-based research to identify patterns and differences between social groups and those living in different countries. Patients' lived experience of digital health technologies is reviewed in Chapter 6, with a particular emphasis on the emotional and sensory elements of these encounters. In Chapter 7 I move to a focus on the health and medical working environment. I begin with a discussion of how healthcare and public health professionals use digital technologies for their work. This is followed by addressing the issue of the (often ambivalent) ways in which patients' use of digital health technologies is viewed by the medical profession, and the implications for medical power and authority and for patient care and medical and health surveillance practices. The book ends with some concluding comments in which I summarise the main themes and findings of the book and outline directions for future research in critical digital health studies.

1

THEORETICAL CONCEPTS

This chapter acts as a foundation for the remainder of the book by introducing some of the theoretical concepts and approaches I find insightful for a critical approach to digital health technologies. I cover perspectives offered by the political economy approach, sociomaterialism, Foucauldian theory, the phenomenology of embodiment, and surveillance and privacy theories, explaining what each has to offer in understanding the social, cultural and political dimensions of digital health technologies. It is important to note here that, while they are presented under discrete headings, many of these perspectives overlap with or inform each other. They provide a rich basis for elucidating the often-unrecognised assumptions, discourses, beliefs and practices that give meaning to the design and use of digital technologies in medicine and public health.

The political economy approach

The political economy perspective is one of the most influential and longstanding in critical approaches to health and medicine. It has its roots in Marxian analyses of the relationship between social class, the means of production and the capitalist economic system. Also known as conflict theory, this perspective views social relations as struggles over power and involving the promotion of the interests of some social groups over others. Political economy critiques have been a central approach in the sociology of health and illness, medical anthropology, media studies and critical health psychology. Writers have drawn attention to such issues as the social determinants of health and illness states (such as social class, gender, ethnicity, age and geographical location), the establishment and maintenance of medical power, the impact and effects of globalisation on healthcare and public health, the role played by commercial entities such as Big Pharma and the biotechnology industry and the implications for social justice.

Many scholars have adopted a political economy approach to examine the nature of scientific medical authority and power and its rise in status in the twentieth century. In his influential book *The Social Transformation of American Medicine* (1982) for example, Starr claimed that (in the US context at least) medical authority had achieved an unparalleled high status and dominance as a profession. The concept of medicalisation has been used by Starr and others to explain the ever-increasing spread of a western medical perspective into social life and embodiment, consonant with an intensification of this profession's power and authority.

Other influential writers on medicalisation include Irving Zola (1972) and Eliot Freidson (1970). They were developing their critiques of western medicine from the late 1960s and into the 1970s, a period in which many powerful institutions, social elites and social norms were being challenged and critiqued. They and others contended that the medical profession had acquired major influence as an institution of social control, taking on the kind of social regulation traditionally offered by the law and religion. Social and moral issues had been redefined as medical problems, requiring the knowledge of the medical profession to diagnose and treat (Baer *et al.* 1986; Conrad 2007; Crawford 1980; Starr 1982). Medical power and the status and authority of the medical profession (often referred to in this literature as 'medical dominance') were viewed as interbound with the extent of medicalisation that had occurred. Once a collection of bodily signs or behaviours are identified as symptoms of a medical condition that can be given an official diagnosis, they become 'medicalised' – drawn into the world of medical expertise for intervention.

There is little doubt that, in the contemporary era, the purview of western medicine has extended well beyond the surgery or hospital, penetrating into many other aspects of everyday life. Over the past quarter-century or so, biomedical innovations have contributed significantly to medicalisation. In addition to technologies such as stem cell, neurological and human genome research, digital technologies are part of these innovations. These novel technologies are part of a new bioeconomy of medicine, health and illness, leading to an intensification of focus on promoting health and preventing illness and disease using technologies, greater medical surveillance of individuals and social groups, a greater reliance on technologies for medical diagnosis and treatment and new forms of medical knowledge and transformations in human embodiment.

Clarke and colleagues (Clarke and Shim 2011; Clarke *et al.* 2010) employ the term 'biomedicalisation' to encapsulate not only the encroachment of western medicine into other areas of life, but also the growing use of technologies to treat, transform and enhance human bodies and profit from them. They also draw attention to the use of medicine and technoscience to develop technologies designed not simply to diagnose, prevent or treat illness and disease, but to optimise human bodies, promising to expand or improve people's capacities and capabilities. These features are strongly evident in the discourses and design of digital technologies for collecting information about people so that they might improve their health, physical fitness and wellbeing.

The political economy perspective literature has further identified the ways in which the practice of scientific medicine tends to depoliticise illness and disease, representing them as individual problems rather than as socially determined, and in doing so serving the interests of the capitalist economic system. Medical discourses and practices are positioned as obfuscating the social and political causes of ill health, including socioeconomic disadvantage, by focusing instead on individual patients' lifestyle choices (Crawford 1977, 1980; Waitzkin 2000). Thus, for example, people on very low incomes living in substandard housing are often positioned as personally to blame for their ill health (by failing to give up smoking, drinking too much alcohol, being fat or not engaging in enough exercise), drawing attention away from the broader conditions of entrenched disadvantage that may be causing their illness (such as poor housing conditions, poverty, unemployment, lack of access to healthcare or social stigmatisation). This viewpoint on health and illness has been referred to as 'victim-blaming' (Crawford 1977).

Exponents of the political economy perspective have also identified a power asymmetry in the doctor–patient relationship. They assert that, in the context of western medicine, medical practitioners possess authoritative knowledge and power, while patients, especially those from disadvantaged groups who lack social status and access to the type of education required to acquire medical knowledge, are not easily able to challenge the claims of their doctors (Baer *et al.* 1986; Conrad 1992; Crawford 1980). Critics contend, therefore, that patients' autonomy is limited or repressed under the western system of biomedicine. They must accept the diagnoses and solutions that doctors decide for them. In response to the unequal power relations of the medical encounter, political economy critics call for more power to be invested in patients and for 'de-medicalisation' to occur. Critics argue that patients should be encouraged and empowered to challenge medical authority and that more attention should be directed towards the social determinants of ill health (Waitzkin 2000). This perspective underpinned many of the consumerist and patient-empowerment activism initiatives originating in the 1970s and which are still evident today (Lupton 1997a, 2012).

Writers critiquing the neoliberal political philosophy of government are the latest to adopt a political economy perspective on health and illness. Neoliberalism, emerging in western countries over the past few decades, involves a focus on the free market and a move away from state-sponsored interventions into social support systems. As a development in capitalist economic rationales, neoliberalist politics tend to focus on deregulation and individualistic solutions to social problems (McGregor 2001; Ventura 2012). Critics have noted that, under neoliberalism, ever-greater emphasis is placed on citizens taking responsibility for their own wellbeing, including educating themselves about the best strategies for self-improvement and productivity and achieving and maintaining good health (Lupton 1995a; Mooney 2012; Petersen and Lupton 1996). As part of the austerity politics adopted by many western nations in the twenty-first century in response to various economic crises and the effects of globalisation, the move towards emphasising citizens' autonomy and self-responsibility over state intervention and support has intensified. From the political economy perspective, such strategies serve to entrench further socioeconomic disadvantage and inequalities contributing to states of health and ill health (De Vogli 2011; McGregor 2001; Mooney 2012).

When applied to analyses of the social meanings and impact of digital technologies, political economy approaches have highlighted the power differentials and the potential for creating or perpetuating socioeconomic disadvantage that are part of digital society (Fuchs and Dyer-Witheford 2013; van Deursen and van Dijk 2014). From a critical approach to digital health, analyses of the disparities in the ways in which people from different social groups and living in different geographical locations use digital health technologies are important. The potential of digital health technologies to entrench further rather than ameliorate socioeconomic disadvantage, stigmatisation and discrimination against minority groups should be uncovered.

Another key feature of digital health requiring attention is the exploitation of people's personal digital data for commercial profit. A global knowledge economy has developed that relies in part on the generation and use of the data that are collected by digital technologies. What is constituted as knowledge and the ways in which knowledges are used for commercial, research, managerial, security and governmental purposes have become intertwined with digital forms of data generation. Indeed, it has been contended by some theorists that power now operates principally via digital modes of communication. In this context, the software, hardware devices, the digital data that they generate and the algorithms that make sense of these data have become key actors in constituting and exploiting knowledges (Amoore and Piotukh 2015; Kitchin 2014a; Lash 2007; Thrift 2005).

Despite the rhetoric of participatory democracy and sharing that characterises much discussion of technologies such as social media sites (Beer and Burrows 2010; John 2017), these media are not the open, collaborative spaces they once were. The ethos of sharing personal details and connecting and communicating with other people online originally underpinned the establishment of such social media as Facebook, Instagram and Twitter, while offering users the opportunity to find content easily online was the initial purpose of search engines like Google Search. Over the past decade or so, however, many actors have realised the economic potential of the personal details that people enter online when they use these types of technologies.

Indeed, the creators of these data are often excluded from full access to their own details, while the internet empires and smaller companies, including the plethora of data scraping, mining and profiling businesses that have sprung up to analyse digital data sets, profit from these data. They have become commodified and bent to commercial interests. As a result, new forms of power have emerged, embodied in internet empires such as Facebook, Google, Apple, Amazon and Microsoft (Andrejevic 2013, 2014; Fuchs 2011, 2014; Fuchs and Dyer-Witheford 2013; van Dijck 2013a). Digital health data are prime resources for commercialisation and commodification by these and many other corporations, including pharmaceutical and biotechnology companies and health app and wearable self-tracking device developers.

Sociomaterialism

The sociomaterial theoretical perspective focuses on the entanglements of humans and other non-human actors. This approach has been most commonly articulated in science and technology studies and, in particular, actor-network theory (Latour 2005; Law and Hassard 1999), as well as cultural studies and material anthropology (Coole and Frost 2010; Harvey and Knox 2014; Ingold 2000). Exponents of sociomaterialism emphasise the role played by material artefacts in social relations and the construction and negotiation of meaning. They acknowledge that bodies/selves are dynamic assemblages of flesh, affect, others' bodies, objects and space/place. They draw attention to the interdependence and physicality of this relationship and accord agency to material artefacts. Objects are represented as participating in specific sets of relations, including those with other artefacts as well as people.

Space and place – the physical environments in and through which people move – are also key to sociomaterial perspectives. People are always located in place and space. Their bodies contribute to and draw from these spatial contexts as part of interactions between human and non-human actors (Ingold 2000). These spaces can have profound implications for people's wellbeing and states of health. Some social scientists have employed the term 'therapeutic landscapes' (Conradson 2005; Gesler 1992) to refer to the ways in which some spaces, whether natural or built environments, work to encourage feelings of wellbeing and safety in people who are ill, mentally distressed or receiving medical care. Bell *et al.* (2017), for example, have researched the important role played by 'green' (including plants and trees) and 'blue' (bodies of water) environments in alleviating stress and anxiety.

Scholars adopting a sociomaterialist perspective are interested in the practices that are undertaken as part of private and communal life: how people use objects like digital technologies, incorporating them into habitual routines. They also often acknowledge the wider contexts in which these object–subject relations are configured, such as geographical location, the age, gender, ethnicity and socioeconomic status of consumers and the influence of these relations upon contexts. The concept of the 'assemblage', also derived from science and technology studies as well as Deleuze and Guattari's writings (Marcus 2006), is often employed in the sociomaterialism literature as a way of acknowledging the material and non-material, the human and the non-human, the fleshly and the ideational in ever-changing configurations. The assemblage concept also emphasises the spatial aspects of the relationships between humans and non-humans: that these assemblages extend beyond flat networks of connection into three-dimensional associations.

When the sociomaterialist approach is taken up to examine humans' relationships with technologies, it is contended that human actors (the users of these technologies) participate in configuring the meaning and uses of the technologies, just as technologies themselves enact human action, embodiment and meaning.

Scholars emphasise the dynamic nature of people's interactions with technologies in a world in which the digital is increasingly part of everyday lives, social relationships and concepts of subjectivity and embodiment, creating new practices and knowledges (Lupton 2015a, 2016a). These approaches develop a critique of digital media and technologies, acknowledging their materiality and political dimensions. They recognise the mutual interaction between human actors and the software and hardware they use.

From this perspective, digital data assemblages are configured via interactions of humans with other humans, devices and software. Digital data themselves are objects in digital data assemblages that have their own social worlds and agency. Digital data practices configure multiple identities and subjectivities that, due to the continuous and heterogeneous nature of digital data generation, are dynamic, constantly shifting and changing. This approach recognises the entanglements of personal digital data assemblages with human action. Not only are personal digital data assemblages partly comprised of information about human action, but their materialisations are also the products of human action, and these materialisations can influence future human action (Gillespie *et al.* 2014; Lupton 2016a, 2017a, 2017b; Marres 2012; Marres and Weltevrede 2013; Ruppert *et al.* 2013).

As sociomaterialist scholars argue, when people interact with digital devices they do so in ways that are structured by the affordances (or capabilities) of these devices, the codes and software that structure these affordances, the transmission technologies that send the digital data that are generated to other people or to repositories and the panoply of other actors and agencies that seek to make use of these data (Gillespie *et al.* 2014; Marres and Lezaun 2011). For example, search engines like Google Search (easily the most highly used search engine) use algorithms that customise searches for each individual user, based on considerations such as what other searches that person has conducted and the person's geolocation. Search returns are also shaped by factors such as whether website developers have paid Google to promote their site and the volume of searches for the same topic by other Google users. Search engines and their algorithms, therefore, are active participants in meaning making, defining how people can access information according to their inbuilt assumptions, orderings and values (Roberge and Melançon 2015; Rogers 2013).

Digital devices that generate personal data participate in the formation of digital data assemblages, in which technologies and humans work together to create new configurations of information. Given the mobility and ubiquity of contemporary digital devices, they may be understood as lively technologies, inhabiting and accompanying us in our physical spaces and residing on or with – and indeed, as in the case of some digital medical implants, sometimes in – our bodies. These devices have become co-habitants with humans. The digital data that these devices generate may also be conceptualised as lively (Lupton 2016a, 2017a, 2017b). First, these data are generated from life itself by documenting humans' bodies and selves. Second, as participants in the digital data economy, they are labile and fluid, open to constant repurposing by a range of actors and agencies, often in ways in which the original generators of these data have little or no knowledge. Third, these data are lively due to the advent of algorithmic authority and predictive analytics that use digital self-tracked data to make inferences and decisions about individuals and social groups. These data, therefore, have potential effects on the conduct of life and life opportunities. Fourth, by virtue of their growing value as commodities or research sources, the personal data that are derived from self-tracking practices have significant implications for livelihoods (those using these data in the data-mining, insurance and data science industries, for instance).

In its focus on materiality, the sociomaterial perspective on technologies offers valuable insights into ways of thinking about the relationship between humans and non-humans in the context of digital health. Digital health technologies directly and obviously relate to human bodies, used to deliver medical care, diagnose illnesses, monitor bodies and communicate information about bodies. However, as outlined in sociomaterial studies, any technology (digital or otherwise) is inevitably embodied as human users engage with non-human objects, place and space. Many social scientists have drawn upon the sociomaterial approach to theorise medical technologies. The term 'materialities of care' is sometimes employed to describe a research focus that seeks to place emphasis on how humans and non-humans interact at moments of medical (and other) caregiving: in other words, how care is a sociomaterial practice (Harbers *et al.* 2002; Mol 2008; van Hout *et al.* 2015).

Scholars adopting sociomaterial perspectives contend that humans' enactments of technological practices facilitate modes of knowing the body and disease. Changes in medical technologies represent transformations in how bodies are conceptualised, touched, managed and visually displayed (Law and Singleton 2005; Lupton 2012; Mol 2002, 2008). Multiple enactments of bodies are generated via the different ways in which they are represented and treated (Harbers *et al.* 2002; Mol 2002, 2008). Patients' knowledge of and practices related to their bodies, and therefore their body ontologies, may differ radically from those of their healthcare providers. Even among healthcare providers, different specialities can see bodies and their ills in a range of ways. This is because a human body and all its dimensions – states of health and ill health and disease, symptoms, signs, activities and movements – are messy, constantly changing and uncontained. They can never be fully disciplined into coherent phenomena (Maathuis and Oudshoorn 2015; Mol 2002; Pols and Willems 2011).

Foucauldian theory

Foucauldian perspectives draw on the far-ranging work of Michel Foucault to focus on the discursive construction of knowledge and matters relating to biopolitics and biopower, governmentality and surveillance of the human body. His work has been taken up in many sociocultural analyses of medicine and public health as well as scholarship on digital technologies and has strong relevance for a critical analysis of digital health.

Foucauldian perspectives adopt a different approach to power relations from that put forward by the political economy approach. Rather than viewing medical power as repressive and controlling, seeking to subject patients, the Foucauldian approach attempts to identify the productive nature of power: how it brings knowledges and practices into being and how these work across a diffuse range of sites to maintain social order in ways that frequently involve the voluntary participation of lay people rather than their subjugation. Foucault and his followers focus on identifying the relationships between discourses, or the modes of speaking about or representing phenomena, and practices, as they operate together to give each other purpose and meaning. Foucault's (2008) concepts of biopolitics and biopower highlighted the ways in which power is exercised via discourses about and practices of managing, regulating and monitoring human bodies (Lupton 1995a, 2012; Petersen and Lupton 1996). He contended that, where once coercion and violence were used to discipline bodies under regimes of sovereign power, more subtle and dispersed forms of power now operate to encourage citizens to conform to expectations and norms.

In his historicophilosophical work on the development of scientific medicine in France, *The Birth of the Clinic: An Archaeology of Medical Perception*, Foucault (1975) wrote about the development and extension of the clinical gaze of the medical profession on the bodies of patients. He remarked on the power of medical practitioners to make distinctions between the normal and the pathological and to work to discipline bodies in certain ways. Practices of examination and mapping of the body that were carried out by doctors constituted the clinical gaze. These practices operated to bring the human body into a field of visibility. These include the use of technologies to listen to or visualise aspects of the body such as the medical dissection, the stethoscope, microscope and X-ray. Outside of the clinic, human bodies were rendered the subjects of other forms of regulation via techniques of monitoring and measuring in domains such as schools, the workplace, the military and the prison. These forms of bodily knowledges intersected with medical data to generate new knowledges about individuals and populations that could be used to govern and manage citizens (Armstrong 1995; Foucault 1991, 2008; Lupton 1995a, 2012; Petersen and Lupton 1996).

In Foucault's work, the power of the medical profession is conceptualised as a form of knowledge production, bringing into being the subjects of 'the doctor' and 'the patient' and the phenomena of 'illness' and 'disease'. Rather than power being experienced by its subjects as repressive (although this may happen in some contexts), the diffuse and heterogeneous ways in which it is exercised renders it productive, generative of knowledges, practices and forms of sociality. Both doctors and patients act as links in the set of power relations that constitute the field of medicine. Adopting this perspective, if power is viewed as relational and processual rather than a possession, neither patient nor doctor can be viewed as possessing power as such, but instead as operating as the agents through which power passes. Rather than patients being oppressed by medical dominance, as the political economy perspective sees it, for Foucauldians patients and doctors are viewed as colluding in the medical encounter to defer (in most cases) authority to the doctor as the person with medical training and expertise (Armstrong 1983, 1995; Lupton 1997a, 1997b,

2012; Måseide 1991). In this way, medical power and expertise are productive and necessary, generating understandings and interpretations of the body from a certain discursive viewpoint (Måseide 1991; Turner 1995).

As Foucault (1979) points out, the Christian model of the confession, involving revealing private thoughts, feelings and actions to another person, became a key technology of the self in many areas of personal life and institutions, including the clinic. When patients visit doctors, they are encouraged to reveal details about their bodies and their lives so that the medical gaze might be most effective and doctors can effect an accurate diagnosis and prescribe treatment (Armstrong 1995; Måseide 1991). The confession is viewed as a means to generate truth, so that either the confessor can achieve psychological relief and absolution or the person to whom she or he confesses can render a judgement or assessment. The confession is a practice of working on the self in which people make themselves knowable to themselves and others.

A therapeutic ethos often accompanies the practice of the confession. It is assumed that emotional turmoil may be relieved or expert advice better provided if the confessor details inner thoughts and feelings (Turner 1995). The confession is usually achieved by the means of verbalising (talking or writing), but images are also increasingly important to revealing elements of the self. In contemporary societies in the Global North, for example, the selfie (self-portait) that is uploaded to social media sites or the graphics of personal data that are generated from self-tracking can be used as ways of revealing elements of selfhood to others. These informal images of bodies, as well as those generated by medical technologies, can also operate as artefacts for generating or provoking the action of confessing the secrets of the body.

Foucault's use of the Panopticon metaphor has been influential in the scholarship on the social dimensions of health and illness as well as critical perspectives on digital technologies, particularly in theorising the ways in which citizens conform to the dictates of the state and other authorities. The Panopticon is a literal architectural structure, a prison first proposed by eighteenth-century reformer Jeremy Bentham. The concept of the Panopticon is used metaphorically by Foucault in his well-known work *Discipline and Punish: The Birth of the Prison* (Foucault 1995) to suggest the operations of power in contemporary societies. The Panopticon prison was a structure designed so that the monitoring gaze of those in power could operate centrally to observe inmates in their separate cells, who were unaware of when exactly they were being watched. This design allowed a small number of those in authority to observe a large number of individuals. The concept included the idea not only that prisoners should be observed by those in authority, but also that they should ideally develop self-surveillance and self-disciplining strategies in response. This approach to the management of problematic populations was also taken up in other institutions, such as the hospital and the school.

For Foucault, the Panopticon was representative of a new form of power, one in which central surveillance and monitoring of individuals were combined with the development of voluntary self-management techniques or, as Foucault puts it, 'technologies of the self' (Foucault 1988). Here it is important to emphasise that, while some of the technologies of the self may be imposed by other people or agencies (think of the practices required of children by their teachers in schools or those demanded by employers as part of working conditions), many others are self-imposed as part of pursuing the individual's own interests. People accept expectations in the sociocultural context in which they live about taking on responsibility for monitoring and managing their bodies in their efforts to optimise and improve their lives and act as 'good' citizens (Lupton 1995a, 2012; Petersen and Lupton 1996).

In Foucault's work, governmentality relates to forms of management of populations, often employing medical and related knowledges, such as epidemiology, that specify how citizens should comport their bodies. In their focus on population health, public health interventions operate at this level, again often seeking to conduct surveillance of citizens' bodies to generate effective strategies for disease prevention and control (Foucault 1984, 1991). Biopolitics operates at both the level of individuals, in terms of how they respond to these expectations and norms as part of their everyday practices, and at the level of populations, in relation to how large groups of citizens are regulated to maintain social order and productivity. Issues of health and illness, life and death, are central to biopower and biopolitics, as are the scientific and other knowledges that are configured by the information generated about these topics.

Foucault's writings have also been taken up in scholarship on the sociocultural aspects of digital technologies. His ideas about technologies of the self and the confession have been used to theorise the presentation of selfhood in social media (Marwick 2013; Sauter 2014; van Dijck 2013b). Perhaps the topic for which his work has been most influential in relation to digital technologies, however, is research on digital surveillance. The two topics of enquiry, digital health technologies and digital surveillance technologies, come together when examining the social impact and meaning of digital health technologies that work to monitor and measure human bodies. The medical gaze that developed from the monitoring and examination of patients' bodies and the diagnosis of health and illness in the clinic served both to reproduce and contribute to medical knowledges about the body (Foucault 1975, 2008). This is a specific form of bodily surveillance, undertaken as part of the medical encounter for the benefit of the patient. Elements of the medical gaze and governmentality have become progressively digitised, generating new forms of surveillance and knowledges about the human body and health and disease. (I have more to say on theories of surveillance later in this chapter.)

Recent Foucauldian positions on big data and the algorithms that manage and interpret these data are valuable in understanding the impact of digital data in health and medicine. The algorithms that collect and manage digital data contribute to certain ways of categorising and producing subjects and bodies; or algorithmic assemblages (Hallinan and Striphas 2016; Striphas 2015; Totaro and Ninno 2014). These assemblages exert algorithmic authority when they are used to construct data profiles or make inferences about people. The algorithmic identities

(Cheney-Lippold 2011) configured using algorithmic manipulation of digital data now influence many aspects of everyday life: what special offers, advertisements or recommendations people are given, whether they are assessed as good or bad credit risks, as safe to board aeroplanes or likely to commit criminal acts (Amoore 2011; Crawford and Schultz 2014; Rosenzweig 2012). Algorithmic authority also plays a part in the types of digital data about themselves that people are offered and the subsequent technologies of selfhood. Algorithmic authority and algorithmic identities are highly evident in the ways in which digital technologies generate information about human bodies which is subsequently used in health and medical domains. They may therefore be conceptualised as contributing to a new mode of biopolitics, shaping concepts and technologies of selfhood and embodiment and the governance of populations (Lupton 2016a, 2016b).

The phenomenology of human embodiment

One critique of the Foucauldian emphasis on discourse and the political econ-omy focus on the ways in which social structures and group membership structure health and illness is that they tend to neglect aspects of the phenomenology of the body, or the lived experiences of corporeality. Sociomaterialist perspectives, in their emphasis on embodied practices and objects, go some way to addressing these aspects. Yet this approach, in its turn, sometimes fails to consider the affective and sensory dimensions of humans' encounters with non-humans.

Understanding the role of the emotions and the senses is vital to the phenom-enology of embodiment. As the French philosopher Merleau-Ponty (1962, 1968) reminds us, we are embodied subjects and experience the world through our bod-ies and our senses. Our experiences and our judgements are always part of our 'being-in-the-world'. For Merleau-Ponty, 'being-in-the-world' is always intersub-jective. Our embodiment is always inevitably interrelational or intercorporeal. We experience the world as fleshly bodies, via the sensations and emotions configured through and by our bodies as they relate to other bodies and to material objects and spaces. We touch these others and they touch us. The senses and emotions are integral to embodied perceptions and experiences of the constituents of space and place, which may include other people, non-human animals, natural and built envi-ronments, climatic conditions and objects such as technologies. Bodies and selves are not contained to the fleshly envelope of the individual body, but extend beyond this into space and connect and interconnect with other bodies and objects. These processes are inevitably relational because they involve embodied interactions and affective responses (Labanyi 2010; Lupton 2015d, 2016a).

Social scientists have identified the mutual dependencies, ambiguities and ambivalences of the doctor–patient relationship, the fact that lay people are often feeling highly vulnerable when they need healthcare. Particularly if they are elderly, from a socioeconomically disadvantaged or marginalised social group or very ill or suffering severe pain, patients may find it difficult to challenge medical authority or simply do not wish to do so (Andreassen *et al.* 2006; Lupton 1997a, 1997b; Lupton *et al.* 1991; Salander and Moynihan 2010). People may harbour very strong emotional investments in allowing their doctors to 'take control' when they are ill, suffering or anxious about their health. Lay people frequently shift between adopting a consumerist perspective and wanting to invest their trust in their doctor, depending on the context (Lupton 1997a, 1997b).

A critical analysis of digital technologies, therefore, requires an understanding of how people engage with them using their bodies, including their senses and emotions. It is here that scholarship on the senses and emotion can offer some insights. The sensory studies literature includes contributions from sociologists, anthropologists, historians, social psychologists and cultural geographers. They focus on the social, cultural and political dimensions of the human senses. These scholars show that the ways in which we understand the world through our senses are the products of acculturation working with physiology, and are therefore historically, cross-culturally and socially contingent. In other words, different cultures have different sensory experiences, practices, definitions and meanings (Classen 1999; Howes 2010, 2015). Sensory responses are also integral to the ways in which people respond emotionally. Sensory experiences can generate very strong emotions across the affective spectrum. Olfactory sensations, for example, can be extremely evocative in eliciting happiness and comfort in some contexts, but in others disgust, disquiet or fear. There are strong connections between smell, place and memory, in which emotion plays a key role (Low 2013).

In cultural studies and material culture studies within anthropology there has long been an interest in the ways in which people 'appropriate' and 'domesticate' objects: that is, how they take new and often unfamiliar objects and incorporate them into their everyday lives. In the process, the objects become customised to the uses and needs of the users. Emotion and the senses can be viewed as central elements in which people interact with digital technologies and incorporate them into their lifeworlds (Lupton 2015a, 2016a). Emotions take place within and around bodies as they move through space and interact with other bodies and with objects. Emotions are 'a crucial element of the body's apprehension of the world' and 'a vital part of the body's anticipation of the moment' (Thrift 2004: 67).

Emotions are located both in bodies and in spaces. They are therefore only understandable, made sense of, in the contexts of particular spaces, in what has been termed an 'emotio-spatial hermeneutic' (Davidson and Milligan 2004: 524). The interactions and movements of human and non-human actors in space and place generate 'affective atmospheres', or feelings that are sensed when people enter a particular physical environment (Anderson 2009). Affective atmospheres are diffuse and constantly changing as actors enter and leave. They are shaped by their material and multisensory properties: visual aspects, touch, sound, smell and taste all contribute to affective atmospheres. A place can feel dangerous or reassuring, calming or anxiety-inducing, therapeutic or harmful, for example (Andrews *et al.*, 2014; Duff 2016).

When considering these aspects of digital technology use, the materiality of human and non-human encounters is foregrounded. These include the sensory, tacit or hidden aspects that may not be directly talked about but are evident when people are observed carrying out habitual activities. Given that digital health technologies are directed at monitoring, representing and diagnosing the human body (including the senses), that the senses are employed in using digital devices and interpreting and acting on the digital data that are generated from these technologies and that digital devices communicate with their users via the senses, understanding these processes is an important element of a critical approach to digital health. Müller (2015: 36) observes that 'affect and emotion [make] the socio-material hold together or fall apart. They are what pulses through assemblages and actor-network and what constitutes their power'. Emotions combine with objects, habitual or improvised practices and discourses to configure an affective atmosphere in which things 'feel right' or 'feel wrong'. Digital technologies can thus be understood as simultaneously social, digital, material, affective and sensory (Farman 2013; Moores 2012; Pink *et al.* 2016a).

The senses have long constituted a major element in medical training, the doctor–patient encounter and other aspects of healthcare work. The act of medical diagnosis, for example, is traditionally undertaken by doctors, nurses and other healthcare providers using sensory information such as viewing patients' bodies and demeanour, touching them, smelling them, hearing the sounds of their bodies (often using a stethoscope) and listening to their accounts of their symptoms (Draper 2014; Goodwin 2010; Harris 2016; Schubert 2011). Medical student training in understanding the human body in previous eras involved their embodied interactions with living and dead human bodies (as in the dissection of cadavers to learn anatomy) (Prentice 2013). Healthcare practitioners' assessments of the efficacy of the therapies they have suggested and general states of patient wellbeing or illness are also typically based on intuitive understandings conducted via embodied interactions with patients (Carmel 2013; Draper 2014; Harris 2011, 2016).

The use of technologies is not separate from these judgements. From the stethoscope onwards, technologies have been employed in the medical setting as tools to facilitate sensory knowledges of patients, working together as a technological assemblage with professionals' bodies. Healthcare trainees and workers are constantly interacting with, using and negotiating the information they derive from the technologies they use in concert with their embodied sensations (Carmel 2013; Gardner and Williams 2015; Goodwin 2010; Harris 2016; Prentice 2013). Indeed, it has been argued that medical work should be described as a 'craft', given that it involves the interactions of bodies (patients and healthcare professionals) with material objects, including physical environments and technologies (Carmel 2013). Healthcare providers engage in a continual interpretation of the information provided to them by their embodied senses and that generated by the devices they are using. Whether the technology used is a stethoscope, an X-ray machine, a pulse oximeter, a blood pressure cuff or an ultrasound imaging device, healthcare providers actively assess and interpret the bodies they are examining with their accumulated knowledge and expertise and their sensory responses at the moment of interaction in relation to the information relayed to them by the technology (Maslen 2015; Schubert 2011).

The emergence of digital representations of phenomena has stimulated profound questions concerning how people make judgements about the nature of the 'real' and the 'virtual', the 'material' and the 'intangible' and the role of the senses in this process. When such digital technologies are introduced as virtual reality for medical training or video or messaging services for telemedical consultations, the full range of sources of medical knowledge and assessment usually conducted through the practitioner's senses is removed. This potentially has significant implications for how medical knowledge is acquired and applied (Mort *et al.* 2003; Oudshoorn 2009; Pols 2012; Prentice 2013). Nonetheless, while some sensory engagements are restricted or cast aside in digital health, it is important to acknowledge that the monitoring properties of new digital technologies offer new ways of sensing, interpreting and enacting the human body and states of health and illness and different ways of interacting with technologies and incorporating them into lifeworlds.

Thus, for example, the opportunities that are now available for people to touch their digital devices present new possibilities for affective engagement with these devices, representing a significant shift in ontologies of human–technological assemblages. In their recent work, Pink and colleagues (Pink 2015; Pink *et al.* 2016b) bring together the anthropology of the senses with digital anthropology. They call for a tactile digital ethnography, involving close observation of how people use touch (and their hands, in particular) when they are interacting with digital technologies. They focus on people's everyday practices to demonstrate that incorporating the knowledges offered by digital data with that achieved by the human senses provides a rich appreciation of how people learn and go about their everyday lives. Their study, involving observations of the embodied aspects of using mobile devices (Pink *et al.* 2016b), revealed that people use their hands not only to tap out messages and open apps and other software but also as a way of connecting with friends and family and with experiences. Touching the screen is a form of social connection and communication, quite apart from any content that may be delivered or generated.

This approach also offers a nuanced concept of digital devices and digital data. Digital technologies enable the digitised locating of the human body in time and space via the use of geolocational sensors and mapping devices. Mobile devices include global positioning systems (GPS) and sensors such as accelerometers and gyroscopes, all of which are locational, and mapping technologies that can identify the physical location of the user. The term 'locative media' (Farman 2013) is sometimes used to describe the types of digital devices that are location-aware. Some of these devices may be mobile, carried with people as they move around in place and space, while others are embedded in the spaces and places in which people move. The concept of code/space, as outlined in the work of Kitchin and Dodge (2011), develops the idea of geographical space, human bodies and software as working together to generate new knowledges. This can be further extended if human bodies are considered, so that we can start to think about the possibilities of bodies–technologies–code–data–space as assemblages.

Digital data assemblages are inextricably entangled with people's concepts of selfhood and embodiment, constantly changing as more data are generated and acted on. Digital data assemblages are distributed selfhoods and bodies. Our identities are not confined to or solely made up of these assemblages, but they are components of selfhood and embodiment. These data have the potential to influence people's lives and self-understandings in significant ways and thus have a different moral status from other forms of information.

Just as we might reflect on how our lively companion devices live alongside us, we might also think about how our lively personal digital data assemblages co-habit with us (Lupton 2016b). As we co-habit with our devices and our data, we co-evolve with them. The design of the devices is conceptualised bearing in mind how users may interact with them, and users' habits of practice as they appropriate the devices into their everyday lives are responses to the devices' designs. So too, humans co-evolve with their personal digital data assemblages. The data are configured in response to, and about, humans' experiences and bodies. In turn, humans may change their modes of being and concepts of selfhood in response to their data assemblages. With both our devices and our data, we are interembodied and intersubjective.

Theories of surveillance and privacy

The role played by digital technologies in watching people is a central feature of contemporary data practices, including those related to health and medicine. As scholars in surveillance studies have emphasised, there are many different modes of veillance (watching). In its simplest terms, surveillance means watching from above or watching over, usually undertaken by people in powerful roles who watch the less powerful to monitor, manage and control them better (Mann and Ferenbok 2013). The term 'surveillance society' is used by some writers to denote the increasing ubiquity of surveillance technologies in everyday life, used to record, survey, monitor and discipline people (for example, Gilliom and Monahan 2012; Lyon 2010; Mann and Ferenbok 2013). It has been argued by these and many other scholars that surveillance is a condition of modernity, essential to the development of the capitalist economy and the contemporary nation state and central to forms of disciplinary power and the maintenance of social order. Various kinds of social relations and interactions, including power relations, are created in and through surveillance technologies. These technologies may be considered part of the production and government of citizens in neoliberal societies.

In the context of digital technologies that generate information about users, dataveillance (watching using data) (van Dijck 2014) is integral. The fastest-growing and most controversial specific type of surveillance is that using the processing of personal data gathered from people's use of digital technologies. These include the use of social media sites, search engines like Google, loyalty cards offered by businesses to their customers, personal information numbers (PINs), information gathered by websites and apps when they are accessed by users and ticketing systems at airports. Geolocation data are generated by mobile devices and sensors embedded in public spaces or in patient self-care or body monitoring devices. The digital data produced by these forms of surveillance serve to individuate users, distinguish them from others and identify them by a series of criteria. Their behaviour is then analysed, to produce 'surveillance knowledge' (Lyon 2010: 108) and in some cases to construct detailed profiles on people. Not only is personal information gathered via the use of surveillance technologies, but individuals can easily be grouped or sorted into discrete categories and classes based on this information and then subjected to assessments based on prior assumptions. Through the sorting and typing of individuals, allowing the development of profiles and risk categories, policies and strategies of inclusion and exclusion operate. Different specific types of individuals are identified as requiring greater forms of disciplinary control (Haggerty and Ericson 2000; Lyon 2002, 2010).

Some modes of digital dataveillance are covert and non-consensual: the subjects of these modes do not realise that they are being watched and have not given their permission. These covert modes include the dataveillance conducted by national security agencies of their citizens (as revealed in the documents released by whistle-blower Edward Snowden from mid-2013), many forms of commercial collection of personal digital data by companies and the dataveillance that is conducted by hackers or cybercriminals. Other modes of dataveillance are open and voluntary.

Recent sociological theories of veillance about new forms of digital media have identified the range of practices in which people engage consensually as part of watching themselves and each other. The mode of panoptic surveillance draws on Foucault's Panopticon metaphor, outlined earlier in this chapter. It involves the few watching the many: as in the use of closed-circuit television cameras in public spaces, for example (Hier 2004).

Synoptic veillance is the inversion of panoptic surveillance. Instead of the few watching the many, synoptic veillance involves the many watching the few. This can take place on social media platforms, in which the activities of public figures or celebrities can be watched and commented on by multitudes of platform members (Doyle 2011). The term 'sousveillance' (literally meaning watching from below) has been used to describe people watching each other and also monitoring those in positions of authority (Mann and Ferenbok 2013). Digital technologies can be employed for sousveillance: for example, people using cameras in their phones to record wrongdoing and sharing these incidents to large audiences on social media or ranking and rating sites that give public assessments of professional services.

Self-surveillance using digital technologies involves people actively gathering information about themselves in the interests of achieving better self-knowledge and (often) self-optimisation (Lupton 2016a, 2017a, 2017b). Sometimes the personal details that are collected are reviewed only by the individual engaging in self-surveillance. On other occasions, people may choose to make their details available to others to view. When they do so, they are engaging in 'social surveillance': the watching that people undertake of each other on social media, personal blogs and discussion sites as part of forming or maintaining social relationships (Marwick 2012). On these sites, when users upload personal information about themselves (concerning what they are doing and how they are feeling in both verbal and photographic formats), they invite others to view and comment on or make a judgement about 'liking', 'favouriting' or sharing their material. Indeed, users of such sites invite visibility, and high levels of responses from others is viewed as a marker of social success and strong relationships (Gerlitz and Helmond 2013). These types of mutual watching can be important to users' presentation and performance of selfhood and identity (Lupton 2016a, 2017b; Marwick 2013; Sauter 2014; Smith and Vonthethoff 2017; van Dijck 2013b).

The term 'intimate surveillance' has been adopted to describe the mode of watching that takes place when people observe other people who are close to them, such as friends, spouses, sexual or romantic partners, children and other family members (Levy 2015; Lupton and Williamson 2017). Intimate surveillance may be a part of social surveillance but may take place less publicly and even covertly (when those who are being watched have no knowledge of it). Many forms of intimate surveillance are benign, undertaken as a means of establishing and maintaining social relationships and engendering mutual feelings of closeness and knowledge of each other. Some are intertwined with caring practices, such as the monitoring parents may undertake of their children's health, wellbeing and development or adult children's practices of tracking the health and wellbeing of their elderly parents. Other uses of intimate surveillance can be coercive or even abusive: as when it is involved in stalking or attempts to control partners (Levy 2015).

All of these digital dataveillance practices generate personal digital data assemblages that are constantly changing as new data points are created and (often) shared online. Novel modes of digital surveillance are dispersed, rapidly changing and productive of new forms of knowledge (Lyon and Bauman 2013). As I noted earlier in this chapter, when digital dataveillance involves the uploading of personal information from digital devices to corporate databases, as is generally the case, these data become open to repurposing for commercial, research, governmental, managerial, security and criminal actors and agencies as part of the global digital knowledge economy. The use of people's personal details, therefore, extends well beyond any original intention that they may have had in gathering them.

Many of the digitised forms of watching I have described are employed for health and medical purposes. The medical surveillance described by Foucault as integral to medical practice and the production of the patient now extends well beyond the clinic, via the emergence and use of technologies such as telemedicine, digital self-monitoring and patient self-care devices and apps and social media forums promoting the discussion of health and medical topics. Health and medical information, like other personal data, is imbricated within forms of dataveillance and social sorting. It is also among some of the most valuable forms of information that are collected by and about people using digital technologies, used not only in legal ways but also in cybercriminal activities. Dataveillance involves what Zuboff (2015) refers to as 'surveillance capitalism', or the exploitation of people's personal information for profit. These data are particularly valued because they are collected as a byproduct of behaviour rather than directly via purposive surveys or interviews, and also because they can be collected in real time.

People have few opportunities to challenge the inferences and predictions that are made by algorithmic calculations. They often have little knowledge about how corporations are exploiting their personal details and using them to construct detailed individual profiles. Given that many forms of dataveillance are partly or fully covert, these assemblages and their movements are often hidden. People can access some of the digital data that are generated on them, but they are often not able to monitor how their data are used by other actors and agencies (Lupton and Michael 2017a). The algorithmic manipulation of these data and their on-selling processes tend to be 'black boxes', or hidden from view (Pasquale 2015).

These issues raise important questions concerning the privacy of people's personal health and medical data. Privacy issues have often been raised in discussions about new digital media, including social media platforms and mobile devices. Some writers have questioned whether the current era of always-connected mobile media, the culture of sharing and confession on social media sites and widespread dataveillance in public places has meant 'the end of privacy' (Lyon 2010; Lyon and Bauman 2013). Can the spatial meanings of privacy, which represent privacy as a kind of personal zone from which others are excluded unless given permission to enter, remain meaningful in a context in which people are available for surveillance and data gathering for much of their waking day (Bennett 2011)?

Recent writings in information ethics and internet studies suggest that concepts of privacy in relation to personal data and dataveillance need to be re-evaluated and calibrated. The term 'networked privacy' (boyd 2012; Marwick and boyd 2014) describes the distributed forms of self-disclosure and intimate relationships developed on online forums. This concept of privacy recognises that such interchanges and content creation and sharing take place in a context in which the revealing of personal details is not only encouraged but expected as a participant. It is not that people 'do not care' about privacy, but that their privacy practices have been reconfigured in response to using new media. Concepts of privacy are highly contextual to the situation and the technology that is being used (Nissenbaum 2011). Users make choices about what technology to employ, what type of content should be shared and how others should use their personal details (Kennedy *et al.* 2015; Marwick and boyd 2014).

Unlike many other forms of information or objects that people use and commodify, these kinds of details can be considered inherent to personhood and individual identity. Writers in information ethics have contended that, because personal health and medical data are about people's bodies, their state of wellbeing and their experiences of health and illness, it is not a question of people 'owning' this information as if it were an object external to them. Rather, the information should be viewed as part of them, just as their bodies or their feelings are (Floridi 2005; Sax 2016).

★★★

I have covered extensive theoretical ground in this chapter. Taken together, the perspectives and concepts I have outlined in this chapter raise central topics and directions for a critical analysis of digital health. They highlight the importance of considering the power relations and political philosophies that influence how digital health technologies are used by lay people and healthcare and public health professionals. The chapter has also emphasised the importance of identifying not only influential ideas and discourses but also the experiential dimensions of human embodiment and humans' encounters with material objects, computer code and place and space and how these encounters are enacted via practices. The key focus of all of these perspectives is the human body: how knowledges are developed about it, how these knowledges are mobilised and how people experience corporeality in the context of their engagements with digital health technologies. Digital health technologies are directed at monitoring, measuring, defining, visualising, diagnosing, therapeutically treating, managing, optimising and controlling human flesh, capacities and vitalities. These aspects of digital health are addressed in further detail in the chapters to come.

2

THE DIGITISED HEALTHY CITIZEN

Many digital technologies are directed at encouraging lay people to seek and generate information about health and illness, engage in medical self-care practices and activities directed at connecting with other patients, improving or promoting their health and avoiding illness and disease. In this chapter, I review these types of technologies and research that has sought to identify patterns of their use. I end the chapter with a critical consideration of the broader implications for ideas and expectations about appropriate patient behaviour and good citizenship.

Websites, online forums and social media

With the advent of personal computing, followed by the World Wide Web and the internet late last century, it soon became obvious that these technologies were being incorporated into many people's information-seeking practices for health and medical topics and issues. An extensive body of research in medicine, public health and the social sciences was published in the late 1990s and into the first decade of 2000 on the ways in which lay people conducted online searches for health and medical topics, blogged about health and medical issues and experiences and constructed online support groups and communities. In investigating the use of such online health sites, researchers addressed such topics as how support groups, discussion boards, blogs or chat rooms operated socially and the kinds of messages portrayed on such forums. This research documented the increasing importance of web-facilitated platforms in providing information and support to lay people. It also highlighted the various ways in which internet-based health and medical information were accessed and used in different ways by people from different social groups (for overviews of this literature, see Kivits 2013; Lupton 2016c; Ziebland and Wyke 2012).

Online searching for health and medical information and using health-related websites remain very popular pursuits. Google has acknowledged that searches for health information using its Search tool are among the most popular (it cites one in 20 searches as being related to this topic) and the company has worked to facilitate user access to such information. In February 2015 Google announced that it had updated its search returns for users in the USA to provide information about the symptoms and treatment of hundreds of diseases and medical conditions upfront. The company worked with a team of doctors to provide this informa-tion (Google 2015). By mid-2016 Google had gone even further in attempting to provide information that had been validated by medical experts, partnering with Harvard Medical School and the Mayo Clinic to ensure that these sources received top billing in health and medical search returns (Husain 2016).

The top medical website, WebMD, attracts an estimated 80 million unique visi-tors per month (as of February 2017), followed by the American National Institutes of Health (NIH) with 55 million, Yahoo! Health with over 50 million, MayoClinic with 30 million and MedicineNet with over 25 million (eBizMBA 2017a). Wikipedia is the most highly used reference source globally. It features a large number of entries on health and medical topics (estimated at over 26,000 articles in many different languages as of January 2014). Its content tends to be ranked at the top of search engine queries for health and medical topics so that it is the first source many searchers would look at (Rasberry 2014). It was estimated that medi-cal Wikipedia entries received 6.5 billion views in 2013 (Heilman and West 2015).

While traditional websites and online discussion forums about health and medi-cine are still numerous, they have been supplemented by social media platforms. The most popular social media sites by a long way are Facebook (established in 2004) and YouTube (2005), followed by Twitter (2006), LinkedIn (2003) and Pinterest (2011) (eBizMBA 2017b). Social media are now frequently used by patients with specific conditions to communicate with each other. Many disease- or condition-specific Facebook pages exist for patient support and information exchange (Bender *et al.* 2011; De la Torre-Díez *et al.* 2012; Zhang *et al.* 2013). Twitter is also often employed to search for health information (De Choudhury *et al.* 2014) and facili-tate information sharing among people interested in specific health and medical topics or conditions, including lay people and healthcare professionals and officials as well as pharmaceutical and medical device companies (Beykikhoshk *et al.* 2015; De la Torre-Díez *et al.* 2012; Murthy 2013; Oh *et al.* 2013; Robillard *et al.* 2013). YouTube features thousands of videos relating to patient experiences (Basch *et al.* 2015; Del Casino and Brooks 2015; Harris *et al.* 2014a; Mazanderani *et al.* 2013b; Naslund *et al.* 2014) while the visually oriented Pinterest offers a forum for shar-ing and curating images about health, illness and medicine (Ahmed *et al.* 2016; Guidry *et al.* 2015; Whitsitt *et al.* 2015). Tumblr (De Choudhury 2015; Kelleher and Moreno 2016; Tembeck 2016) and Instagram (Andalibi *et al.* 2015; Gauthier and Spence 2015; Ging and Garvey 2017; Tiidenberg 2015) are now also frequently used by people to discuss or visually portray their bodies and experiences of illness and medical treatment.

In addition to these general social media sites, a multitude of platforms have been established that specifically invite patients to contribute personal information about their bodies, medical conditions, treatments and healthcare experiences. The most well-known of these types of platforms is PatientsLikeMe. Others include CarePages, HealthUnlocked, CureTogether, Smart Patients and Treato. The Patient Opinion websites (in the UK, Australia and Ireland) invite users of their services to discuss their experiences anonymously (or 'share their stories'), both positive and negative. These narratives are then passed to the relevant area health services in the interests of improving healthcare. It is claimed on the UK Patient Opinion site that 'We pass your stories to the right people to make a difference' (Patient Opinion 2016). In the UK, the National Health Service (NHS) has developed an initiative to fund libraries, community centres and pubs to act as 'digital health hubs'. These are designed to provide training and support for people to learn about accessing health and medical information online and use websites such as NHS Choices, which offers information and advice on a range of conditions, online patient support communities and healthcare services. As the title of the website suggests, the focus is on supporting lay people to make 'choices' about their health and healthcare: 'Your health, your choices', as the tagline has it (NHS Choices 2016).

Organisations such as the World Health Organization and the Centers for Disease Control and Prevention have social media accounts with large numbers of followers and have used these accounts effectively to disseminate health information to the public (Hart *et al.* 2016). Commercial enterprises also offer websites, social media pages and discussion forums as part of their promotional and patient education efforts. For example, major pharmaceutical companies have established their own websites, in which they employ various strategies to seek to engage patients and potential consumers and promote their brand. The Merck company offers its MerckEngage website, which features a combination of information for people taking medication and those assumed to want to engage in personal health promotion activities to prevent illness. The range of information offered on the site includes details on medication safety, the pharmaceutical products offered by Merck and how medicines are made, as well as recipes for healthy meals, motivational tips and messages for activities such as weight loss and fitness programmes and even advice for caring for pets (Merck also manufactures medicines and vaccination materials for pets). The website also provides special offers for patients, such as the opportunity to use coupons to access cheaper medication and to engage in drug trials, as well as software tools to help patients remember to take their medications and caregivers to provide care for loved ones. The 'Our Mission' statement on the website states: 'To cheer on the healthy choices you make every day and give you new ideas and tools to help keep you on the right path' (MerckEngage 2016).

Telemedicine and patient self-care devices

Telemedicine employing digital technologies has been used in some countries since the early days of personal computing. Telemedicine literally refers to 'medicine practised at a distance', or healthcare that is effected using media rather than traditional face-to-face encounters. Originally using telephones, closed-circuit television and other plugged-in devices, telemedicine has increasingly incorporated video services like Skype, wireless devices, software platforms, apps and data analytics into its repertoire. The latest versions of telemedicine, like other recent digital health technologies, offer continuous real-time monitoring, wireless data transfer and cloud computing storage facilities that reduce the expense and expertise required for the proprietary systems that were characteristic of earlier technologies. In several countries, including the USA, the UK and some parts of continental Europe, telemedicine has become a significant part of healthcare delivery. In the USA, 72 per cent of hospitals and 52 per cent of physician groups have telemedicine programmes, and 74 per cent of large employers offer telemedicine to their employees as part of their healthcare programmes (Beck 2016).

Corporate organisations have entered the digital healthcare market. The US giant retailer chain Walmart now provides interactive, self-service health kiosks, encouraging shoppers to check their eyesight, weight, body mass index and blood pressure and access health-related information (as well as showing advertisements for related products stocked by Walmart which can be targeted to users based on their responses). Other US providers are offering cubicles where lay people pay a set sum to engage in a video consultation with a doctor or nurse practitioner (Appleby 2013). Such cubicle-based telemedicine often involves the remote use of stethoscopes, thermometers and other medical tools by the patient (sometimes with the help of an attendant) to take the patient's vital signs and communicate this information to the remote healthcare worker. In the USA, hundreds of employers offer telemedicine kiosks to their employees, often supported by their health insurers. The instalment of the kiosks is viewed by employers and insurers as offering employers benefits by reducing workers' time off to seek medical attention, facilitating preventive care before more intensive medical treatment is required and reducing health insurance costs as a result (Kaiser Health News 2016).

Also in the USA, a range of apps and platforms now offers lay people opportunities to locate medical practitioners and other healthcare professionals and make appointments. Platforms like ZocDoc (with associated apps for mobile devices) help patients find doctors and dentists in their local area and make appointments online, as well as read reviews of doctors by other users. In addition to ZocDoc, there is Vitals, which uses a quality indicator and Castlight Health, which presents billing information for various healthcare services. Apps like Pager allow users in some parts of the USA to contact healthcare professionals and arrange an at-home visit. Other apps, such as Doctor on Demand, involve remote telemedicine consultations. Patients consult with the doctor using video calls on their device (described by the platform as a 'video visit'). Using the DrEd platform ('your online doctor'), after completing a questionnaire users are able to have medications prescribed by doctors working for the platform and sent to them by mail.

One important element of contemporary telemedicine is the range of digital devices used for patient self-monitoring at home for chronic health conditions. The

Alere MobileLink is an example. Patients take their readings from testing devices that are compatible with the system (blood coagulation monitoring, glucose meters, weight scales, blood pressure monitors and pulse oximeters) and the data are sent wirelessly to their healthcare provider. Cases or attachments for smartphones can be purchased that turn the phone into a digital health-monitoring system. Another device is the iPhone Wello case, which has sensors enabling the user to measure blood pressure, heart rate, body temperature, blood oxygen levels and heart electrical activity and includes an attachment that users can blow into to measure lung function. All of this tracking can be carried out by any user, under medical supervision or not, once the case has been purchased.

Digital devices integrate with the body in various ways. In the case of smartphones and wearable devices, they are carried or worn on the body. Some medical devices may be inserted into the body for short periods of time, like those used to monitor the strength of women's pelvic floor exercises. Others are surgically implanted into the body, becoming part of the body more or less permanently. These include continuous glucose-monitoring devices, heart pacemakers, insulin pumps and cochlear ear implants. Digital medication (sometimes referred to as 'smart tablets' or 'ingestibles') is also available, designed to increase patient compliance with drug regimens. It involves tablets embedded with microchips that are swallowed, react with chemicals in the stomach, produce a slight voltage which is transmitted to a patch worn by the patient and then sent to the patient's doctor or carer. In these cases, incorporation becomes literal: users may not be able to remove the devices even if they want to.

Another range of medical devices embedded with sensors is part of the physical environment in which people move. There are many sensor devices designed for the care of the elderly: tracking their routines, activities and vital signs at home and in assisted care facilities. These include 'smart' mattresses, chairs or floors that can detect the movements of residents as a way of monitoring their wellbeing. Digital emergency response systems are worn on the body or are wired into the home to provide alerts in case of an accident or sudden onset of a medical problem. These are connected to family members, healthcare providers or emergency services. One of the latest of such devices is CarePredict, a wearable tracking system which uses sensors embedded in a band worn on the wrist and the walls of the older person's home to track the individual's movement around the house, including identifying which room the person is occupying. The data are uploaded wirelessly to the internet, where they can be accessed by caregivers. In some countries, and particularly Japan, robotic care providers have been developed to provide bodily care for elderly people in their homes or in community care or hospitals such as hygiene tasks and lifting them out of bed or chairs. These robotic assistants are viewed as a way of alleviating shortfalls in human caregivers. Some also incorporate sensors to measure the user's biometrics and movements and send out emergency alerts.

With its promise of reducing healthcare costs, this approach to medical care and preventive medicine has been bestowed with new importance following the global financial crisis occurring in the early 2000s and the resultant strain on the economies of many developed countries. These actions are promoted as having the potential to relieve the financial burden on the healthcare system in the current era of austerity (De Vogli 2011; Greenhalgh *et al.* 2012; Veitch 2010). For example, the new model of healthcare funding proposed by the US Patient Care and Affordable Care Act (otherwise known as 'Obamacare'), that was signed into law in 2010, moved healthcare away from the traditional fee-for-service model to one that rewarded preventive care activities by financially penalising hospitals with high patient readmissions (Malykhina 2013). Telemedicine and digitised patient self-care systems were viewed as contributing to this objective by reducing face-to-face interactions of patients with healthcare providers and hospital visits.

The NHS in the UK is also working towards expanding telehealth initiatives, with then Health Secretary Jeremy Hunt announcing in early 2016 his goal to ensure that 25 per cent of patients with a chronic condition like hypertension or diabetes will be monitoring their health remotely by 2020. Other plans include facilitating patients to be able to book medical appointments online and to consult doctors using digital technologies (Misra 2016). The Australian Government is also adopting new digital health initiatives. In 2016 it introduced a new statutory authority, the Australian Digital Health Agency, that according to its website is 'tasked with improving health outcomes for Australians through the delivery of digital healthcare systems and the national digital health strategy'. One of its key missions is to introduce successfully electronic patient records nationally (the My Health Record system). The Health Care Homes model has also recently been introduced by the Australian Government, in which patients with chronic health conditions will be encouraged to use digital at-home self-care, medical management and telemedicine technologies.

Health and medical apps and wearable self-tracking devices

The introduction of smartphones and tablet computers that could be easily carried around and connect to the internet in most locations provided further opportunities for people to go online (the iPhone was released in 2007, the iPad in 2010 and the first Android smartphone in 2008). Apps for mobile devices, first introduced in 2008, have provided further opportunities for lay people to access, create and share health and medical information. Over 1.5 million apps have been placed in each of the top two app stores, Apple App Store and Google Play (Statista 2015b). The developers of apps, wearable devices and health and fitness tracking software are finding ways of connecting with other digital media, especially social media. A survey of health and medical apps published in 2015 found that recent apps were more likely, compared with apps available two years ago, to offer the functions of connecting to another device or wearable device or social media site (Comstock 2015). In mid-2016 the NHS announced plans to give millions of patients free access to health apps and wearable devices for the self-management of chronic illness in the interests of saving money on treatment and rehabilitation costs (Campbell 2016).

A detailed review of health and medical apps found that, by late 2015, 160,000 health and medical apps had been placed on the market (IMS Institute for Healthcare Informatics 2015). The review found that a diverse range of publishers were responsible for developing these apps, including digital entrepreneurs, healthcare institutions, fitness and weight control companies, health insurance and pharmaceutical companies and independent doctors. Over half of all health and medical apps had limited functions, mostly providing information. One in ten had the capability to connect to a monitoring device or sensor, while a third could connect to social media networks. Most health and medical apps (65 per cent) focused on promoting wellness, diet and exercise, with nearly a quarter directed at the self-management of chronic diseases such as diabetes, high blood pressure and mental health conditions.

Many types of wearable devices are offered on the market for this type of health and fitness tracking, including the Fitbit, Jawbone UP and Misfit ranges. Such body functions, sensations and indicators as blood glucose, body weight and body mass index, physical activity, energy expended, mood, body temperature, breathing rate, blood chemistry readings and even brain activity can now all be monitored using portable wearable and internal sensors that have been embedded in wristbands, headbands or shoes or woven into clothing. These technologies produce detailed data that may be readily communicated to others via social media platforms or transmitted to caregivers and medical or public health professionals.

In mid-2014, Apple announced its new Health app for iPhones and iPod Touch devices. The app automatically counts the steps taken by its user and can also incorporate health and physical activity information from third-party apps and consolidate them into a comprehensive health profile or dashboard (iOS8 Preview: Health 2014). By employing the associated HealthKit platform software developed by Apple, when the user opts in to the system the app both collects data that are generated from the phone and sends them to other apps and collates the data that other apps generate. Thus, for example, if a person uses an iPhone to record her or his blood pressure, this reading can be automatically sent to a third-party app installed on the phone.

Smartwatches also often include health and fitness tracking sensors and apps. The Apple Watch, released in 2015, includes a range of sensors, such as geolocation, accelerometer, gyroscope and heart rate monitors that facilitate self-tracking. It offers two pre-loaded apps, Workout and Fitness, that work with the embedded sensors (heart rate sensor, global positioning system (GPS) and accelerometer) to track users' physical activities and body metrics. Samsung has similarly developed the Galaxy Gear smartwatch which includes biometric monitoring capabilities. The Google Fit program is directed at health and fitness self-tracking. The tagline on the website announces that Fit will help people 'Get to a healthier you' and 'Stay motivated' through its range of goal-setting and body-monitoring tools. It provides a platform where different self-tracking data can be integrated and accessed from any type of device, including the Android Wear smartwatch, and from a range of other platforms.

Some apps and devices enable people to engage in self-diagnosis. A study of self-diagnosis apps I conducted with Annemarie Jutel (Lupton and Jutel 2015) found that the app developers used various claims to entice users. Their app descriptions asserted that they will save lay people's time and money (by potentially allowing them to avoid a visit to the doctor), allay their anxieties, improve their health by allowing them to diagnose a medical condition and then seek treatment, educate them by enhancing their medical knowledge and support patient empowerment by bestowing information about diagnoses. There were frequent references to these apps helping lay people to access medical information, assess their own symptoms and make decisions about whether or not to seek medical help. Some self-diagnosis apps are linked into systems of medical referral and health insurance coverage. The iTriage app, for example, provides a database for users to search for their symptoms, suggests possible causes, provide details of medical practitioners in the user's area and even personalised cost information for recommended tests and treatments that take into account the insurance plan to which the user belongs. The app description suggests that 'iTriage puts you at the center of your healthcare so you can make confident decisions'.

Apps for helping people with mental health conditions are also available (Donker et al. 2013; Tucker and Goodings 2015). Some target depression by monitoring the user's movements using GPS and accelerometer technologies as well as interactions via phone call, email and social media. If the user appears not to have moved much from home or is not making contact with others via the device, then the app registers that something may be wrong. Other apps allow people with depression to join a community of others with the same condition and to log their feelings each day ('mood tracking') to post and share with the community (how happy they feel on a sliding scale), as well as follow the mood statuses of other users. Some offer 'health coaching' to users, to provide motivation and advice. Still others allow users to complete questionnaires to screen themselves for conditions such as depression.

Children are the focus of several health-related apps, websites and wearable devices designed to encourage them to engage in physical exercise and monitor their progress, teach them yoga and meditation techniques or eat healthy foods. Schools are beginning to use self-tracking devices such as heart rate monitors in physical education programmes (Lupton 2015b; Lupton and Williamson 2017). Apps have been developed for children that use games to provide therapy for conditions such as attention deficit-hyperactivity disorder or help them manage their diabetes or asthma. The Eli Lilly pharmaceutical company has partnered with Disney to produce a website marketed to children with type 1 diabetes. T1 Everyday Magic offers 'real-life' videos telling the stories of children and their families, digital books featuring Disney characters designed to help young children learn about their condition and its treatment, resources such as stickers and colouring-in pages that can be downloaded and recipes for family meals, snacks and special-occasion food.

Workplace wellness programmes have become increasingly digitised in response to the development of wearable self-tracking devices and apps (or 'digital wellness tools'). Mobile apps and software programs that remind employees to get up from their desks and take exercise breaks and to help them manage stress and sleep better are becoming more often used in the workplace (Zamosky 2014). These technologies facilitate the blurring of the health and medical sphere with the domestic domain and the workplace, so that, for example, employees may be encouraged to track their sleep patterns as well as other biometrics such as their diet and exercise habits as part of a corporate programme that seeks to ensure that they are productive because they are well rested and in good health (Lupton 2016a; Moore and Robinson 2016). Wearable technology manufacturers such as Fitbit are brokering deals with employers and insurance companies to sell their fitness and activity trackers and data analytics software as part of these wellness programmes.

Public–private sector collaborations are also expanding. An example of government health organisations attempting to leverage the products, customer base and high profile offered by large internet corporations is the partnership between Amazon and Public Health England. As part of the One Health public health campaign, Amazon has established the One You Health Hub on its British website, offering products for sale such as wearable self-tracking devices, digital body weight scales and products to achieve a better night's sleep, as well as hints and tips 'to help you live a healthier lifestyle'. By virtue of this partnership, Amazon is rendered into a health promotion site – an offshoot of Public Health England.

Persuasive computing and gamification

Many digital health approaches, particularly those conforming to the 'persuasive computing' approach that has been developed in human interaction studies, draw on psychological models of behaviour change. One writer whose work is constantly cited in this literature is B.J. Fogg, a behavioural psychologist who has concentrated his research on designing computer systems for behaviour change (Fogg 2002, 2009). While Fogg claims that his model of behaviour change for persuasive computing is new, it has strong similarities to many other social and cognitive behavioural change models that have been used for decades in health education and health promotion (Lupton 1995a). Fogg argues that for a person to carry out a particular behaviour, three aspects must combine. The individual must be sufficiently motivated, have the ability to perform the behaviour and be triggered to perform the behaviour. All three of these factors must be present for behaviour change to occur. He calls this model the 'Fogg Behaviour Model' (Fogg 2009).

Behavioural models such as these rely upon a psychology of motivation and change that view behaviour as hierarchical and linear: one stage leads to the next and so on in a logical and rational progression. For example, Li and colleagues (2010) use what they call a 'stage-based model of personal informatics systems' to outline five stages that they identify in the process of engaging in self-monitoring as part of health promotion efforts. The stages are preparation, collection, integration, reflection and action. Each stage, from preparation on, leads to the next, with 'barriers' identified as affecting each stage and possibly preventing a person from moving on to the next. These barriers include factors such as lack of time, difficulties in interpreting the data, forgetting to collect the information, motivation and lack of accuracy in the data collected.

Mainstream health psychology researchers interested in digital health likewise tend to be preoccupied with using psychological models of behaviour change to encourage people to take up certain practices, overcome barriers to change or explain why they resist exhortations to change their behaviours. In focusing on individualistic models of behaviour, failing to question taken-for-granted assumptions about the need to persuade people to adopt practices that are imposed on them and ignoring the political dimensions of digital health, health psychology reflects broader trends in psychology as a discipline. Health psychology has evolved to act as a handmaiden to the medical and health education professions in their efforts to encourage lay people to take responsibility to protect and promote their health, to the exclusion of consideration of the sociocultural contexts in which health practices are taken up and the lived experience of health and illness (Lyons and Chamberlain 2006; Mielewczyk and Willig 2007; Murray 2015).

This approach remains evident in much of the contributions to the contemporary health psychology literature that has sought to address digital health topics. If there are attempts made to understand people's health beliefs and behaviours related to digital technology use, these tend to be contextualised by how interventions may either be successful or not work. Thus, for example, the editors of a special issue on digital health in the journal *Health Psychology* express their concern in their introduction that approaches to using digital technologies tend not to employ health behaviour theory (Borrelli and Ritterband 2015). The articles published in this special issue focus on how to conduct more effective health behavioural change using digital technologies. It is simply assumed across these contributions that first, digital health technologies should be adopted by their target audiences; and second, health psychology theories of human behaviour are valid and appropriate to use in designing digital health 'interventions'. Indeed, the very use of the oft-used term 'intervention' in health psychology accounts of digital health assumes that digital media and devices should be used as tools for introducing and persuading behavioural change in targeted groups.

Ethically and politically questionable interventions have been used in this type of health psychology research: including, for example, testing a facial-morphing app with young women smokers to determine whether seeing their faces digitally altered to look old and wrinkly (purportedly the effect of smoking) would deter them from continuing to smoke. The authors of this study approvingly note that some of the young women were disgusted (even to the point of nausea) by the sight of their faces becoming old as they were digitally manipulated, and advocate using this approach accordingly (Grogan *et al.* 2011). In such initiatives, the simple objective to change people's behaviour to conform to health-promoting ends appears to overcome any consideration of the ethics and politics of eliciting emotions such as disgust in response to older women's faces and evoking ageist and sexist responses to motivate behaviour change.

Gamification is a strategy that has been frequently employed in digital technologies directed at promoting or improving users' health. Gamification has been described as 'the use of game design elements in non-game contexts' (Deterding *et al.* 2011: 9). The term originated in the digital media industry to describe the incorporation of features into digital technologies that are not explicitly designed as games, such as competition, badges, rewards and fun that engaged and motivated users to make them more enjoyable to use. Gamification is now often used in literatures on marketing strategies, persuasive computing or behaviour modification.

Many dimensions of embodiment have been gamified using apps. Some gaming technologies (sometimes referred to as 'exergames') use sensors to generate digital data on players and encourage them to exercise and lose weight. These include games for Wii consoles such Wii Fit, which calculates players' body mass index and provides data on their fitness levels. Xbox Fitness offers users the opportunity to work out under fitness coaches and receive personalised feedback on their exertions. The Xbox Kinect technology includes features such as seeing which muscles have been engaged in the activity, measuring the user's exertion and heart rate and providing a physical energy expenditure meter. Some digital gaming technologies, such as Kinect 2.0 on the Xbox One, now have sophisticated sensors and software that are able to measure biometric features such as heart rate variability (by detecting changes in the colour of the user's skin) (Calbucci 2013).

A range of apps has been developed that attempt to combine fun and fitness, including the popular Zombies, Run! This app uses augmented reality in the attempt to motivate people to run further and faster. It includes game strategies such as missions that users must achieve to progress and a storyline involving zombies chasing runners which they listen to as they run. Run logs and statistics such as calories burned are also collected to track users' progress. At the other end of the age spectrum there are 'brain-training' game apps to help prevent or alleviate the symptoms of memory loss and dementia in the elderly.

Corporate public relations and marketing for pharmaceutical and biotechnology companies are beginning to use gamification in apps directed at promoting their products. One example is the app game for children made by the biotechnology company Genentech. The Ralph's Killer Muenster game involves players saving San Francisco from a mutant cheese using an understanding of DNA and genetics. The game is the centrepiece of a marketing campaign by Genentech, which also involves a website and blog by the fictional protagonist Ralph the cheese-maker, a Twitter account, a YouTube video and even a real-world food truck that drives around San Francisco offering Ralph's Killer Grilled Muenster Sandwiches. The purpose of the campaign is to portray biotechnical innovation as important and intriguing (Taylor 2013).

Numerous apps also seek to gamify pregnancy (Lupton and Thomas 2015; Thomas and Lupton 2015). Apps directed at pregnant women invite them to generate time-lapse videos of their expanding bellies, for example, to share on social media, while other apps claim to help them predict the sex of their fetus. Other apps are marketed at little girls, involving users giving make-overs to pregnant women or helping them give birth. Yet another genre of apps lets users engage in pregnancy-related pranks: presenting fake ultrasounds, for example. There is even a genre of apps that invite users to monitor their sexual activities and compete against other users to see who is the best lover or has the most conquests (Lupton 2015c).

Gamification has also crept into healthcare initiatives. For instance, health-care providers in the USA have begun to invite pregnant women to engage in gamified software in the attempt to ensure that they seek appropriate healthcare. UnitedHealth offers BabyBlocks, a program to encourage low-income women to attend prenatal appointments. After signing up to the program the women unlock online 'blocks' in the game by attending appointments and then are eligible to receive rewards such as gift cards.

The three-dimensional interactive virtual world Second Life and others like it have also been identified as offering health promotion possibilities. These platforms allow users to create avatars and interact with other users employing real-time com-munication tools. Health promoters have realised the potential for disseminating educational materials to lay people and providing virtual training environments for healthcare workers on virtual worlds (Beard *et al.* 2009; Ghanbarzadeh *et al.* 2014; Kamel Boulos *et al.* 2007). One study of health-related activities on Second Life conducted in 2008 found a considerable number of sites whose purpose was to disseminate health information (Beard *et al.* 2009). Second Life and other virtual worlds have been used for activities such as weight loss, diabetes management and obesity prevention programmes (Ghanbarzadeh *et al.* 2014).

Gamification strategies serve to encourage people to engage in self-surveillance, physical activity or self-care because such practices give them pleasure. Thus, for example, many practitioners of self-tracking enjoy features such as rendering vari-ous aspects of their everyday lives into metrics, comparing these metrics as they change over time or competitively with those generated by others, uploading these data and sharing them on social media and creating data visualisations to show off these data (Fotopoulou and O'Riordan 2017; Lupton 2016a, 2017a, 2017b; Stragier *et al.* 2015; Sumartojo *et al.* 2016;).

Health promoters have investigated ways to employ these digital games for pro-moting increased exercise, particularly for young people and the elderly (Kamel Boulos and Yang 2013; Millington 2014a, 2014b; Öhman *et al.* 2014). Thus, for example, a research team drew on Fogg's work to develop software for mobile phones to persuade healthy eating behaviour in children (Pollak *et al.* 2010). The design included a virtual pet that responded to information children uploaded about their eating habits (using a photo they take of their meals and snacks) and sent them reminders via email to eat well. The pet also reprimanded children via an email message if they seemed not to be eating according to healthy guidelines and showed either a happy or sad face. The researchers claimed that using this game involving caring for a pet would motivate children to eat well, providing incre-mental rewards as well as admonishments if they were not well enough 'persuaded' by the game format and reinforcing the idea that children were being monitored by the pets. As this example demonstrates, it is often considered appropriate in the persuasive computing literature to attempt to surmount resistance to 'persuasion' by using emotional triggers (rewards as well as punishments), or to suggest to people that their behaviours are under surveillance by others.

Health and life insurance companies, workplace wellness programmes and healthcare organisations are also developing ways to encourage people to use digital devices to collect information on themselves that involve persuasive computing and gamification strategies. Again, the USA leads the way here. Welltok's CafeWell 'Health Optimization Program' is one such technology, marketed to health insurance companies, health systems, accountable care organisations and other 'population health managers'. The focus on the platform is to provide 'an engaging and rewarding way for consumers to take control of their physical, emotional and financial health'. This includes a range of services, including the provision of information and advice and self-tracking technologies. Members of the programme received a 'personalised health itinerary' including tailored articles, videos and condition management programs, earn rewards for completing health challenges, are encouraged to join conversations or support groups on specified health topics and engage with coaches and health experts providing advice (Welltok – Solutions – CafeWell 2014). This is described as 'incentive driven health care' (Welltok – Solutions – CafeWell Rewards 2014).

Workplace wellness programmes frequently employ competitive motivations to encourage employees to participate. For example, the Jawbone company (Jawbone 2016) offers the 'Up Group' package to employers seeking to institute wellness programmes. On its website, Jawbone argues that promoting competition between different teams in an organisation will motivate individuals to exercise more, sleep better and eat healthier food. Team members are encouraged to view the data on their apps showing how their team is performing against other teams and to upload supportive comments and emoticons to motivate other team members.

Patient engagement and the healthy citizen

When discussing the apparent imminent revolution in healthcare driven by the new digital technologies, the terms 'patient engagement' or 'patient empowerment' (Barello et al. 2012; Greenhalgh et al. 2012; Morden et al. 2012) or even 'participatory biocitizen' (Swan 2012) are frequently used. In this discourse, the 'patient' or 'lay person' becomes a 'participant' who is actively involved in self-care: 'at the centre of action-taking in relation to health and health care' (Swan 2012: 97). More specifically, and particularly in the USA, the term 'patient activation' is employed, often in relation to a bureaucratic model representing patients as being 'more effective managers of their health and health care' (Greene and Hibbard 2012: 520). Patient activation is further described as involving lay people in activities to promote their health and prevent illness, teaching them to use the healthcare system appropriately (for example, not delaying care), encouraging them to research doctors' qualifications, prepare questions for consultations and seek out information about their condition as well as engaging in self-management of their illnesses or chronic health conditions (including monitoring of their symptoms) (Greene and Hibbard 2012).

These perspectives represent the latest version of the 'patient as consumer' approach that has circulated in various formulations since the 1970s. In the wake of consumerist and health activist movements emerging during that decade, there were calls from some quarters for healthcare to become 'democratised', for lay people to become more conversant with health and medical issues, engage in preventive health behaviours and seek to position their doctors as providers whose knowledge and expertise should not simply be taken for granted (Lupton 1997a, 1997b; Lupton *et al.* 1991). At that time, lay people had little access to alternative sources of medical knowledge other than coverage of health and medical issues in the news media, books written for a lay readership and patient support groups that may have shared information in face-to-face meetings or by distributing photocopied newsletters.

In contemporary discussions of patient consumerism, the discourse of patient engagement is brought together with that of digital medicine when lay people are advised that they should use digital technologies as part of patient engagement practices to construct the figure of what I term 'the digitally engaged patient'.

For some commentators, novel digital technologies have heralded new ways of encouraging patients to be more engaged in healthcare and preventive health endeavours that go well beyond using websites to seek out health information or participating in patient support groups. As part of the discourse of the digitally engaged patient there is now much talk of 'collaborative' relationships between patients or lay people and healthcare professionals and providers in terms of producing and sharing data on medical and health topics. One author has gone so far as to use a pharmaceutical metaphor to describe patient engagement as 'the blockbuster drug of the century' (Dentzer 2013: 202). Related to this metaphor is the new discourse that has emerged of 'prescribing' digital technologies and their associated platforms such as smartphones, Facebook and apps to patients. This discourse is often accompanied by the assertion that using such technologies will 'truly empower patients (and their families) and help them better understand their treatment and what's going on with their bodies' (Husain 2012).

As I outlined earlier in this chapter, in addition to 'empowerment' and 'engagement', words and phrases like 'better' and 'healthy' 'choices', 'taking control' and 'keeping on the right path' recur in discourses on digital health. These emphasise the notion not only that lay people have the opportunity to exercise choice and make informed decisions about their health and healthcare, but that they should take advantage of this opportunity. The corporate developers of many health and medical apps, self-care and self-tracking devices and other software constantly draw attention to their products' functions in providing consumerist values of choice and control over healthcare decision making as well as self-management of one's health. So too, government documents and spokespeople continually employ this language when describing healthcare and preventive health policies and strategies.

The figure of the digitally engaged patient is one element in the concept of the idealised healthy citizen that also receives expression in health education and health promotion discourses and strategies. Both may be viewed as part of a neoliberal political orientation to patient care and personal health promotion. They position lay people as ideally willing to seek relevant health and medical information actively, engage in their own healthcare and take up behaviours that preserve and maintain good health, in the attempt to shift the burden of such responsibilities from the state to the individual (Lupton 1995a; Petersen and Lupton 1996; Tulloch and Lupton 1997). These discourses suggest that 'empowerment' may be achieved by using sophisticated digital technologies for seeking medical knowledge and advice and for self-monitoring and self-care. Programmes directed at preventive medicine, patient self-care and health promotion have traditionally relied on a discourse of ideal citizenship that melds private objectives with the public good, the self with the community. Idealised healthy citizens are also willing to share their data for the interests of others or to provide encouraging feedback about other people to help motivate them. These discourses further imply that control over the recalcitrant body and its ills can be better achieved via technological means.

The apps and platforms I have described in this chapter adopt an approach that champions the ideals of self-responsibility in the quest for self-optimisation. Whether they are school children or elderly people, users are expected to accept and take up the assumptions that people should 'take control' of their health and be entrepreneurial in achieving and maintaining good health and high levels of physical fitness and mental wellbeing. Various strategies are employed to achieve these ends, including providing information in readily accessible formats, offering software (platforms and apps) that facilitate patient-to-patient communication, equipping patients or the elderly home with self-care devices or self-tracking apps, installing biosensors in their homes, representing participation as playful or competitive or encouraging people to engage in 'wellness' programmes at school or at work.

Certain design features, such as gamification or the use of happy, smiling, attractive (and assumed 'healthy') images of people on apps and platforms work towards privileging and idealising health, wellness and physical vigour and representing these goals as easily achievable. In some cases, it is assumed that people will take up practices of information seeking, self-care and self-monitoring voluntarily for their own purposes, either privately or as part of communal endeavours to share information. In others, these practices are 'pushed' or imposed on people, with little choice offered to them (Lupton 2016a).

Contemporary strategies and perspectives concerning behaviour change in digital health often conform to the 'nudge' approach. The nudge approach involves commercial, managerial and government actors and agencies working to elicit behaviour change in individuals and groups (Crawshaw 2013; Lupton 1995a; Pykett et al. 2013, 2014). Rather than seeking to exhort people to engage in certain behaviours (or relinquish those that are considered harmful or risky), the nudge approach involves persuasion (Jones et al. 2010). It is therefore a type of 'soft' or 'libertarian

paternalism' that adheres to the Foucauldian model of the governance of populations, in which coercion is largely forsaken in favour of using psychological models
of behaviour change to encourage people to take up self-care practices voluntarily
for their own health, happiness and productivity (Pykett *et al.* 2013).

When nudge is used for digital health purposes, the idea is to provide devices
or software that can remind people to engage in health-promoting behaviours or
push them towards changing their behaviour. Health education strategies have
long relied on approaches to behaviour change that position professionals as educators who need to convey expert knowledge to the uninformed or ill advised.
The mass media have traditionally provided a mode for conveying information
and using techniques of marketing and advertising to disseminate information and
motivate behaviour change in targeted populations (Lupton 1995a; Tulloch and
Lupton 1997). Digital technologies provide even more opportunities for the mass
dissemination of messages and for opportunities to use nudge. The relatively crude
consumer marketing principles of identifying target groups based on shared socioeconomic and attitudinal attributes and designing health campaigns for the mass
media exhorting them to change their behaviour have become superseded. It is
now possible to send individuals and members of target groups messages that are
individualised and tailored to their personalised characteristics and reach them on
their preferred social media platforms. Behaviour change can be closely monitored
for each individual using apps and self-tracking devices.

Healthcare providers, government health promotion initiatives and commercial agencies take variable roles in supporting digitally engaged patienthood and
digital personal health promotion. In some cases, patients are directed by healthcare providers to use self-care practices as part of therapeutic regimens. In others,
the state directly intervenes in seeking to align people with self-care or preventive health objectives by employing targeted advertising or messaging campaigns.
Strong elements of paternalism are evident in the persuasive computing, nudge
and gamification literature, particularly when these approaches are employed in
relation to adopting strategies that encourage behaviour change for responsible self-
management, such as persuading people to give up smoking or excessive drinking,
comply with their prescribed medical regimens or take up physical fitness activities. Indeed, many representations of digital health initiatives portray lay people as
recalcitrant and passive, requiring the help of experts to educate, 'activate' them or
persuade them to engage in and continue behaviours that are deemed appropriately
health-protective.

By focusing on the individual, these technologies tend to reduce health problems to the micro, individual level. Such approaches do little, therefore, to identify
the broader social, cultural and political dimensions of ill health and the reasons
why people may find it difficult to respond to such messages. These practices are
emphasised to the exclusion of other ways of caring for human subjects, such as collective or state-supported initiatives (McGregor 2001). This is despite the current
emphasis in health promotion policy and the new public health that seeks to take a

broader approach to alleviating socioeconomic disadvantage and inequities, develop communities and challenge political interests (Baum 2008; Baum and Fisher 2014; Puska 2007).

★★★

All the digital health technologies I have discussed in this chapter generate continual streams of digital data about human bodies. Concepts such as the digitally engaged patient and the responsible healthy citizen tend to focus on shifting responsibility for care from the clinician to the patient, placing new expectations upon people to manage their health in ways that were traditionally viewed as the preserve of healthcare professionals. The rhetoric of such accounts uses terms such as 'patient empowerment' as well as cost-efficiency as positive outcomes of this shift of responsibility. So too, health promotion discourses represent members of the public as ideally willing to take on responsibility for promoting their health using the latest digital technologies, to the point that they are happy to receive regular messages on their smartphone 'nudging' them into preventive health behaviours or to have their health habits and practices continuously monitored and assessed with an app or wearable device. This is a body/self configured as requiring, and in fact desiring, constant dataveillance. The next chapter addresses the topic of the digitisation and datafication of bodies, health and disease.

3
DIGITISED EMBODIMENT

In this chapter, I address the manifold ways in which human bodies have become increasingly datafied via the use of digital technologies for health and medical purposes. When people engage in activities such as searching online for health and medical information, interact on and upload material about themselves to social media platforms and online discussion forums, use digital patient self-care devices, consult healthcare providers using remote communication technologies, use health and medical apps, play console exergames, employ self-tracking devices to engage in the digital monitoring of their bodies or undergo digital medical scanning tests, they are constantly generating streams of detailed digital data about their bodies. This information can be used to generate a panoply of images and other representations that portray what human bodies look like, how they feel, where they go and what they do.

Imaging and imagining the body in medicine

Digital health initiatives are the latest point in a long history of the use of devices for monitoring and visualising the human body in medicine and public health. Writers in sensory studies have pointed to the growing dominance of the visual in western cultures (Howes and Classen 2013). This turn towards the visual has also been a trend in medical ways of knowing the body. There are many intriguing accounts in medical histories and science and technology studies analysing the ways in which knowledges of the human body have been developed in medicine via visual imagery, often sidelining other sensory modes of knowledge (for example, Burri 2013; Cartwright 1995; Duden 1993; Stafford 1993; van Dijck 2011). Like any mode of representation, medical images are social constructions that are underpinned by tacit assumptions about the value of certain forms of information and modes of representation. They can possess great persuasive power in highlighting some elements of embodiment over others as well as providing explanation and justification for strategies of action in response (van Dijck 2011).

Historically, artists as well as medical scientists have attempted to portray and map the exterior of human bodies and also to look inside them, rendering them more visible, and therefore knowable (Amoore and Hall 2009; Stafford 1993). This included the introduction of anatomical dissections of the body in the Renaissance, in which corpses were cut apart to determine how the inner structures of the body looked and worked. Dissection of the body was viewed as a way of contributing to scientific knowledge and better still to exert authority over disease and death (Richardson 2006). Medical dissection sought to map and contain the human body just as cartographies of landscapes sought to develop authoritative and precise visual images of previously unexplored territories (Amoore and Hall 2009). Amoore and Hall (2009: 449) refer to these images as revealing 'a dark enthralment with bodily surfaces, depths, and interiors which later claims to objectivity and learning ... could not fully mask'. They identify a morality evident in the pleasures of exposing bodily interiors to others, connected to Calvinist doctrines of rigorous self-examination.

By the Enlightenment period, this desire for rendering bodies knowable by amassing information about their visual form and structure took on a more metricised form, as medical researchers sought to impose scientific certainties on the body (Stafford 1993). The development of photography in the mid nineteenth century led to a proliferation of images of the body, both medical and popular. What was considered to be the neutral and scientific accuracy of the photographic image began to achieve primacy in ways of knowing the body (Fox and Lawrence 1988). With these changes in visualising technologies available to document both the interior and exterior of the body, the focus on what could be seen began to take precedence over other sensual ways of knowing, documenting and understanding human embodiment. Medical perception shifted from a multisensory engagement with the patient, including touching, hearing and smelling the body, to focusing on viewing it. Physicians became trained in the operation of the clinical gaze using visualising technologies (Duden 1993; Foucault 1975; van Dijck 2011). Many of these technologies appeared to make the body transparent by producing images of the phenomena that lie beneath the skin: imaging technologies such as the X-ray, the ultrasound, endoscope, electron microscope, computed tomography (CT) and magnetic resonance imaging (MRI) worked to render the interior of the body more visible. They led to a mentality that assumed that the more information that can be gathered about the interior of the body and its physiology, the better (Burri 2013; van Dijck 2011).

With the advent of websites, social media platforms and apps, the internal organs and workings of the body have moved from being exclusively the preserve of medical students and surgeons. Digital medical devices have entered into the public arena of the internet, offering new possibilities for lay people to gaze inside the spectacle of the human body. A vast volume of computerised medical images of human life from conception to death are now readily available online. Tapping in keywords such as 'human anatomy' will call up many apps on the Apple App Store or Google Play which provide such details. While these apps have been explicitly designed for the use of medical and other healthcare students and trainees, they are readily available to any person who may wish to download them.

The Visible Human Project developed by the US National Library of Medicine is an earlier example of how human flesh can be rendered into a digital format and placed on the internet for all to view. The developers of The Visible Human Project used digital technologies to represent in fine detail the anatomical structure of two cadavers (one male and one female). Each body was cross-sectioned transversely from head to toe. Images of the sections of the bodies using MRI and CT scans and anatomical images were uploaded to the Project website. They can also be viewed at the National Museum of Health and Medicine in Washington, DC. A similar web-site, the Visible Embryo, displays images of embryos and fetuses from fertilisation to birth, with a week-by-week display showing the stages of fetal development. The data used for this website were drawn from digitising microscopic cross-sections of human embryo specimens held on slides in the National Institutes of Health's Carnegie Collection of Embryos as well as from three-dimensional (3D) and 4D digital fetal ultrasound images.

Many opportunities are provided on the internet for people who want to view detailed images of surgical and other medical procedures in their full gory detail. YouTube has become a major provider of anatomical and surgical technique vid-eos for medical training. Some medical specialists and surgeons upload images and videos of their work to Snapchat and Instagram, mostly in the effort to promote their services (cosmetic surgeons are in the forefront in this practice). Instagram does not allow users to upload images that are considered too explicit (such as those portraying surgery on breasts or genitals), so some doctors have turned to Snapchat as an alternative forum. One infamous such specialist is Sandra Lee, a dermatologist known as 'Dr Pimple Popper'. Her Instagram photos and YouTube videos showing her at work have received many millions of views. Perhaps the best-known Snapchatting medical specialist is the cosmetic surgeon 'Dr Miami' (Michael Salzhauer), who uploads detailed photos and videos of his surgical procedures (including controversial procedures like labiaplasties, or surgery designed to reshape women's external genitals). 'Dr Miami' is unafraid to Snapchat images of himself brandishing a wad of body fat he has just excised in a tummy tuck. He employs two full-time staff members to manage his social media accounts (Wischhover 2016).

The use of web-streaming services is employed by a number of hospitals to host webcasts of surgical procedures for any interested person to view. The US National Library of Medicine provides a list on its website of several such webcasts with hyperlinks, from numerous different hospitals (US National Library of Medicine 2016). Lay people may now even view live-streamed surgical procedures using a smartphone app and wearing a virtual reality headset to provide a 3D immersive effect, as offered by the Medical Realities company in April 2016. This technology is designed principally for training medical students, but also allows lay people who participate to feel as if they are present in the operating theatre.

Pinterest, an image-curating and sharing platform, features many collections of images related to medical matters. Several of these relate to patient experiences of health (see Chapter 2), but others are curated by medical and nursing students and practising healthcare providers. Some are humorous, featuring memes, cartoons or other images designed to appeal to medical and nursing students and other trainees in the health professions. Other Pinterest photographs feature novelty commodities, again clearly directed to the same audience (for example, anatomical heart or electrocardiogram heart beat cookie cutters, human organ and stethoscope-shaped jewellery, coffee mugs in the shape of spinal vertebrae). While these images are vastly outnumbered by the serious photographs in Pinterest collections that show anatomical images and other medical information (some of which are explicit photographic images that detail flesh, bone and blood), they offer alternative representations of the ways in which human bodies, the experiences of healthcare professionals and students and the practice of healthcare are represented online.

The major differences offered by the latest digital technologies that document and monitor the human body are the continual nature of the surveillance opportunities they present, their expansion from the clinic into domestic and intimate spaces and relationships and their feedback mechanisms, which allow their subjects to 'read' and interpret their own bodies via biometric measurements. Medical practices that were once embodied in the flesh, including the development of doctors' expertise in touching the patient's body and determining what is wrong, have increasingly become rendered into software such as the video conferencing services offered in remote telemedicine technologies. Virtual bodies have been developed for medical training purposes, allowing students to conduct virtual surgery. To achieve this virtuality, the processes by which doctors practise – their customs, habits and ways of thinking – are themselves digitised. Both doctors and patients are rendered into 'informatic "body objects", digital and mathematical constructs that can be redistributed, technologized, and capitalized' (Prentice 2013: 20).

Numerous digital health technologies are directed at illuminating the exterior or interior of the human body with the use of metrics that may represent features of the body as numbers or graphs. The use of apps to collect information about body functions and movements, for example, generates a continuing set of images that represent the body. Biometric data serve first to fragment the body into digitised pieces of information and then to combine these pieces into a recombinant whole that is usually presented in some kind of visual form. Amoore and Hall (2009: 48) use the term 'digitised dissection' to refer to the ways in which biometric whole-body scanners at airports operate. This term is even more apposite when adopted to discuss the fragmentation of bodies in the context of digital health. Digital technologies are able to peer into the recesses of the body in ever-finer detail, creating new anatomical atlases.

The Human Genome Project offers another example at an even greater scale of digital detailing of the human body at the molecular level. This is the world's largest collaborative scientific endeavour to date. Scientists involved in the Project sought to identify and sequence every gene and its variations in the human genome. This was accomplished in 2003. Specialised software has contributed to this mapping and further investigations into human genetic sequencing, including attempts to discover the genetic bases for diseases. Indeed, in some discourses of digital health, the human genetic code is identified as one aspect of digitising the body, given that it represents embodiment as a code. For example, Topol (2012) describes the possibilities of 'digitising humans' by identifying their genomic coding and monitoring and measuring their bodily functions and activities in fine detail using digital technologies.

Social media and self-representation

It is not only medical technologies that have contributed to new forms of digitised embodiment. Many popular forums facilitate the uploading of images and other forms of bodily representations to the internet for others to view. Pregnancy, childbirth and infant development represent major topics for self-representation and image sharing on social media. Since the early years of the internet, online forums and discussion boards have provided places for parents (and particularly women) to seek information and advice about pregnancy, childbirth and parenting as well as share their own experiences. Apps can be now be used to track pregnancy stages, symptoms and appointments and document time-lapse selfies featuring the expansion of pregnant women's 'baby bumps'. Fetal ultrasound images are routinely posted on Facebook, Twitter, Instagram and YouTube by excited expectant parents (Lupton 2013b; Lupton and Thomas 2015; Thomas and Lupton 2015).

Some parents continue the documentation of their new baby's lives by sharing photographs and videos of the moment of their birth (Longhurst 2009) and milestones (first steps, words uttered and so on) on social media. Wearable devices and monitoring apps allow parents to document their infants' biometrics, such as their sleeping, feeding, breathing, body temperature and growth patterns (Lupton and Williamson 2017). The genre of 'mommy blogs' also offers opportunities for women to upload images of themselves while pregnant and their babies and young children, as well as providing detailed descriptions of their experiences of pregnancy and motherhood (Morrison 2011). These media provide a diverse array of forums for portraying and describing details of infants' and young children's embodiment. A survey of 2,000 British parents' use of social media for sharing their young children's images conducted by an internet safety organisation estimated that the average parent would have posted almost 1,000 images to Facebook (and, to a much lesser extent, Instagram) by the time their child reached the age of five (Knowthenet 2015). Contemporary children, therefore, now often have an established digital profile before they are even born, offering an archive of their physical development and growth across their lifespans.

As described in Chapter 2, people with medical conditions are now able to upload descriptions and images of their bodies to social media to share with the world. YouTube offers a platform for such images, but they are also shared on other social media such as Facebook, Instagram, Tumblr, Snapchat and Pinterest. Pinterest offers a multitude of humorous memes and images with inspirational slogans designed to provide support to people with various conditions such as chronic illness or mental health conditions. Humorous memes include one with a drawing of a young woman sitting on a bed with her hand over her face and the words 'Why are there never any good side effects? Just once I'd like to read a medication bottle that says, "May cause extreme sexiness"'. Other images about chronic illness are less positive, used to express people's despair, pain or frustration in struggling with conditions such as autoimmune diseases, endometriosis and diabetes. Examples include a meme featuring a photo of a person with head bowed down (face obscured) and the words 'When your chronic illness triggers depression' and another showing a young woman's face transposed over an outline of her body with the text: 'The worst thing you can do to a person with an invisible illness is make them feel like they need to prove how sick they are'.

Individuals with disabilities have also employed blogs and platforms like Tumblr, Instagram and YouTube to express their experiences publicly as part of seeking to change public perceptions of the disability (Ellcessor 2016; Ginsburg 2012). Disability activists have made extensive use of online forums and social media, particularly Facebook and Twitter in recent years, to agitate for social or political change (Ellcessor 2016; Ellis *et al.* 2015). For example, activists have used online forums to debate definitions of disability (Cimini 2010) and autism (Giles 2014).

The increased visibility offered by online media to the portrayal of human embodiment in all its diversity, states of health or ill health and stages of development means that features of corporeality that may previously have been hidden or considered too private are now on public display. The process of dying and the dead body have also received coverage on digital media. It is now possible for audiences to find images of death and dying at all phases of human life. Social media platforms host images of corpses and first-person accounts of dying. One example that created controversy in the news media was the Instagram account of a US pathologist. She posted hundreds of images of autopsied corpses on her account, claiming it to be a form of public education (Anonymous 2015). Another website, Unidentified Dead Bodies, has been established in India as a public service to assist with the identification of corpses. It features images of the bodies and details about where they were found, asking viewers to contact police or the coroner in charge of the case with any information they may have about the dead people portrayed on the site (Unidentified Dead Bodies 2016). A Chicago medical examiner's office has undertaken a similar exercise, posting photographs on its website of unidentified bodies that have come in for examination (Anonymous 2013).

Many memorial blogs and YouTube videos feature parents mourning pregnancy loss and stillborn infants, often featuring images of the dead fetuses or infants (Lupton 2013b). Some people who have confronted a fatal illness have blogged about their experiences, presenting a textual and sometimes visual portrayal of their last days. There are numerous videos posted on YouTube showing the end-of-life stages of mortally ill people, death and after-death scenes posted by friends or family members of the dead. These are the kind of images of the dying and dead human body that until the advent of the internet would have received little or no exposure.

'Selfie' portraits enable people to photograph themselves in various forms of embodiment. A popular hashtag on Instagram is #fitspo (or 'fit inspiration'), used to refer to images people upload of themselves, including selfies, showing them eating healthy food, engaging in sporting and fitness activities and displaying how fit and trim they look in their exercise wear. The idea behind the #fitspo tag is that others who are interested in improving their physical fitness can follow these very fit-looking people, pay attention to any tips they may have for achieving the levels of fitness and good health that they display and be motivated to aspire to these achievements. Some people who contribute to the #fitspo genre have earned a good living in endorsing fitness wear and other related products.

In stark contrast, another genre of Instagram selfie culture involves people seeking to support body-positive and body acceptance ideals using hashtags like #fatpositive and #fatacceptance. They post selfies showing off their fat bodies in the attempt to challenge dominant assumptions about fatness as unhealthy and unattractive. Some people with disabilities have also posted selfies to draw attention to disabled embodiment. This includes young people showing off their amputated limbs, colostomy bags or insulin pumps and older women baring their chests to reveal their mastectomy scars. Survivors of rape and sexual abuse have also uploaded selfies to public forums as a means of expressing and drawing attention to their experiences and agitating for social change.

There is another genre of selfies showing subjects experiencing ill health or medical treatment. These include self-portraits taken by celebrities in hospital receiving treatment for injuries. A larger category of health and medical-related selfies includes those that show people in a clinical or hospital setting undergoing treatment, experiencing symptoms or in their recovery after surgery. Among the social media platforms available for such representation, Tumblr is favoured as a forum for posting more provocative images that challenge accepted norms of embodiment. One example is Karolyn Gehrig, who uses the #HospitalGlam hashtag when posting selfies featuring her self-identified 'queer/disabled' body in hospital settings. Gehrig has a chronic illness requiring regular hospital visits, and uses the selfie genre to draw attention to what it is like to live with this kind of condition. The photographs she posts of herself include portraits in hospital waiting and treatment rooms in glamour-style poses. She engages in this practice as a form of seeking agency and control in settings that many people find alienating, shaming and uncertain (Tembeck 2016).

People who upload selfies or other images of themselves or status updates about their behaviour on social media are engaging in technologies of the self. They seek to present a certain version of self-identity to the other users of the sites as part of strategies of ethical self-formation (Sauter 2014; Tembeck 2016; van Dijck 2013b). In the context of the 'like economy' of social media (which refers to the positive responses that users receive from other users on platforms like Facebook, Twitter and Instagram) (Gerlitz and Helmond 2013), users of these platforms are often highly aware of how they represent themselves. This may involve sharing information about a medical condition or self-tracking fitness or weight loss data (Stragier *et al.* 2015) as a way of demonstrating that the person is adhering to the ideal subject position of responsibilised self-care and health promotion.

It can be difficult for users to juggle competing imperatives when sharing information about themselves online. Young women, in particular, are faced with negotiating self-representation practices on social media that conform to accepted practices of fun-loving femininity, attractive sexuality or disciplined self-control over their diet and body weight but do not stray into practices that may open them to disparagement for being 'slutty', fat, too drunk or otherwise lacking self-control, too vain or self-obsessed or physically unattractive (Brown and Gregg 2012; Ferreday 2003; Hutton *et al.* 2016).

It is also important to acknowledge that, as part of self-representation, people may also seek to use their social media forums to resist health promotion messages: by showing themselves enjoying using illicit drugs or alcoholic drinking to excess, for example. Fat activists have also benefited from the networking opportunities offered by blogs and social media to work against fat shaming and promote positive representations of fat bodies (Cooper 2011; Dickins *et al.* 2011; Lupton 2013a; N Smith *et al.* 2015). In these and other cases referred to earlier, a more challenging political orientation in the use of social media is discernible, as people seek to draw attention to the illnesses with which they are living and to the deficiencies in broader understandings, funding arrangements, treatment options or government policies concerning these conditions.

More controversially, those individuals who engage in proscribed body modification practices, such as self-harm, steroid use for body building or the extreme restriction of food intake (as in 'pro-anorexia' and 'thinspiration' communities), have made use of social media sites to connect with likeminded individuals (Boero and Pascoe 2012; Center for Innovative Public Health Research 2014; Ging and Garvey 2017; N Smith *et al.* 2015). Most social media platforms have policies in place to prohibit these kinds of interactions, but in practice many users manage to evade them. The platforms have a difficult task, because they want to support people's attempts to communicate with each other about their management of and recovery from health conditions like self-harm or eating disorders but are loath to be viewed as promoting the efforts of those resisting recovery and promoting these behaviours. Their attempts to police the representation of nude human bodies for fear of contributing to pornography are also controversial. Until it changed its policy in 2014, Facebook was the subject of trenchant critique for censoring photographs that women have tried to share on the platform portraying them breastfeeding their infants because of concerns that they were showing their nipples, a body part that Facebook usually prohibits in users' posts because they are deemed to be obscene. Facebook's new policy also allowed mastectomy survivors to post images of their postoperative bare torsos, even when nipples were displayed (Chemaly 2014).

Digital self-tracking

Many people choose to datafy themselves by using digital self-tracking devices to collect detailed information about their bodies and behaviours. Like medical visualising technologies, digital self-tracking devices operate by delving inside the body, eliciting data on internal functioning and then rendering these data visible. As I detailed in Chapter 2, smartphone apps, smartwatches and other wearable devices and digital gaming consoles can digitally document an array of bodily attributes and functions. The most intimate and personal aspects of human bodies are now open to digitisation and datafication. Menstrual cycle and fertility monitoring apps for women are among the most popular in the app stores, as are those for pregnant women to monitor their bodies and those of their fetuses. Insertible vaginal digital devices can be used to track women's pelvic floor exercises, sending data to their smartphone app demonstrating their progress. Another set of apps encourages people to monitor their sexual activity based on factors such as frequency, body movements and sounds emitted during sex. Apps can record details of people's mood and their mental health states. Some apps and platforms now incorporate photographs as part of self-tracking data collection. The athletic self-tracking platform Strava, for example, has a 'Strava Stories' feature which enables members to incorporate photographs they have taken on their cycle, run or walk with their other metric data.

Quantification of bodily features and algorithmic manipulation of personal data are important dimensions of these new forms of datafication. The data collected by these devices and software are rendered into visual form for users to view: often by way of graphs and comparative metrics. According to Apple's announcement of its Health app,

> 'How are you?' now has a really accurate answer … Heart rate, calories burned, blood sugar, cholesterol — your health and fitness apps are great at collecting all that data. The new Health app puts that data in one place, accessible with a tap, giving you a clear and current overview of your health.
>
> *(iOS8 Preview: Health 2014)*

As with many other health-related self-tracking apps the Health app provides 'dashboards' that visualise body data such as sleep patterns and calories burned (yet another mechanical metaphor for representing human embodiment). It is these data, as presented in this way, which are portrayed as denoting what 'health' means. As this description suggests, understanding and articulating how healthy one feels is more accurate if digital data are employed rather than relying on an individual's subjective sense of wellbeing.

A dominant discourse underpinning accounts of self-tracking for health or fitness purposes refers to the importance of generating self-knowledge as part of optimising life. The use of digital devices is portrayed as contributing invaluable insights that otherwise could not be developed using other forms of knowledge production. Thus, for example, the Wellocracy website, which advertises itself as

'Your trusted source for personal health tracking' describes the data generated from self-tracking as follows:

> Your activity tracker data isn't just a bunch of numbers and computer codes: It's an invaluable source of information about YOU. Data catches the hidden moments that have eluded us in the past, shining a bright light on our blind spots, providing us with greater insight about how our behavior impacts all aspects of our lives. Through this new self-knowledge, we can begin to implement positive change. Staying on top of our data can help integrate these good habits into our everyday lives.
>
> *(Understanding Your Data 2014)*

The digitised data assemblages that are configured via self-tracking technologies are the newest forms of 'informatic bodies' (Waldby 2000). When behaviours and body functions are digitised as quantifiable data, indicators and concepts of health and fitness become narrow representations of these phenomena. Health and well-being become represented by certain numbers that are collected by a self-tracking device, game app or sensor-embedded smart object. Accounts of self-tracking for health and medical purposes are beginning to describe a data entity generated from an individual's different personal data sets. Thus, writing recently for *Nature Biotechnology*, Kish and Topol (2015) describe the 'external wisdom of the body' that these data sets comprise while Swan (2013) makes reference to the 'extended exoself' configured by self-tracking data.

In such accounts, using digital technologies for recording details about one's body is represented as offering digitised data that are more reliable than fallible human perception, offering greater truth and meaning. Digital data are privileged over the haptic sensations people feel from their bodies, and represented as able to uncover hidden illness or disease that might otherwise not be detected using phenomenological experiences of embodiment. These portrayals of digital self-monitoring suggest that order and control over what might otherwise be an unpredictable (because unknowable or mysterious) body may be instituted via digital and metric knowledges. Data, metrics and algorithms are represented as neutral and accurate, far removed from the messy contingencies and uncertainties of the body and its ills and the distressing or unsettling emotions associated with these. Human cognition, memory, perception and sensation are represented as unreliable and inaccurate because they are 'unscientific'. They are born of fallible fleshly embodiment rather than the supposedly objective data that are generated by computer software and hardware.

People who use digital devices to track their body metrics voluntarily often upload the detailed data that they have collected to the internet to share with others on social media sites or fitness or weight loss platforms (Fotopoulou and O'Riordan 2017; Lupton 2016a, 2017b; Smith and Vonthethoff 2017; Stragier *et al.* 2015). Self-trackers may invite their friends and followers to comment on their metrics: the net of surveillance is thus expanded around the self-tracker's body. These interactions contribute to processes of datafication of the human body, and distribute modes of watching from self-surveillance to social and intimate surveillance. One example of this phenomenon is a US woman with diabetes. This woman uses social media to help manage her condition, as well as home-based technologies to monitor her blood glucose levels. She regularly reports, on her blog and via Twitter, her daily activities and symptoms: what she ate for breakfast, what her blood readings are or how much exercise she has engaged in that day. This woman's motivation for providing these details to her readers and followers is the support they in turn give her in managing her condition. As she is quoted as saying:

> Because I have people who follow me in Twitter it means I have some kind of audience that is caring for me in the background. It's helpful if I'm having a rough day, if things are not going so well with my blood sugar. I find support there, and it keeps me in line too.
>
> *(Hawn 2009: 365)*

The skilful manipulation and portrayal of personal data can be a key factor of this type of social surveillance. The 'show and tell' presentations on the Quantified Self and other self-tracking forums are often very complex and aesthetically appealing, conforming to the appeal of the 'data spectacle' (Gregg 2015). The pleasures of 'showing and telling' in these formats, therefore, include not only engaging in the opportunity to let other interested people know about the insights about oneself that the tracker has garnered, but also to display prowess in making these data beautiful or easy to understand. Such communications of personal data seek to attract the interest and attention of other people and participate in the communal and sharing ethos that is an integral dimension of the Quantified Self movement. They have strong performative dimensions in revealing both how a presenter's self-tracking efforts have improved that person's life and also how adept she or he is at manipulating self-tracking technologies and data materialisations and thereby facilitating sharing of the data with others (Barta and Neff 2016; Lupton 2016a, 2017b; Nafus and Sherman 2014; Smith and Vonthethoff 2017).

3D printed self-replicas and organs

While digital data materialisations of human bodies tend to be 2D, the development of 3D printing technologies allows for tangible manifestations of personal health and medical information. A new way of representing selfhood and embodiment has emerged in the wake of the development of 3D printing technologies. This is the 3D printed self-replica, a fabrication using digital 3D body scans of people that produces a material artefact of a person's entire body or parts thereof. Full figurines of people made in this way are usually miniature in size, while separate body parts replicas, such as a head-and-shoulders bust, may be life-sized. These artefacts are advertised as promoting opportunities for personal memorabilia and record keeping about people's life events, interests and families. 3D printed self-replicas can be ordered from 3D printing companies and can even be made at home using a soft-ware package developed for the Xbox Kinect game box or a home 3D scanner in conjunction with a home 3D printer. Some commentators have begun to refer to the 3D printed self-replica as a new form of 'selfie'.

Medical imaging technologies can be used to create products for the commer-cial market as novelties. One company offers a service which turns MRI brain scans into full-scale replicas of the brain, which can be mounted on a stand and displayed at home (Grunewald 2014). The company also produces earrings, pendants and cufflinks for customers in the shape of their brains. As the company suggests, this process will allow customers to 'hold your brain in your hands!' and wearing the brain jewellery would be 'great for conferences and talks' (Brainform 2015). Artist Brendon McNaughton offers customers the opportunity to use their MRI heart scans to create a larger-than-life model of their hearts covered in shiny 22-carat gold leaf; enabling them to display their literal 'heart of gold'. 3D ultrasound imag-ing is now being used to produce life-sized figurines of human fetuses for their expectant parents to hold and display. A Californian company calling itself '3D Babies' provides this service, as well as fabricating newborn infant replicas using photographs supplied by the parents. These replicas are marketed on the company's site as offering an 'artistic sculpture for your display case', 'memorabilia for baby's room', 'centrepiece for baby shower', a way to 'share the news of your pregnancy' or to use at a 'gender reveal' party (3D Babies 2014).

The use of what has been dubbed 'patient specific 3D printed organ replicas' (models of patients' organs using data from MRI, ultrasound and CT scans) in sur-gery, medical training and doctor–patient communication is also beginning to be discussed and researched in the medical literature (Moody 2014). Such replicas can be manufactured in separate parts to demonstrate the internal as well as external view of an organ or other body part, and they can be made transparent to allow a better view inside it. They allow surgeons to look closely at the body part's structure and plan or practise surgical interventions before cutting into the patient's body. These anatomical models can also be employed as diagnostic tools. One example is the use of a 3D printed anatomical replica of a diseased infant's brain and part of its skull by a surgeon in Brazil. The surgeon used the replica to visualise the condition for diagnosis, plan the complicated surgery that was required and as a reference during surgery (Krassenstein 2014a). Another intriguing case is provided on a 3D printing blog of a man who was not medically trained but expert in 3D imaging and printing, and thus was able to use the CT scans that had been made of his spine to produce a fabrication of it. Having done so he was able finally to identify a long-term condition for which his doctors had failed to find a diagnosis (Krassenstein 2014b).

3D organ replicas are increasingly employed as part of educational practices, both for medical students or surgical trainees and for patients. Researchers are working on fabricating models of human body parts for teaching anatomy to medical stu-dents in lieu of cadavers (West 2014). Patient-specific 3D printed organ replicas are employed in some hospitals to communicate information to patients about their conditions and assist doctors in obtaining informed consent for procedures (Sher 2014). The replicas are made and shown to patients so that they can not only see but also touch them and their doctors can point to features on the replica to explain the problem and how they intend to treat it. It is contended that such replicas offer more explanatory power to doctors when explaining complex medical matters to their patients than do 2D representations or simply verbal communication (Moody 2014; Sher 2014).

3D fabrication may also be employed to represent more abstract features of human bodies. Human–computer interaction researchers have been experimenting with ways of using 3D digital body objects as an educational tool for assisting people in understanding the personal digital data that they collect from self-tracking efforts. For example, Stusak and colleagues (2014) developed what they entitled 'data sculptures' from participants' running activity data. In a three-week field study, they investigated the impact of four different types of sculptures on the participants' running activity, the personal and social behaviours that the sculptures generated and their reactions to receiving the physical tokens of the runs. The digital data that the participants generated from each of their runs over this period were individually rendered via 3D printing into a discrete unique component that could be added with other components produced in the study to make a larger sculpture. The idea of this was to incite interest and enthusiasm from the participants as they sought to build their own customised sculpture with each piece and to encourage them to reflect on their data.

The 3D material rendering of the human body or parts thereof represents a specific type of code/space; a fabricated bodily form of digital data that may be a miniaturised version (as in 3D self-replica figurines), life-sized (as in the customised anatomical replicas used in medicine) or a non-body shape (as in the data artefacts and sculptures generated from physical activity tracking in the experiments described above). What is particularly intriguing about 3D printed body objects is that they represent the re-materialisation of digital data as solid, tangible objects extruded from a 3D printer. 3D body fabrications, like any form of data visualisation (such as graphs or other 2D portrayals), constitute an attempt to fix these data assemblages at a certain point in time in a specific context. The physical assemblages that are configured of the human body via 3D printing techniques are material manifestations of the coming together of human and non-human actors. These include the human flesh that is rendered into a different form via digitisation and fabrication, but also the human actors who operate and use the technologies that produce this object and the range of non-human actors that bring the object into being, including digital software, the materials that are used to form the shapes and the machinery that extrudes and lays down the materials to form the object.

We can see in the fabricated body in medicine and health a return to the haptic, or the sensation of touch, as part of representing and understanding human bodies. There are limits to the sensory affordances of the non-organic 3D digital body object, however. Non-organic anatomical replicas, of course, do not provide the types of haptic and other sensual cues that organic human flesh and bone does. Unlike the organic objects that are fabricated using 3D bioprinting techniques, while these objects may be touched and held, they are still cold and stiff, lacking the tactile and olfactory properties of human flesh and bone. Interestingly, some of the supporting argument for why such models are superior to cadavers for medical training is the fact that they combine the anatomical accuracy (as in detailed replicas of human organs) and physical materiality (students can handle them) of human flesh, without what is represented as the repugnant features of dead bodies such as their smell, tendency to deteriorate and cultural or religious distastes or prohibitions against using dead bodies for medical training (Monash University 2014). 3D objects of the human body, or parts of it, allow the fleshly body to interact with the digitised physical materialisation of that same body. Flesh and bone are rendered into another material form (usually made of some kind of plastic) that can then be viewed, picked up and handled by the body from which the object is derived.

3D printing technologies offer the possibility of producing fabricated forms of embodiment that are uniquely customised. Patients can not only see but touch and handle a plastic model of their own organs; self-trackers can grasp an object that is a tangible representation of their bodily activities, movements or functions. A circuit of making, meaning and representation, of digital fragmentation of the body and subsequent solidification of these data, is created whereby human bodies emit digital data, which may then be used to construct 2D digital models for 3D printers to turn back into material digital body objects. People who handle these fabricated objects may then change their behaviours accordingly, thus generating a different set of digital data that may produce different objects … and so on. The agency of the non-human actor on which writers who adopt a sociomaterial perspective insist is all too obvious in this circuit.

Digitised cyborg assemblages

In previous eras, the human body was often conceptualised and portrayed as a mechanical object: as a workshop full of instruments and tools, for example, or in the industrial age with metaphors representing the body as a combustion engine (Lupton 2012). With the development of computing technologies, these earlier concepts have not necessarily disappeared, but have been augmented by novel formulations that portray bodies or their parts as digital technologies. Medicine and public health have become increasingly represented and experienced as a digitised information science, creating a new medical cosmology and new forms of technological embodiment. Humans became represented as 'organic computers' (Berman 1989), disease as a form of computerised information malfunction (Haraway 1985) and their genetic makeup as types of computerised codes (Nelkin and Tancredi 1994). The brain and nervous system, in particular, have attracted visual imagery and metaphors that represent them as computerised communication and processing devices (Lupton 2012). Such representations transform humans into information repositories, configured not merely by machine-like parts but now also the aggregation of tiny components that are visible and knowable only by digital technologies.

The concept of the cyborg has often been employed to describe the ways in which human bodies intersect and interact with technologies. This concept acknowledges that the boundaries between humans and technologies are blurred and ambiguous, generating novel forms of assemblages (Haraway 1995; Lupton 1995b). In this era of enhanced and increasing digitising of humans as part of the configuration of digital data assemblages, a new form of cyborg is generated: the digital cyborg assemblage (Lupton 2015d). New formulations of digitised bodies need to allow for the dynamic nature of digital knowledges and practices of embodiment that involve ever-shifting hybrid forms acting cybernetically as data generated in real time lead to responsive changes, which produce more and different data and so on. The concept of the digital cyborg assemblage moves on from the more static concept of the cyborg to represent the dynamic nature of contemporary digitised bodies in the context of lively devices and lively data.

Digital cyborg assemblages are configured when human actors interact with digital technologies. As prosthetic technologies, digital devices extend the capacities of the body by supplying data that can then be used to display the body's limits and capabilities and allow users to employ these data to work upon themselves and present themselves in certain ways. The digital data assemblages that are thus configured comprise new forms of embodiment. They have their own social lives and materiality, quite apart from the fleshy bodies from which they are developed (Lupton 2016a, 2016b). I would contend, therefore, that cyberspace or virtual reality may now be conceptualised as the data that digital devices produce, which can be visualised, algorithmically interpreted and shared with others if we so desire. In other words, the new cyberspace/virtual reality is the data archive of the body that is stored when these data are transmitted to devices, online platforms or the cloud, as well as the myriad of ways of visually representing the body in social media and other digital forums.

Digital data assemblages are constantly created and recreated when information about individuals is derived via surveillance technologies and then reassembled for various purposes. These technologies create and recreate certain types of data assemblages which can then be scrutinised, monitored and used for various purposes, including intervention. Writing about the dataveillance of human bodies, Elmer (2003: 611) contends that:

> The observed body is of a distinctly hybrid composition. First it is broken down by being abstracted from its territorial setting. It is then reassembled in different settings through a series of data flows. The result is a decorporealized body, a 'data-double' of pure virtuality.

Yet it may also be argued that the body as it is produced via digital technologies is far from being 'decorporealised'. While the abstracted data assemblage produced through biometric measurements and health surveillance technologies that are able to identify 'at-risk' individuals may be categorised as a virtual cyberbody, this assemblage feeds back information to the user in ways that are intended to encourage the user's body to act in certain ways. The flow of information, therefore, is not one-way or static: it is part of a continual loop of the production of health-related data and response to these data.

This assemblage also calls into question previous representations of the cyborg, in which utopian ideas about the use of technology in transcending the imperatives and constraints of the fleshly body were often dominant (Buse 2010; Lupton 1995b). The digitised cyborg assemblage configured by digital health technologies, in contrast, supports a reflexive, self-monitoring awareness of the body, bringing the body to the fore in ways that challenge the non-reflexive, absent body (Leder 1990). The body is hardly able to disappear when its functions, movements and habits are constantly monitored and the user of digital technologies is continually made aware, via feedback, of these dispositions.

★★★

There are many implications of the types of datafication practices I have outlined in this chapter. They raise questions, such as how people are coming to understand, manage and represent their bodies and how students and practising professionals in medicine and public health learn about and represent human bodies and intervene in health and illness states. Such practices encourage people to engage in various kinds of voluntary dataveillance, both of themselves and others. They can take up self-surveillance, social surveillance and intimate surveillance by using digital devices and software to monitor, measure, record and share their own and others' personal details.

It is important to emphasise that datafication practices are structured by the affordances of the technologies. Only certain types of information about the bodies and practices of the humans who use them are collected by digital health technologies. This information is returned or presented to the users in specified ways. Users generally cannot manipulate what data are collected or the ways in which data are selected for their viewing beyond the parameters that have been set by the developers of these devices. The same is true for websites, apps and social media platforms. Here again, users must accept the terms and conditions of the software and the structures of use that they offer. In the context of the digital data economy, these structures and affordances have implications for what kinds of personal details users offer up to developers and how various parties access and share these details. The next chapter goes on to investigate these issues by discussing the manifold uses of big digital health data.

4

BIG DIGITAL HEALTH DATA

In the previous chapter, I reviewed the manifold ways in which human bodies and health and disease states have become datafied, or rendered into digital data assemblages. These assemblages come together with other people's personal data to form much larger data sets – or big data – that can be combined in almost endless variations for analysis about illness, disease and health-related behaviours at the population level. Much attention has been paid in recent years to the potential of big data to contribute to medical knowledge, the delivery of healthcare, the practice of health promotion and disease surveillance. Corporate actors also view big data as important sources of information and valuable commodities. In this chapter I address the issue of big health data in more detail, paying particular attention to the various and diverse claims that are made for the possibilities of these data across a range of domains and sectors. The chapter ends with a discussion of the significant privacy and security risks to which people's personal health and medical data are exposed.

Patient data and health informatics

Discussions about the potential of big data about health and illness have had a major impact upon healthcare and public health policy and practice. There is now much focus on the power of the vast data archives gathered by digital technologies, both to inform patients about their own bodies and health states and also to provide information to healthcare providers about the health states of populations and the use of healthcare. The data-utopian viewpoint is aptly suggested in the headline of a post for the digital technology blog Gigaom: 'Better medicine, brought to you by big data' (Harris 2012). The author outlines such medical data activities as: computerised genomic sequencing; the analysis of medical record data by hospitals to help reduce medical errors, facilitate better expenditure, improve patient care and contribute to the planning of medical trials; the use of medical data for research projects; using software to sift through medical journals to review major findings; analysing patient data for early diagnosis and preventive medicine; and identifying patterns in patients' contributions to social media platforms.

The opportunity to collect highly detailed information in real time, aggregate data on one patient across a long period or join up sets of data from many patients and tag these data for ready retrieval are features that did not exist prior to the expansion of ubiquitous mobile devices and sensors embedded in objects and locations. Many details about patients are generated and uploaded to databases when they attend healthcare facilities and providers. Most medical practices use digital forms of record keeping of patient details, including their demographic details and information about their health status, drug prescriptions and treatment regimens. A specialised field of research, health informatics, is devoted to researching the design, development and application of such data-gathering systems in healthcare and for health policy purposes. These data can be employed for purposes such as health profiling for targeting treatment and illness prevention strategies. Thus, for example, in Australia some hospitals are trialling a digital data system, the Patient Admission and Prediction tool, that is designed to predict the days and time of day when demands on their emergency systems are likely to be greatest based on their electronic records. They are using these data to manage their staffing and other resources to ensure that patients' needs will be better and more quickly met and costs will be reduced (CSIRO 2016).

The term 'patient-generated data' has begun to be employed in the medical literature as a part of health informatics. This term refers to the various ways in which details about patients are generated predominantly outside the clinic setting by the patients themselves or by their family members and other caregivers (Wike 2013). These details are generally gathered voluntarily through self-tracking efforts, using remote monitoring self-care devices and uploading material to social media platforms, or as part of routine transactions online, such as searching for health information. Several hospitals in the USA are working on integrating the data from patients' self-tracking devices with their electronic medical records. This step has been facilitated by the availability of these personal data devices, changing models of payment for healthcare in the USA and the development of software which assists hospitals in merging these different sources of patient data. For example, a health system in North Carolina, Carolinas Healthcare, has developed an app platform that allows patients to download their personal data from more than 70 mobile digital devices, including heart rate monitors, blood pressure monitors, body weight scales, physical activity trackers and blood glucose meters. These data are stored in the same portal as the patients' electronic medical record and can be accessed by their healthcare providers or carers if the patients give their consent (Wicklund 2016b).

The concept of 'precision' or 'personalised' medicine is often employed when the benefits of gathering detailed information about individuals' bodies are discussed in the medical and health informatics literature. Precision medicine rests on the idea that the more unique information that can be generated about individuals, including their medical history, current health state, genetic profile, lifestyle and living environment, the better their bodies can be assessed, monitored, diagnosed and medically treated. The Obama administration strongly advocated for the precision medicine approach. President Obama announced a Precision Medicine Initiative in his State of the Union address in January 2015. A press release from the administration described the initiative as 'a new model of patient-powered research that promises to accelerate biomedical discoveries and provide clinicians with new tools, knowledge, and therapies to select which treatments will work best for which patients' (The White House Press Office 2015). The initiative is funding the National Institutes of Health, the National Cancer Institute, the Food and Drug Administration and the Office of the National Coordinator for Health Information Technology to conduct data-gathering projects to contribute to developing better understandings of the individual contributors to disease, prevention and medical treatment.

The ideals of open data and citizen access to data are espoused in such programmes. The White House announcement of the Precision Medicine Initiative made reference to the need for 'open, responsible data sharing' of the medical information that would be collected (The White House Press Office 2015). In November 2015, the White House released a document outlining privacy and trust principles for this initiative. This document notes that participants should have access to the data that they generate for the initiative as well as to the findings of research based on aggregated data from the various projects that are involved in 'consumer-friendly' ways (The White House 2015). US citizens have a legal right to access their patient records and their medical information from other sources, such as their health insurer and pharmacies. The Consumer eHealth Program encourages them to do this and to then to take 'action' on the information as part of the objective 'to help all of us make better choices to maintain and improve health' (Consumer eHealth Program 2016: no page number given).

Recent innovations in online technologies directed at eliciting data voluntarily from patients have explored ways to connect diverse sources of data for the use of both patients and healthcare providers. Initiatives are developing that involve providing lay people with access to the records that their healthcare providers generate on them. Patients are now often encouraged to use web-based personal health repositories like Microsoft HealthVault to keep records of their symptoms and treatments, document progress towards their fitness goals, view their medical test results and facilitate communication with healthcare providers. The Consumer eHealth Program run by the US Office of the National Coordinator for Health IT is directly targeted at patient engagement, as outlined on its website, where it is noted that the program seeks to achieve 'the empowerment of individuals to improve their health and health care through Health IT' (Consumer eHealth Program 2016: no page number given).

The arena of clinical trials for new drugs is one form of medical knowledge generation where crowdsourcing using patient-focused social media platforms has been employed for some years as an alternative to the expensive traditional format of the standard clinical trial. This approach has drawn on the self-interest and voluntary labour of patients and their willingness to self-experiment rather than to be co-opted into the traditional randomised controlled trial to contribute to the innovation process (Cooper 2012).

The recruitment of patients for clinical trials with patient support sites has now become more formalised. PatientsLikeMe, for example, has developed tools for matching registered users with global clinical trials of new therapies and drugs, while SmartPatients provides direct information and information feeds about clinical trials to users. Medical researchers are also experimenting with providing patients with proprietary health- or fitness-tracking wearable devices to gather data for research. Thus, for example, a hospital in the US state of Minnesota is using Fitbit to collect information about the sleeping and physical activity habits of child patients with type 1 diabetes. They are using these data to determine how these habits affect the patients' condition and treatment (Wicklund 2016c).

Major internet companies are also seeking to collect and use big health data in a variety of ways. In 2015, Apple announced ResearchKit, an app framework that enables users to donate their personal data to medical research projects (ResearchKit 2015). In early 2016 the company introduced CareKit, another app framework that allows users to set up a system by which they can track their medical conditions, medications and treatments and transfer their health data to healthcare professionals and caregivers of their choice. According to Apple's press release announcing CareKit, this software framework 'helps developers empower people to take a more active role in their health' (Apple 2016). The developers nominated in the press release as already working with CareKit included Glow, which is incorporating its pregnancy app, Glow Nurture, into the CareKit modules established by Apple. Apple also has a relationship with the direct-to-consumer personal genomics company 23andMe. Under this arrangement, 23andMe sends its genomic data to two ResearchKit apps, Asthma Health and MyHeart Counts. The concept was lauded as allowing data from three separate data sets – genomic data, medical records and self-tracked biometrics – to be combined in unprecedented ways to provide insights into individuals' health and also generate data at a population level.

Google has also introduced a massive initiative directed at health, Verily (formerly entitled Google Life Sciences). According to the project's website, Verily will 'use technology to create a true picture of human health' (Verily 2016). The focus of Verily is on using big data to assist preventive medicine efforts. The company has employed medical, data analytic, chemist and IT engineering experts to engage in projects that involve bringing together health and medical data from different sources to identify patterns in the determinants of illness and disease. It is targeting major conditions such as heart disease, cancer and mental illness (Piller 2015). The project is starting with an initial baseline study, the Cohort Program, in which volunteers contribute their genetic and molecular details and also use biometric tracking devices to collect data on their heart rate, blood oxygen levels and heart rhythms and the contact lens recently developed by Google that monitors blood glucose levels. The researchers will then analyse the data to identify sets of biomarkers that may predict the emergence of disease. The concept is to generate data that will lead to insights into how diseases emerge in healthy bodies. This pilot study is envisaged as the initial point of a much larger study involving a million or more US citizens (Barr 2014).

In the UK, Google has partnered with the National Health Service (NHS) to engage in a data-sharing agreement. Google's DeepMind artificial intelligence company will be using NHS patient data from three major London hospitals, including historical medical records dating back five years. Some of these data will be used to build an app called Streams, which is designed to help hospital staff monitor patients with kidney disease. DeepMind is also building a platform which will provide data analytics services to the NHS, again using patient data accumulated by the NHS, that may be used to identify disease outbreaks and predict the onset of disease using machine learning and algorithmic calculations (New Scientist 2016).

For their part, the IBM company has launched their Watson Health initiative (IBM 2016), which they proclaim to be nothing less than 'pioneering a new partnership between humanity and technology with the goal of transforming global health'. They describe their use of their powerful Watson computing platform as 'cognitive computing', which analyses the use of language and employs machine learning to 'see health data that was previously hidden, and do more than we ever thought possible'. The data from sources such as social media, news articles, medical records and medical research reports that the Watson computer can access and analyse are presented as offering opportunities for a wide range of actors, including retailers, nutritionists, physicians, medical researchers and healthcare administrators to improve their services.

Big data for health promotion and public health

Beyond clinical information about illness and disease, many health-related data are generated by people's use of search engines, social media sites, apps and self-tracking devices. Companies that invite users to upload personal medical and health information when using products such as apps, smartwatches and wearable devices often amass huge databases of these details. This is evident in blog posts uploaded by the Jawbone company, which offers devices and software that facilitate self-tracking of sleep, diet and physical exercise habits. On its blog, Jawbone regularly publishes posts that provide insights into the patterns that the data of their hundreds of thousands of users upload to their databases. Thus, for example, one post compared the sleeping and exercise habits of commuters aged 25–35 compared with non-commuters of the same age (Mandel 2015). It was demonstrated that long-distance commuters both sleep and exercise less than non-commuters, while short-distance commuters (those travelling less than 5 miles to work) achieve the highest step counts. The data also showed the times of day that users exercised more formally or 'worked out'. Other analyses from Jawbone data have shown the sleeping habits of users across international cities (those living in the Australian city of Melbourne get the most), how the sleep of students at a number of major US universities compare (apparently, Columbia University students go to bed the latest and, not surprisingly, those at military academies awake the earliest) and the relationship of sleep, exercise and time of day to mood.

These reams of health and medical data have potential uses for health promotion and public health initiatives. The potential for data mining this type of personal health information to contribute to knowledges about the behaviour of social groups is beginning to receive attention in health promotion and public health. Part of the valorising of big data is the notion that bringing diverse data sets together will enhance understanding and contribute to knowledge. In an article on the use of big data in medicine and public health, for example, the authors outline ways in which digital data sets may be combined productively to produce insights:

> do grocery shopping patterns obtained from stores in various areas predict rates of obesity and type 2 diabetes in public health databases? Does level of exercise recorded by home monitoring devices correlate with response rates of cholesterol-lowering drugs, as measured by continued refills at the pharmacy?
>
> *(Weber et al. 2015: 2479)*

The authors provide a figure in the article that demonstrates how they think data from many different sources can be linked to provide information on an individual for healthcare purposes, including police records, social media networks, status updates and posts, genetic testing, fitness club membership details, credit card purchases and climate and weather data.

In a medical journal commentary entitled 'Community vital signs: taking the pulse of the community while caring for patients' (Hughes *et al.* 2016), the authors refer to the importance of aggregating patients' data for population health management. They describe these big data sets as able to monitor such 'vital signs' of a patient's community as the socioeconomic status, education attainment levels and distribution of age, gender, ethnicity and race and so on of its members. The idea they propose is to incorporate community large-scale data into electronic health records, so that clinical information and broader socioeconomic indicators can be brought together to provide better knowledge of the individual patient's living circumstances. In turn, aggregated clinical data from electronic health records can feed into measures of distribution of disease across communities.

A growing number of medical and public health researchers have conducted content analyses of social media interactions focusing on health and medical material in recent years. Twitter is particularly favoured as a source of material for this type of big data research, as it is a more public platform than Facebook and provides a high volume of material in real time. It is also often assumed by health and medical researchers that the comments people make on social media tend to reveal their otherwise hidden concerns or health-related behaviours. Indeed, for one commentator tweets are portrayed as 'a goldmine for the field of epidemiology in that people are often very open and candid in their tweets' (Reddy 2015).

Studies using Twitter have frequently used massive data sets in their analysis, involving hundreds of thousands or even millions of tweets. Thus, for example, researchers have investigated topics such as what health-related topics health professionals discuss on Twitter (Alnemer *et al.* 2015; Lee *et al.* 2014b), the extent to which personal health issues are disclosed on the platform (Yin *et al.* 2015), the content of tweets about sexually transmissible diseases (Gabarron *et al.* 2014) and whether the topics of health and medical tweets are representative of the incidence of medical conditions (Weeg *et al.* 2015). Most of this research is preoccupied with evaluating how 'factual', 'serious', 'testable', 'representative' or 'evidence-based' the posted content is.

Another type of big data analysis for health research is work using content analysis of social media status updates to attempt to discern states of ill health and disease. This approach often uses 'sentiment analysis', a method that mobilises software to track the use of specific words, phrases or images in people's updates on social media, with a particular focus on the expression of emotion. Researchers using this method claim that it allows them to track and predict the incidence of health and medical conditions and that healthcare services and policy can then be developed to intervene. Examples of studies taking this approach include analyses of social media material referring to sleep problems (McIver *et al.* 2015), pain (Tighe *et al.* 2015) and health topics in general (Sadah *et al.* 2016).

Researchers and public health workers have also begun to use large digital data sets as a form of disease surveillance (sometimes referred to as 'infodemiology' or 'digital epidemiology'). Here again, social media material and the content of other digital data such as search engine queries are harvested in the attempt to discern outbreaks of epidemic diseases (Salathé *et al.* 2012; Yin *et al.* 2015). There was some excitement for a while about Google Flu Trends, used to develop systems to track influenza outbreaks by monitoring online queries conducted employing Google's Search tool. This enthusiasm has since been attenuated by the realisation that Flu Trends was not very accurate: high numbers of searches for flu may be caused by media coverage of outbreaks, for example, rather than reflecting the searches of people experiencing the symptoms of flu (Lazer *et al.* 2014). Some platforms and associated apps have been specifically established to collect and display information about infectious diseases. These can be used by members of the general public wanting to check where outbreaks are occurring as well as by public health workers to map disease. These platforms also often work as a forum for crowdsourcing these data. Platforms such as HealthMap and Sickweather encourage users to contribute information about their own or others' illnesses. They also draw on search engine traffic, online news reports and government alerts, blogs and social media comments to identify outbreaks of infectious diseases in geographical regions.

Crowdsourcing has also been proposed as a way of helping people with disabilities learn about public spaces that are accessible for those with mobility difficulties, or to assist people with impaired sight to locate bus stops. The European Wheelmap and J'accede platforms, for example, encourage members of the public to upload information about accessible amenities in cities to create comprehensive databases that can be used by people with limited mobility. The much larger travel websites TripAdvisor and Yelp offer opportunities for users to input information about wheelchair-accessible places (Captain 2016).

Bringing together diverse data sets to inform and promote public health also operates at the city level. The notion of the 'healthy city' has been part of health promotion discourses and strategies for some time. The healthy city concept was initiated by the World Health Organization's European Office in 1986. The idea was to move away from a focus on individuals and their lifestyles to viewing health promotion as a community initiative that required structural planning and policies that used the city as a unit of focus. Special attention is paid to environmental conditions, such as housing and air quality, the provision of public open spaces and public transport arrangements as well as encouraging strong social ties to support good health and alleviate or prevent disease (Goldstein 2000).

In recent years, a new version of the ideal city – that of the 'smart city' – has begun to enter public discourse. The smart city concept incorporates the integration of various kinds of digital technologies that operate to generate information about the inhabitants and physical spaces of the city that can be used to inform policy and enhance the liveability, efficiency, sustainability and productivity of the city. The concept includes the idea that digital innovation and entrepreneurship will be facilitated by 'smart' people living in the city. In this model of the smart city, the generation of big digital data sets and their analysis are considered vital to improving the operation and management of the city (Kitchin 2014b).

The concepts of the 'healthy city' and the 'smart city' are beginning to come together (in what might be called the 'smart healthy city') in some attempts to use digitised sensing and monitoring technologies for health-promoting purposes. The smart healthy city concept brings together personal biometric data collected on individuals with digital data sets on the cities' populations and environs. It sometimes includes citizen science initiatives (Kamel Boulos and Al-Shorbaji 2014; Kamel Boulos et al. 2011). One example is the initiative announced by New York University in 2014, involving collaborating with the developers of a new residential area in that city, Hudson Yards, to create a 'quantified community' to promote energy efficiency and residents' health and wellbeing. Information on factors such as pedestrian traffic, air quality, energy production and consumption and health and physical activity levels of residents was to be routinely collected as part of this project, employing self-tracking sensor technologies used by the residents and embedded into the built environment (Anuta 2014).

Another project by the MIT Senseable City and the Alm Lab has suggested the idea of the 'smart sewerage platform'. The Underworlds project collaborators are doing just that (Underworlds 2016). They suggest a future in which sewerage can be mined for the information it contains about the bacteria and viruses in human waste, thus pointing to the level of infectious disease in the community. The information from waste water analysis in sewerage systems will be combined with demographic data to generate detailed maps of local health statuses in neighbourhoods.

Most discussions of the use of big data for health promotion tend to take an individualistic approach, focusing on using persuasive computing combined with the insights of big data to target better and more accurately individuals and 'at-risk' groups for behaviour-changing messages. Big health data initiatives seeking to move away from changing individual behaviour to broader initiatives such as community development and challenging the political status quo remain in the minority. There are currently few published accounts in the health promotion literature describing projects that seek to use digital technologies to develop healthy public policy, confront poverty and substandard living conditions and support grassroots political initiatives aimed at changing the status quo. Nonetheless, some citizen science, citizen sensing and citizen data programmes that are community-initiated are beginning to emerge that go beyond simply asking citizens to contribute data as part of crowdsourcing efforts. These involve community groups working to access open government data sources or generate their own digital data on aspects such as crime levels, traffic conditions, waste disposal and environmental pollution in their local environs to use in political activism for change (Conrad and Hilchey 2011; Gabrys 2014; Kamel Boulos *et al.* 2011; Purdam 2014). These initiatives acknowledge that digital media should not simply be viewed as tools for communicating health messages by those in power but can also act as spaces that provide the opportunity for contestation and resistance to top-down directives.

The commodification of personal health and medical data

In Chapter 2 I described a range of platforms and apps that have been developed that are specifically designed to attract patients to contribute accounts of their health states and healthcare experiences. Patient support platforms also often highlight the opportunities for patients to share their personal information not just with each other but also with other actors. The discourses of sites focusing on patient support and the democratic sharing of information highlight the opportunities afforded to participants by allowing contributors to benefit from others' knowledge and experience of their medical conditions.

Thus, for example, on the PatientsLikeMe website, people are invited to register as members to gain access to others' uploaded data on their disease or health condition and to upload their own data by creating their personal health profile. This then allows users to compare their own experiences with others. Physiological markers such as severity of symptoms, quality of life, mood, triggers of symptoms, responses to new drugs or therapies and side-effects may be tracked on the website and shared with other users. The website aggregates the data from all users with the same condition as well as providing personalised graphs and charts that allow users to identify patterns in their experiences. The focus is on quantifying these markers as much as possible, in what the website's co-founder, Jamie Heywood, describes as 'measurement-based medicine' (Marketwire 2013).

Many of these websites have attracted large numbers of regular users. The developers of HealthUnlocked (which they describe as 'the social network for health'), for example, claim that it is the most well-used patient support site in the UK, with over 500 patient communities and more than 2.5 million entries to date from members (HealthUnlocked 2016).

With the advent of these kinds of platforms, healthcare providers and organisations are increasingly subjected to digitised representations of their services and assessments. These sites often encourage members of the public to make comments about their experiences with healthcare providers and even formally to evaluate and rank them online. In countries like the UK, Australia and Ireland, the Patient Opinion platforms provide a forum for patients to tell their stories of their experiences with the state-provided healthcare systems that are then conveyed to local health services as a way of providing feedback. However, it is in the USA, where universal healthcare is not offered to all citizens and there is, therefore, a greater commercial emphasis on healthcare delivery, that these rating and ranking apps and websites are most prolific. The consumer review platform Yelp is frequently employed for rating medical services and individual doctors, while more specific apps and platforms like ZocDoc, RateMDs and HealthGrades publish patient reviews and rankings of individual doctors and hospital services.

The HealthTap website and related app are explicitly directed at both patients and doctors. It provides information to patients and connects them with healthcare providers, allowing them to ask questions about health and medical issues that are answered by doctors, and to search for doctors in their area and make appointments online. The doctors who participate answer questions and at the same time are able to build a professional profile and online reputation and advertise their services. Medical practices, clinics and hospitals and digital technology developers are also encouraged to participate, providing information on their services and reaping the benefits of the data that are produced by the contributions of patients and doctors. Doctors' answers to patients' questions are aggregated so that the patients can see the level of agreement and seek second opinions, while doctors are ranked according to the quality of their responses. Such platforms, therefore, represent both patients and doctors as the generators and beneficiaries of the data collected. In this digital data economy, there is a mutual exchange of data, each reliant on the other party to participate in the exchange to produce the value of the data.

Many patient support and patient opinion platforms and apps draw on a discourse idealising information sharing, social support and mutual benefit. In their memorably entitled article, 'The gift of spit (and the obligation to return it)', Harris and colleagues (2012) emphasise that the mentality of the gift often underpins such social sharing in online platforms. They use the 23andMe company as an example, pointing out that on its website the company represents the participation of consumers in contributing their genetic material and answering a questionnaire about their health and other personal details as a form of gift exchange, implying a social bond or norm. On the PatientsLikeMe website (2016), the site's developers similarly argue that using the platform works towards 'Making health care better for everyone through sharing, support, and research'. As part of a general 'rhetoric of democratisation' and 'participatory cultures' (Beer and Burrows 2010), it is suggested on such platforms that individuals become 'good citizens' by participating in these technologies and contributing their experiences so that they may be aggregated for the greater good (Adams 2011; Harris *et al.* 2012; Wyatt *et al.* 2013).

Being a digitally engaged patient, therefore, involves considering the benefits offered by one's participation to others as well as to oneself. This concept of sharing personal information excludes the use of these data for commercial purposes (John 2017). Despite this overt discourse of altruistic sharing, in many cases the developers of these apps and platforms incorporate a financial as well as a philanthropic motive into the data-sharing project that they seek to establish. As part of the 'new media capitalism' (Gehl 2014: 15), prosumers' unpaid labour that is contributed as part of their engagement with digital media is exploited for economic gain on the part of others (Gehl 2014; van Dijck 2013a; Zuboff 2015). The developers have a bottom line to pursue: monetising patient opinion and personal health and medical data. Indeed, a major difference between many of the newer patient support websites that have emerged in the contemporary internet era and earlier patient support and information sites is that they have been established not by patient communities themselves or by charities or other non-profit organisations addressed at supporting specific medical conditions, but by web entrepreneurs or pharmaceutical companies specifically seeking to use the data collected for commercial reasons.

In the past, pharmaceutical companies have established or financially supported some patient support websites. This support is not always readily apparent to visitors to these sites (Ball *et al.* 2006; Read 2008). The newer patient support websites are building on this commercial involvement in other ways, particularly in the use of the data uploaded by the sites' users. While the initial impetus for making the website may have come from personal experiences of illness or those of a family member (as is the case of PatientsLikeMe), many of the more recent sites have been established with a predominantly commercial motive. These motives include selling advertising, goods and services to users and on-selling data from their archives to third parties.

Other websites promoting patient engagement and support using social networking are funded by companies that then use the websites to sell advertising and the data collected to interested parties, such as health product marketers. This is the strategy developed by Alliance Health Networks (2016), for example. The Alliance Health company has established chronic illness condition-specific social networks on websites with related apps that encourage patients to share their experiences with others, ask questions of experts, access news articles on their condition, post product reviews and so on. The owners are quite open in their website about their use of these social networks to provide information to health marketers and help them engage in 'relevant, productive conversations' with patients who are members. This information, however, is found on a page directed at potential commercial clients rather than at the patients who use the site.

In a further development, some platforms have been developed specifically to 'scrape' the web for patients' accounts of their experiences in blogs and forums. Web scraping (also referred to as 'data harvesting' or 'data mining') involves sourcing and gathering data from online archives for specific purposes. The Treato platform (2016) is one such example. It focuses on harvesting patients' accounts of drug therapies across the spectrum of social media and other digital platforms, including seeking out accounts of how well drugs work, their side-effects and why patients may switch one brand for another. It uses a form of semantic analysis called 'natural language processing' to convert the written accounts of patients into quantified data. Treato provides free access to the general data that are collected but also offers a more targeted service to pharmaceutical companies that incurs fees. This company is merely one of many engaged in data brokering and web scraping for commercial reasons in what is a rapidly expanding industry.

Other commercial uses of medical and health big data are expanding rapidly. By virtue of the over one million saliva samples sent to them by people wanting to know details of their genome, the 23andMe company possesses the world's largest repository of DNA data. The company estimates that its customers supply it with up to two million pieces of information about themselves per week, including their genetic makeup and answers to the company's questionnaire about their medical and health details. These sources of information can be examined to identify relationships between DNA and health conditions. The company has sold access to its users' DNA and health-related questionnaire database to more than 13 drug companies and has opened its own drug lab to test some of the treatment ideas originating from its user data (Regalado 2016).

Pharmaceutical and biotechnology companies view the information that people share on social media sites as opportunities for learning about how their and their competitors' products and services are viewed and discussed. The term 'unbranded social media engagements' is used in industry circles to refer to biopharma companies 'seeding disease education' and 'priming the market' for a new product, for example, by setting up Twitter accounts or engaging on social media and linking to a website with information about the disease and the product (Evans 2014; Robinson 2014).

Sometimes government agencies seek to profit commercially from the patient data they collect and manage. In the UK, the care.data program was developed to compile data from NHS services. According to the NHS, this program was planned to allow the NHS to discern how healthcare is offered across its sites and the health needs of patients and to find more effective ways of delivering healthcare and preventing and managing illnesses, identifying those most at risk of developing an illness and guiding decisions about use of the resources. On the care.data website, the NHS also claimed that the program would allow 'the public to hold the NHS to account' because citizens would be able to access the information generated (Better Information Means Better Care 2014). The NHS also planned to use the big data sets in the care.data program for commercial purposes by selling the data to third parties. However, this intention to sell the data, as well as concerns about patient privacy and the potential for re-identification of anonymised data, created a high level of controversy, to the point that the rollout of the care.data program had to be postponed twice (Boiten 2014). The plan was eventually abandoned in mid-2016 due to these concerns.

Personal data and biovalue

Sociologists and other social researchers have begun to cast a critical eye over the ways in which people's personal medical and health information is commodified and even stolen by cybercriminals. A detailed book-length account by US sociologist Mary Ebeling (2016) of her investigations into how her personal health information was used by data harvesters and data brokers reveals the full extent of the commodification of such data. Ebeling suffered an early miscarriage when she was only six weeks pregnant. Despite the loss of the pregnancy at such an early stage, she found that she was targeted aggressively by marketers seeking to sell her products for her future baby. Ebeling uses the term 'data phantom' to describe this virtual infant, who did not exist in real life but continued to live in numerous databases as a marketable subject. Few people knew about the pregnancy, save Ebeling's husband and her doctor's office. She had not announced the pregnancy on social media or undertaken online searches for pregnancy or bought pregnancy-related goods or services. Despite this, information about the pregnancy had been distributed across a wide range of agencies.

Ebeling's book exposes the complex and often hidden workings of data broker companies, which specialise in locating personal information in publicly available databases or data that they purchase from other companies. They use these diverse data sources to create marketable data commodities such as detailed consumer profiles. These data commodities can be sold to other agencies for purposes such as marketing, conducting credit checks and research. In the USA, patients' electronic health records are often on-sold by the companies who provide the software and storage for these data. In the USA, where most healthcare is privately funded, healthcare providers frequently use databases to determine whether patients are credit risks. In these ways, private medical information can leak into the digital data economy, unbeknownst to the patient. As Ebeling points out, the people whose data are used for these purposes have no opportunity to discern what is happening, as data brokers do not have direct contact with the public but rather access databases from other 'consumer-facing' companies.

The commodification of personal data about people's health states and medical conditions is part of a wider move in medicine to an economy based on human bodies and their products and an increasing capitalisation of medical knowledge and practice. Several scholars have addressed the topics of bioeconomies, biocapital and biovalue, concepts that are closely related to biopolitics, biopower and medicalisation. Biovalue and biocapital are produced from the surplus commercial value that is attributed to biological objects such as human body tissues, cells and organs (Mitchell and Waldby 2006; Rose 2007, 2008; Waldby 2002). Questions of value for money and the economic value of medical knowledge and research findings are now central to modern medicine. So too, human bodies and their parts have become viewed in some contexts as possessing economic value. Dimensions of human life have been broken down into units that may be stored, changed and commoditised: transformed into the exploitable knowledge of vitality (Rose 2007).

While these objects of vitality are generally material – human bodies and their products, medical technologies, pharmaceuticals and so on – data on human bodies may also be included into the economy of biocapital as intellectual property: the results of clinical research or the data produced by the Human Genome Project or direct-to-consumer genetic testing, for example (Levina 2010; Webster 2012). These forms of biocapital contribute to the bioeconomy. The social media platforms and self-monitoring devices and apps that have been developed to promote the uploading of personal health data, the sharing of these data and their subsequent entry into the digital data knowledge economy provide routes for the translation of biodata into a new form of biovalue that generates digital biocapital.

Scholars contributing to the literature on the bioeconomy have identified the diverse ways in which the biological products that are commodified in this economy are derived and used (Rose 2008; Waldby 2002). In some contexts, they are donated as part of altruistic gifts, for example, unpaid ova donation. In other contexts, biological phenomena such as human cells, blood or tissues may be taken from people without their knowledge or consent, or repurposed and commercialised without the donors realising. For example, stem cell lines have been cultured in laboratories using original cells that were taken from the donor many years previously, thus taking on a life of their own that may continue indefinitely (Mitchell and Waldby 2006). In many cases donors receive no financial compensation for their body products, while others profit from them (Clarke *et al.* 2010). There are many parallels between the bioeconomy of human bodily matter and that of the digital data that their bodies generate. What particularly distinguishes digital data as biocommodities is the sheer diversity and range of the ways in which they are generated, which can be combined to generate different data sets and profiles on people and populations and can be capitalised. They offer biovalue on an unprecedented scale.

Data privacy and security

Digitised methods for collecting, sharing and using health and medical information about people raise many questions concerning privacy and ethics with which social norms and regulatory bodies are only just beginning to grapple. These include the extent to which people give their informed consent when allowing access to their health and medical data, the potential for data-mining and data-profiling practices to de-anonymise this information, inadequate measures to protect data security and prevent breaches and hacks, questions about ownership of personal data and the ways in which their data may be used to perpetuate social disadvantage (Lanzing 2016; Mittelstadt and Floridi 2016; Mostert *et al.* 2016). Data mining and profiling methods, in combining diverse data sets on people, can begin to reveal very detailed and sensitive information about them in ways these individuals may not have anticipated when they granted consent to the use of their data (or without their knowledge).

Since 2013, various scandals involving data breaches and hacking into often very intimate personal information have received a high level of coverage in the news media. These include Edward Snowden's revelations about the dataveillance carried out on citizens by national security agencies, the celebrity nude photo on iCloud hacking event, and various sex dating sites hacks, in which millions of users' sexually explicit details were released by the hackers on to the internet. These events have drawn attention to the precarious status of the protection of people's often very sensitive and intimate details that are contained in digital data repositories.

Cloud computing provides great opportunities for ease of data storage, sharing and access from diverse locations. However, it also poses significant data privacy and storage risks. During transmission and storage, many opportunities exist for data leakage, breaches and hacking to occur (Ali *et al.* 2015). There is a multitude of privacy threats involved with uploading personal health and medical information to social media platforms, including the misuse of the data, accidental data releases, disclosures to third parties and user profiling across sites (Li 2015; Thilakanathan *et al.* 2014). It has been found that healthcare providers, app developers and social media sites often do not adequately encrypt users' data to protect their security. Malicious or incompetent insiders working in cloud computing providers have been identified as one major health data security risk, by either deliberately sharing these data for financial advantage by selling them to third parties or by allowing data leakages. Many digital remote health monitoring systems, for example, have not been designed with patient data protection in mind (Thilakanathan *et al.* 2014).

Data breaches and leakages are common in healthcare organisations and developers' archives of personal data, including those generated by health and medical apps (McCarthy 2013; Wicks and Chiauzzi 2015). A study of over 80,000 health-related web pages found that 90 per cent leaked user information to outside parties, including commercial data brokers (Libert 2014). A report published by the US Privacy Rights Clearinghouse found that mobile health and fitness app developers often have no privacy policy and send the data uploaded by app users to undisclosed third parties. Few of these developers encrypted all data connections and transmissions between the app and developer's website (Ackerman 2013).

A detailed analysis of the data privacy and security of selected wearable fitness trackers was conducted by Open Effect, a Canadian not-for-profit research organisation (Hilts *et al.* 2016). It found that nearly all of the fitness trackers emitted geolocation data that could be accessed by third parties so that the location of the wearer could be identified (the Apple Watch was the only exception). Two trackers did not encrypt their data well enough to prevent third parties accessing or tampering with the data. Data input into several devices could be falsified, calling into question their validity and accuracy, particularly if used for customising insurance premiums or as legal evidence. The authors' analysis of the terms and conditions and privacy policies of the fitness tracker software found that in many cases the developers stated that they held the right to share or sell these data to third parties. In the case of acquisition of the developer's company by another entity, these data could be included as assets that could be used, traded or sold by the company that acquired them. Individual users were granted far less access to their own data, with most developers limiting their opportunity to export their personal information from the developers' databases.

Digital data sets on personal health and medical details have become a key target of cybercriminals (Ablon *et al.* 2015). The value of this information on the black market is high. As a result, hackers often target medical databases when conducting cybercrime. Hackers can make tenfold the profit from hacking individuals' medical information than from accessing their credit card details. When they are able to steal names, birth dates, diagnosis codes, billing information and health insurance policy numbers, cybercriminals can create fake IDs to buy medical equipment or pharmaceuticals for resale on the black market or to file fraudulent insurance claims. Hackers often target the US healthcare and health insurance industries because their ageing software is not adequately protected (Humer and Finkle 2014; McCarthy 2013). In early 2015, for example, confidential information about 80 million patients was accessed illegally on the database of the US healthcare provider Anthem Inc., which had failed to encrypt this information (Symons 2015).

Public understandings of data privacy and security issues

People are not offered, and nor do they receive, financial compensation for sharing their experiences on online platforms and apps. The value contributors derive is non-commercial, while the exchange value of the data they create is accumulated by the for-profit companies that provide the platforms for patients to share their experiences or trawl the web to harvest the data and render it into a form that is valuable for commercial entities. It often not until people access the fine print in sections of the sites, such as their terms and conditions of use and their privacy policy, that the ways in which the sites' owners employ users' data in various ways for commercial purposes is made apparent to them. While some sites include a direct statement concerning 'how we make money', this is not always made entirely clear. For example, it is noted on several patient support websites that the data aggregated on the site by users' contributions are used 'to conduct scientific studies' or 'research', with no direct mention made of the fees that the developers may receive for providing these data to their clients. On some sites, it is not until an individual begins the 'sign up' process to become a contributing 'member' that the terms and conditions and privacy policies are revealed.

Given that the information about the commercial uses to which data archives are put is often buried in lengthy terms and conditions or privacy policy statements and must be actively searched for, or else is couched in ambiguous terms, it is likely that many of the people who upload their medical and health data for personal or altruistic reasons are not fully aware of the extent to which their accounts have become valuable commodities. Nor do users have control over the products of the affective and altruistic labour that they invest in sharing their experiences on online sites. The use value of the information created by users is restricted by the limits imposed by the platform they are using. Indeed, it can be extremely difficult for people to retrieve for their own purposes the data they upload to apps or platforms, enter as part of their electronic medical records or that are generated as part of their participation in clinical trials. A 'digital data divide' has opened up between internet companies and other owners of big data sets and ordinary citizens, whereby the former have access to massive, potentially commercially valuable personal data and the latter have very little access even to their own information (Andrejevic 2014; Pasquale 2015; Zuboff 2015).

The benefits of engaging in self-tracking health and collecting medical information for the purposes of self-knowledge, reflection and self-optimisation are therefore countered by the potential for these details to be used by other parties, sometimes in ways that may be detrimental to the person who generated the data (Lanzing 2016; Lupton 2016a). Mary Ebeling (2016) describes her feelings of 'betrayal' and feeling 'violated' when she realised that information about her pregnancy that she thought was confined to her doctor's office was in fact circulating in the digital data economy and used for others' profit. As she points out, people prefer to be able to choose the context in which their private details are disclosed and to know what the implications of such disclosure are.

Several studies have been published on public understanding of personal digital data, including my own research with Mike Michael in Australia (Lupton and Michael 2015, 2017a) as well as other Australian research conducted by Andrejevic (Andrejevic 2014; Andrejevic and Burdon 2015), a focus group study located in England, Norway and Spain (Kennedy *et al.* 2015) and various surveys in the USA undertaken by the Pew Internet Research Center (Madden and Rainie 2015; Rainie 2015; Rainie and Duggan 2016). These studies have revealed that, for most users of online technologies, the ways in which their interactions are monitored by companies for targeting them with customised advertising are obvious. Many people across these wealthy countries are now becoming aware of the manifold ways in which their personal data are being collected, monitored and reused for the purposes of others. They support some of these uses if they benefit themselves or others, but are also unsettled by not really knowing how their data are used by others. People tend to feel powerless to control how others collect data on them and how these data are used, and express concerns about the fairness of personal data use.

Market research on consumers' attitudes concerning with whom they want to share their health and medical data has also demonstrated that the public is becoming aware of possible risks of others gaining access. For example, Australians who were asked about who should receive access to their electronic health records agreed that their primary doctor should have access to their electronic health record (79 per cent) but were not willing to allow their employer (1 per cent) or a government organisation (5 per cent) to have access. Nor were they very supportive of family members (16 per cent) or caregiver (15 per cent) being allowed access (Accenture Consulting 2016b).

The Wellcome Trust (2013) conducted qualitative interviews with Britons about public attitudes to the use of their personal data. The interviews revealed that the participants could identify many benefits of other actors and agencies using their personal data, such as protecting national security and improving government services and the allocation of resources as well as time saving while shopping and engaging in other online transactions. However, they were highly concerned about the possibilities that their personal information might be stolen, leaked, hacked or shared without their consent. A later study commissioned by the Trust focused on the public's attitudes to commercial access to health and medical data (Ipsos MORI 2016). This research found that participants believed that they owned their health and medical data and that they should be able to provide informed consent if this information is shared. They were concerned that their data could be de-anonymised, leading to possible discrimination or financial loss. The participants struggled to identify what was happening to their health and medical data in a situation in which data sharing across a range of agencies was becoming more prolific.

Patterson (2013) found, in her interviews with people living in New York City and the San Francisco Bay Area who were using the fitness tracker Fitbit, that many are simply not aware of how their fitness data and other personal details entered into the app (such as their geographical location, real name, date of birth, height, gender, email address and so on) could be accessed by other parties. They talked about their Fitbits as an intimate device that had become part of their everyday routines and lifestyle, part of what they wore each day (some never took them off). Patterson's participants were very wary about such actors as their employers (or prospective employers), health insurance companies or marketing and advertising companies accessing their Fitbit data. They thought twice about sharing their Fitbit data with social media friends (apart from those on fitness-tracking platforms) for fear of being viewed as obsessive, compulsive or narcissistic by their friends, or simply boring them with the information.

Patterson's research revealed that, despite the fact that users were able to make inferences about other users' behaviours and geolocation from observing their activities on the platform, they seemed not to realise fully how their own details could easily be viewed by others (including members of the public who were not users of Fitbit) and assumptions made about their movements and health status. They typically underestimated the extent of the information that Fitbit or other users could access about them. Because the participants wanted to use the device to learn about their bodies and track their progress towards fitness or athletic goals, they uploaded a lot of detailed information to the device. They rarely read through privacy policies and had little incentive to think twice about how these data might be accessed by other parties because they were focused on the use value of their Fitbit and had grown habituated to its use. They also tended to trust the Fitbit developers because it was a device that had been developed overtly to help people with achieving their health and fitness goals, and therefore seemed benign rather than exploitative.

These studies on public attitudes to personal data mining suggest that a moral economy of data management is developing, in which moral meanings and value judgements are ascribed to specific ways of collecting, managing, sharing and interpreting personal data. These meanings and judgements are socially, culturally and politically inflected, raising questions about what is the right or fair (morally justified) way of managing personal data that are related to ideas of identity, self-responsibility, good citizenship and social group membership (Vertesi *et al.* 2016).

Corporate and policy makers' responses to data privacy and security

In the wake of the numerous scandals and events that have highlighted vulnerabilities in personal data privacy, there are a growing number of indications that digital technology developers are beginning to recognise that the public is becoming more concerned about data privacy and security issues. Apple's CEO Tim Cook has made repeated public statements over the past few years about the importance his company places on protecting the personal data collected by Apple devices. He has emphasised that Apple profits from selling its devices, not its customers' personal data.

Apple's public position on the importance of their users' data privacy was further highlighted by the stance the company took in February 2016 when the US Federal Bureau of Investigation (FBI) sought to have the company provide assistance to unlock the iPhone of one of the people involved in the December 2015 San Bernardino shootings. Apple refused the FBI's request, citing its policy about protecting personal data stored on iPhones. Companies like Google and Facebook, however, have a completely different business model that relies on profiting from users' data. Google exercises strong security features to protect users' personal information against access by unauthorised outsiders, but retains its right to access users' data readily for its own purposes. Facebook has a similar stance. For its part, Microsoft, renowned in the past for lax data security, lodged a lawsuit in the USA directed at forcing the US Government to allow it and other companies that store customers' digital data to disclose to their customers when warrants have been issued that require the companies to release their data (Fleishman 2016).

In late 2015, the Consumer Electronics Association published a set of voluntary guidelines outlining how technology companies should approach privacy and security for what was termed 'personally identifiable wellness data' collected by their devices (Consumer Electronics Association 2015). Major companies involved in making such devices, like Apple, Google and Fitbit, as well as around 2,000 other companies, contributed to and agreed on these guidelines, which were developed in the attempt to win consumer trust in the companies involved. The principles enshrined in the guidelines included that companies should: take steps to protect consumers' data privacy; offer a clear and easily understandable written privacy policy for collecting, storing, transferring and using personal wellness data; obtain affirmative consent from consumers before transferring their wellness data to an unaffiliated third party; not knowingly disclose these data in ways that might be unfair or prejudicial to consumers (such as limiting their access to credit or insurance coverage); and write privacy policies that describe how the companies respond to requests for users' personal data from legal and civil enforcement authorities.

Various regulatory and policy bodies have also released guidelines for developers concerning data privacy and security protection. In June 2016, the European Commission submitted a Code of Conduct on privacy for mobile health apps to a European Union (EU) independent advisory group, the Article 29 Data Protection Working Party, for comments (European Commission 2016). The Code was based on EU data protection legislation, and once approved will act as guidelines for app developers to follow voluntarily. It outlines advice on issues such as how app developers should gain consent of the users of their app to process their personal data, limitations around the purpose of using their data, including the extent to which developers should seek to exploit these data commercially, the anonymisation of the data, transparency of explanations to users about how their data will be collected, stored and used (including by third parties), protecting the privacy and security of these data as well as ensuring that users have the right to access all of the data they have created using the app and know what to do in the case of a personal data breach.

★★★

While the active creation and sharing of online content, including personal information, have been features of capitalist economies for some time, new digital media technologies have provided the conditions for an expansion of these activities and introduced novel ways of commoditising the data generated. Representations of the value of 'digitising' oneself and 'measurement-based medicine' suggest that data in themselves are more powerful and accurate sources of knowledge than are other means of collecting information about people's behaviour, experiences and opinions. Such discourses also participate in a more general privileging of the measurable and the quantifiable in contemporary societies (Beer 2017). Collecting as much data as possible on patients and healthcare provision underpins a wider effort on the part of governments and commercial entities to gather masses of data on populations via digital media technologies to inform service delivery and the development and marketing of products (Kitchin 2014a; Zuboff 2015). Some social groups benefit from these dataveillance strategies, while others are disadvantaged or marginalised. The next chapter takes up the topic of the social structuring of digital health technologies and the implications for social inequality and marginalisation in greater detail.

5

THE SOCIAL STRUCTURING OF DIGITAL HEALTH USE

Any critical analysis of digital health needs to acknowledge the social determinants of technology use. Different social groups often have variable access to and use digital health technologies in different ways. This chapter reviews these aspects of digital health, acknowledging that factors such as geographical location and socioeconomic status influence digital technology use in general and that the social determinants of health beliefs and behaviours and health status are also contributing factors to the ways in which social groups take up digital health technologies.

Digital social inequalities

Digital social researchers have demonstrated for many years that those with lower levels of income, education and understanding of how to use digital technologies, as well as people with disabilities and those living in rural and remote regions and less wealthy countries, are less likely to want to go online, possess the skills to do so or have access to the internet. The term 'digital divide' is often used to describe these differences (van Dijk and Hacker 2003). However, some researchers prefer to refer to 'digital social inequalities', contending that this term better acknowledges the complexity of the intersections and co-constitution of socioeconomic status, embodied capacities, access and infrastructure issues in shaping digital technology use (Halford and Savage 2010).

The differential use of social groups' participation in internet and digital device activities involves features such as lack of basic knowledge, skills and experience, low interest or anxiety about learning how to use digital technologies, design elements that discourage use in some social groups, lack of access to devices or reliable wi-fi and lack of time to learn about or use these technologies (van Dijk and Hacker 2003). The most recent research demonstrates that, although access to the internet has gradually improved for most social groups and geographical locations, these differences still persist (Robinson *et al.* 2015). The UK Digital Exclusion Heatmap website (2016), which combines measures of social and digital exclusion from a variety of sources, shows that geographic areas in the UK with low levels of broadband adoption also have lower levels of education, digital skills and economic growth, as well as poorer health status. These areas are concentrated in Scotland and the north of England.

In the USA, smartphone owners are more likely to be younger, more affluent and highly educated, although there are no differences between racial or ethnic groups (Anderson 2015). Fifteen per cent of US adults do not use the internet at all, and this group is dominated by those aged 65 years or older. While the expense of internet access and lack of availability are factors shaping this lack of use, more significant on the part of this social group are lack of interest and a perception that the internet is not easy or is risky to use (Zickuhr 2013). Some people simply do not see the relevance of digital technologies to their lives. This is particularly the case for socioeconomically disadvantaged older people (Olphert and Damodaran 2013; Robinson *et al.* 2015).

Social media use is also strongly differentiated between social groups and geographical location. A Pew Research Center survey in the USA (Duggan 2015) found that younger people (aged 18 to 29) are much more likely to use messaging apps, online discussion forums like Reddit and social media platforms such as Tumblr and Instagram than are older adults. Urban dwellers and university-educated people are also more likely to use messaging apps, while Instagram and Twitter are more popular among urban dwellers. The same survey revealed that Facebook is more popular among Hispanics than other ethnic/racial groups (white non-Hispanic and black non-Hispanic) but that Instagram has more black non-Hispanic users than the other ethnic/racial groups compared, especially white non-Hispanics.

Major differences in access to devices such as smartphones and wi-fi continue to exist between wealthy and less wealthy countries. The Pew Internet Research Center showed that, in 2015, people in advanced economies such as South Korea, Australia, Canada, the USA, the UK and Germany were far more likely either to own a smartphone or report using the internet at least occasionally. For example, in South Korea 94 per cent of the population reported using the internet compared with only 8 per cent in Ethiopia. Interestingly, however, the most avid users of social media are in countries with lower internet use: 76 per cent of Africans who use the internet, for example, say that they use social media, compared with 71 per cent of US people and 65 per cent of people living in six European nations who use the internet. The same study found that those aged 18 to 34 were far more likely than those aged 35 or above to use the internet or own a smartphone in nearly all of the 40 countries surveyed (Poushter 2016).

While it is important to document patterns of use across geographical regions, countries and social groups, a focus on individual decision making fails to acknowledge the broader social, cultural and economic factors contributing to choices about using digital technologies. Differences in the use of digital technologies are not only about access, but are also related to group or community norms and cultural beliefs. Cultures of participation, therefore, are important when considering differences in digital media use (Halford and Savage 2010; Sims 2014). It is important to acknowledge that digital technologies are themselves invested with norms and meanings that represent their use for different social groups in specific ways that can be difficult to overcome (Dunbar-Hester 2010). For example, even if their access to the internet and digital devices is similar, people with different educational backgrounds and income levels tend to use these technologies differently. Privileged people use digital technologies in ways that bolster their existing socioeconomic advantage and status (Halford and Savage 2010; Sims 2014; van Deursen and van Dijk 2014).

Gendered expectations and norms also structure people's engagement with digital technologies. The information technology (IT) industry is dominated by white, middle-class men. Far fewer women are employed in this industry (Cozza 2011; Robinson *et al.* 2015), partly due to the strongly masculinist culture associated with digital technologies, both in the industry and in everyday use (Paasonen 2011). As a result, it is characterised by specific cultural norms that tend to be blind to perspectives from outside this demographic when devices and software are designed and marketed (Dunbar-Hester 2010; Oudshoorn *et al.* 2004, 2016) and reproduce stock gender stereotypes (Lupton 2015c). Thus, for example, when the Apple Watch was first released, it was subject to criticism from women, who noted that although it was equipped with a range of self-tracking sensors and apps, none had been included for menstrual cycle or ovulation tracking (Eveleth 2014).

Globally, more men than women use the internet. In most wealthy countries, there is little gendered difference, but there are far greater disparities between male and female use in developing countries (Measuring the Information Society 2013). The Pew survey of 40 countries referred to earlier showed that in half the nations surveyed, and particularly in African nations, men were more likely than women to use the internet. In many of the less wealthy countries, men also had higher rates of smartphone ownership (Poushter 2016).

While there is now little or no gender difference between countries in the Global North in terms of access to and use of the internet and mobile devices (Measuring the Information Society 2013; Poushter 2016), women and men continue to use these technologies differently. The gendered difference between men's and women's technical skills and confidence in using digital technologies begins in childhood, as do distinctions between what activities they use digital technologies for (de Almeida *et al.* 2015; Dunbar-Hester 2010). In adulthood, women tend to use the internet for activities related to maintaining social and family connections and for domestic duties, while men tend to engage more in gaming and other forms of entertainment online (Ahrens 2013; Joiner *et al.* 2012). Women are more likely to use some social media platforms than men. In the USA, 77 per cent of women use Facebook compared with 66 per cent of men, and 31 per cent of women use Instagram compared with 24 per cent of men. However, men are slightly more likely to be Twitter users (25 per cent compared with 21 per cent of women) (Duggan 2015).

The types of responses that people receive from other users on online discussion forums and social media are also strongly differentiated along the lines of gender and ethnicity or race. Women and non-whites are subjected to greater levels of discrimination, threats of violence, trolling, hate speech and other forms of online harassment than are white men, as are members of social minority groups, such as people with disabilities and gays and lesbians (Citron 2009; Daniels 2013; Ellis and Goggin 2014; Humphreys and Vered 2014). One study of women bloggers based in Germany, Switzerland, the UK and the USA who write about politics or identify as feminist found that almost three-quarters of them reported being subjected to online abuse (Eckert 2017). These experiences may lead members of such groups to use digital media differently: for example, exerting more caution over the material they upload or the social media sites they frequent.

Bodily capacities can also be major contributors to digital social inequalities. Many people with disabilities find digital technologies offer them opportunities to communicate with others and provide and receive support and information, thus alleviating social isolation for those who may find it difficult to meet and talk to others offline (Caron and Light 2015; Dobransky and Hargittai 2012, 2016; Ellcessor 2016; Ellis and Goggin 2014; Ginsburg 2012). Disability activists have campaigned for decades to draw the attention of developer companies and policy makers to the importance of considering accessibility issues (Goggin 2015).

Some features of digital technologies have helped people with disabilities to access them, such as sound-based technologies that can turn Twitter or smartphone texts into audible messages for people with visual impairments, or text-based communication for people who have difficulty with speaking. For example, a study with participants who had amyotrophic lateral sclerosis, which made it difficult for them to speak intelligibly, found that social media were very important to them as a form of communication both with others with their condition and with friends and family (Caron and Light 2015).

In many other ways, however, the design of digital technologies can lock out people with disabilities. Many people with disabilities find that the design of digital technologies does not address their needs, which can have the effect of excluding them from participation (Caron and Light 2015; Ellis and Goggin 2014; Goggin 2015; Kent and Ellis 2015). Changes in the design and affordances of software or devices can entail restrictions of the access that people with disabilities have to them. Now that Twitter incorporates far more visual imagery, for example, its content is less accessible to users with vision impairment. The term 'digital disability' has been employed to describe these aspects of restricted use of digital technologies on the part of people with disabilities (Kent and Ellis 2015). Kent and Ellis (2015) give the example of the increasing use of digital disaster and crisis communication using social media. As people with disabilities are often excluded from using popular social media sites because their disability may preclude access to the internet or being able to read social media content, they may not be able to receive this information and respond appropriately to protect themselves from the threat.

Social group membership and relative socioeconomic advantage also play influential roles in patterns of health and illness. It has been well established in social and public health research (Bleich *et al.* 2012; Braveman *et al.* 2011; Marmot and Allen 2014) that people in disadvantaged social categories, such as those with low levels of education and income, or those in minority ethnic or racial groups, are more likely to become ill and die younger compared with people who are socioeconomically advantaged. Less privileged groups also have lower access to quality healthcare services. Across wealthy and developing countries, Marmot and Allen (2014: S518) note: 'There is a striking social gradient in health and disease running from top to bottom of society'. At the global level, wealthy countries are able to devote more resources to providing healthcare, while nations with emergent or depressed economies, dealing with violent conflicts or dictatorships and severe income inequality, struggle to meet their citizens' healthcare needs (Davies 2010; Ghobarah *et al.* 2004).

Cultural health beliefs and practices

When reviewing the ways in which social groups take up, resist or ignore digital health technologies, it is also important to consider the concepts of health and illness they hold. Healthism, or the idea that good health should be prioritised over other aspects of everyday life, is strongly embedded in norms and expectations among the socioeconomically advantaged living in western countries (Crawford 1977, 1980; Fitzpatrick and Tinning 2013; Lupton 2012). Other social groups often have different priorities, such as access to better housing, avoiding being a victim of crime or obtaining regular employment. A focus on achieving and maintaining good health may be well down the list. Furthermore, as many researchers have shown (for example, Chamberlain and O'Neill 1998; Savage *et al.* 2013; Tilki 2006; Warin *et al.* 2008), people of lower socioeconomic status often express less confidence in exerting control over their health status and a great sense of fatalism about health and illness. They perceive health-promoting behaviours to be less effective, come under more social pressure to engage in behaviours like cigarette smoking, overeating or excessive alcohol consumption, or are more likely to do so to alleviate the stresses of a difficult life compared with more socially advantaged people.

Health beliefs, understandings of the human body and associated behaviours, also vary significantly between cultures and geographical regions. Immigrants or refugees to countries in the Global North or indigenous citizens, therefore, may not subscribe to the dominant biomedical culture (Lock and Nguyen 2010; Spector 2002). Designers and developers often fail to incorporate health beliefs and concepts outside of dominant western biomedical perspectives and neoliberal political mentalities. In Chapter 2 I asserted that the concept of the responsibilised healthy citizen that underpins most digital health rationales and design is an atomised actor, operating to fulfil the requirements of self-care and personal health promotion. Cultural understandings of embodiment, health and illness beyond these concepts are not acknowledged or recognised.

This point was made by Christie and Verran (2014), who evaluated the responses by members of a remote Aboriginal community to an iPad app designed to teach them about the human body and illness. They discovered that this app, based as it was on western biomedical concepts of anatomy and disease, was incomprehensible to people in this community. Their medical cosmology incorporated assumptions of embodiment that recognised bodies as always part of communal groups and relationships with other people and with the physical environment, and of health and illness states that were affected by these relationships. Taken-for-granted medical visualisations with which western people are familiar did not make sense to this group of Aboriginal people.

There are often many complex issues contributing to social groups' patterns of digital media and device use, and these patterns may not be linear or fixed. An in-depth four-year study based in remote outposts in Australia (Rennie *et al.* 2016) identified a range of sociocultural and infrastructural factors explaining why many Aboriginal people living there sometimes chose not to use the internet, even when it was available. Cultural factors such as community norms about internet use, resource sharing and social reciprocity were integral in these people's decisions. So too, infrastructural issues, such as the quality of people's housing conditions, frequency of movements of visitors between houses and their household dynamic, as well as electricity supply and billing difficulties and inconvenience in dealing with retailers related to language barriers or lack of a home telephone, were significant factors in people's internet practices.

Little detailed research is available that focuses on cultural and geographical factors that influence digital patient self-care practices, particularly in countries outside the Global North. One exception is a study based in rural India (Nahar *et al.* 2017), in which the method of anthropological fieldwork was employed to investigate to what extent older people with diabetes or depression living in a rural Indian district used mobile phones to help with their conditions. The researchers observed that, despite official policies that often valorise the possibilities of improving access of rural Indian populations to healthcare using smartphones, many barriers stood in the way of achieving these goals. Although most people owned a mobile phone, these were basic models that did not offer access to the internet and facilitated phone calls and texts only. They therefore did not use any apps at all on their phones. Broader cultural trends included patients' resistance to seeking out government-run health services, preferring to access local services, a desire to defer to medical authority rather than take on the 'engaged patient' role, view of health status that sees it as a collective and relational rather than individualistic and atomistic phenomenon, and people with depression's reticence to acknowledge their illness or seek out a digital solution to treatment in a context in which this condition is highly stigmatised.

Patterns of digital health technology use

Online search engines and websites

While many people may well use digital technologies in the ways envisaged by the designers, developers and promoters of these technologies, a high degree of diversity in use is evident from research addressing digital health use. There is no doubt that some forms of digital engagement for health and medical topics and issues are popular across social groups. As I noted in Chapter 2, the use of search engines to find information about health and medicine online attracts many internet users. A Pew Research Center survey conducted in 2012 (Fox and Duggan 2013a) found that almost 60 per cent of their US respondents had searched for health information online in the past year. Of these, 88 per cent had started their search using a search engine like Google Search. One in three respondents had gone online specifically to find information about a medical condition they or someone else might have. One-third of mobile phone owners and half of smartphone owners had used their devices to obtain health information.

Pew's survey showed that, among online health information seekers, 16 per cent had searched for others with the same condition or health concern, 30 per cent had consulted online reviews or rankings of healthcare providers or treatments and a quarter had read or watched someone else's experiences of health or medical issues over the past year. Pew's research (Fox et al. 2013) also found that four in ten people are caring for an adult or child with significant health problems. Of these respondents, 87 per cent owned a mobile phone; of these, 37 per cent said that they had used it to look for health information online. Research conducted in other countries in the Global North has similarly found that online searching for health information is very common. These include surveys conducted in France (Beck et al. 2014), Poland (Bujnowska-Fedak 2015), Germany (Bidmon and Terlutter 2015) and Australia (Rowlands et al. 2015).

There are some significant differences in the ways that different social groups use these technologies, however. The Pew Research Center survey (Fox and Duggan 2013a) found that women, white people and those with a high education level and income were more likely to have sought health and medical information online. Among all mobile phone owners, Latinos, African Americans, those aged between 19 and 40 and university graduates were more likely to use their phones to find health information (Fox and Duggan 2012).

Other research has identified that people from disadvantaged social groups possess less knowledge and fewer skills in using digital health technologies, and this can exacerbate existing social inequities that contribute to poorer health states and higher levels of poor health. Thus, for example, a study using focus groups comprised of Australians of low socioeconomic status (Baum et al. 2014) revealed that their low income, factors such as housing instability as well as lack of cultural capital (or knowledge) or social contacts who could teach them how to use digital media restricted their access to health and medical information and other resources online.

They expressed lack of confidence in gaining the skills and literacy level to find and understand such information, due to poor English language levels or limited educational opportunities. Other research has similarly found that people from non-English-speaking backgrounds may struggle with the language skills or education level to use digital technologies for health and medical purposes (Gibbons *et al.* 2011; O'Mara *et al.* 2012).

The US National Cancer Institute representative survey of the US population (Kontos *et al.* 2014) found no evidence of differences in online health information seeking by race or ethnicity, but significant differences for gender, age and socioeconomic status. Female respondents were more likely to use online technologies for health-related information, as were younger people (those under 65 years of age) and those of higher socioeconomic status. This survey discovered that women were more likely than men to go online to look for a healthcare provider, use email or the internet to connect with a doctor, track their personal health information online, use a website to help track diet, weight or physical activity or download health information to a mobile device and use social media sites to access or share health. Being younger in age was influential in health information-seeking activities online. This survey also revealed that people of low socioeconomic status were less likely to go online to look for a healthcare provider, use email or the internet to connect with a doctor, track their personal health information online, use a website to help track diet, weight or physical activity or download health information to a mobile device. However, they were more likely to use social media sites to access or share health information.

A large survey of over 26,000 respondents in all 28 member states of the European Economic Union undertaken in 2014 identified some interesting differences between countries. For example, Finnish, Swedish and Dutch respondents were much more likely to search for health and medical information online compared with Bulgarians and Romanians (Hone *et al.* 2016). More specifically, in relation to how people access or share user-generated health and medical content online (such as people recounting their experiences of disease and illness), the authors of a UK-based survey noted that only one-quarter of their internet-using respondents reported doing so, and more than 20 per cent were unaware that these resources were available. Even those respondents who did report accessing or sharing health-related user-generated content for the most part did not do this often: almost 80 per cent did this less than weekly. The minority who did so daily (only 7 per cent) were predominantly young (16 to 25 years), employed and male (O'Neill *et al.* 2014).

It would appear that, while searching for online information is popular, other modes of finding information or engaging in self-monitoring are less commonly used. A US study using representative data collected by the National Cancer Institute in 2012 (Kontos *et al.* 2014) found that, across the sample as a whole, fewer than one in five had used email to contact a doctor, bought medicines or vitamins online or tracked their personal health information online. Thirty-eight per cent reported using the internet to search for a healthcare provider. Higher numbers reported using the internet to access health-related information. Nearly 80 per cent of respondents had searched online for themselves and 57 per cent had done so on behalf of someone else. Forty-three per cent had used the internet in the past year to help with tracking diet, weight or physical activity but only 12 per cent had downloaded health information to a mobile device.

This survey found that only a small proportion of respondents had engaged in online health support groups or with a health-related blog (3–5 per cent), while 17 per cent had visited social media sites to read about or share health-related information. In a seven-country survey (Australia, Brazil, England, Norway, Saudi Arabia, Singapore and the USA) conducted by a research consultancy (Accenture Consulting 2016a), more than half of the respondents across the countries said that they used websites for health information, but only 27 per cent said they used social media for this purpose while 16 per cent used online support communities.

As outlined earlier in this chapter, health status and level of physical ability are important structuring factors in internet use: people with disabilities and chronic health conditions are less likely to use the internet than others due to lack of access and expertise and physical conditions that make internet use difficult (Choi and DiNitto 2013; Ellis and Goggin 2014; Fox and Boyles 2012). A national survey of US people with six types of disabilities (Dobransky and Hargittai 2016) found that, with the exception of those with hearing impairment, these respondents were less likely to use the internet. However, the respondents who did go online used the internet in similar ways to the general US population, and found this access very beneficial: particularly sharing their own content, accessing reviews of products and services and facilitating communication with the wider community.

The Pew Research Center (Fox and Duggan 2013b) investigated how people living with chronic conditions used digital technologies for health-related purposes. It was found that, of the 45 per cent of respondents who reported living with one or more chronic conditions (such as high blood pressure, diabetes, lung conditions, heart disease or cancer), 72 per cent used the internet compared with 89 per cent of respondents without a chronic condition. However, those among the chronically ill who did use the internet were more likely than people without a chronic condition to go online to access health and medical information, consult online reviews about health services and treatments and read or watch something online about other people's health or medical conditions.

Telemedicine and electronic patient records

While little recent research is available on the numbers of patients taking up telemedicine, at least one study has discovered that only a minority of people in the USA are using it. *The Wall Street Journal* commissioned a survey of US adults for an article on telemedicine (Beck 2016). The survey found that, while 61 per cent of respondents were open to the idea of using telemedicine services, only 15 per cent had done so. Their concerns about using telemedicine included that their health insurance would not cover the service (43 per cent), their personal medical data might not be secure (37 per cent), loss of a personal relationship with their healthcare professionals (35 per cent) and problems with internet connections (34 per cent). On the more positive side, the top benefits of telemedicine identified by respondents were convenience (59 per cent), potential cost savings (40 per cent), ease of prescription refills (35 per cent) and the possibility of more frequent communication with healthcare professionals (26 per cent).

The Accenture Consultancy seven-country survey (2016a) similarly found a low use of telemedicine across these countries. As a whole, only 15 per cent of respondents had used remote consultations: ranging from a low of 8 per cent of Australians to a high of 24 per cent of Saudi Arabians. For the most part, respondents viewed remote consultations as offering less quality care, even though they may be more convenient and less expensive. The majority in every country far preferred in-person care over remote care.

The potential of electronic health records has also received a high degree of attention for some years now. Advocates claim that the full introduction of this manner of recording patient information will streamline health service delivery, ensure that patients' information can be consolidated and archived in one place for better patient management and care, reduce time spent in consultations with doctors, improve diagnosis and provide patients with better information about their health. Despite these apparent benefits, health services have experienced major difficulties in rolling out comprehensive electronic health record systems. Questions have been raised about whether they do improve the quality of care and about data privacy (Buntin *et al*. 2011; Classen and Bates 2011; Tang *et al*. 2006). The Accenture Consulting seven-country survey (2016a) revealed that, even where patients do have access to their electronic health records, few bother to look at them.

Health and medical apps and wearable devices

Apps in general are highly used by many mobile device owners. Billions of app downloads have now been recorded by the major app stores (Statista 2015a). One market research study found that the average US smartphone user used 26 apps per month, and the time spent on using them per month was increasing (Nielsen 2015). The numbers of downloads of health and medical apps have increased each year, from 1.7 billion in 2013 to 2.3 billion in 2014 and 3 billion in 2015 (Wicklund 2016a). Only a select group of these, however, receive high downloads, while the rest languish with little interest paid to them. The very popular, highly downloaded apps include fitness-tracking or calorie-counting apps, period trackers or medical information apps provided by reputable medical information companies such as WebMD (IMS Institute for Healthcare Informatics 2015).

In contrast, apps offered by healthcare services are rarely used. A market research survey (Accenture Consulting 2015) found that two-thirds of the 100 largest hospitals in the USA had developed their own apps, but hardly any of their patients (less than 2 per cent) used them. This survey showed that users consistently rate healthcare provider apps lower than the popular independent digital health apps. This is largely because these apps fail to match the quality of those offered by commercial developers in terms of their content, ease of use and functions. Patients want apps that offer access to their electronic health records or allow them to make medical appointments or prescription refill requests: few of these apps met any of these requirements.

The Pew Research Center survey (Fox and Duggan 2013a), discussed earlier, found that one-fifth of the US respondents who used smartphones had downloaded health apps. The most popular apps were for monitoring exercise, diet and weight. Regarding monitoring health or medical status, this survey found that 69 per cent of respondents said that they tracked at least one health or medical indicator (such as symptoms, body weight, exercise, sleep patterns or diet) for themselves or a loved one. People with chronic health conditions were more likely to be tracking a health indicator. It is interesting to note, however, that most people did not use an app or other type of software to engage in self-monitoring their health. Of those who did track health indicators, half did so by committing the information to their memories. One-third made records using pen and paper and only one-fifth said that they used some kind of digital technology to track health indicators (Fox and Duggan 2013c).

A more recent study of mobile phone users in the USA (Krebs and Duncan 2015) revealed a far higher proportion who had downloaded health and medical apps. The researchers found that almost 60 per cent of respondents had downloaded a health or fitness app for their phone. Fitness, nutrition and weight-loss apps were the most frequently used, with most of those who had them using them daily. The most common reasons for not using health-related apps included lack of interest, cost and concern about data privacy and security. Of those who had initially used health apps, about half of the respondents had stopped. The reasons they gave for relinquishing use included the burden of entering data, loss of interest, hidden costs, because the apps were confusing to use, or they did not like the apps sharing data with their friends.

When asked what type of health or medical apps they would like to use, most people in this survey responded that they appreciated apps for contacting their doctors or making medical appointments, as well as apps designed to access their medical records. In relation to apps for nutrition, weight loss or fitness, the respondents wanted apps that could provide personalised advice to help them meet their goals and to motivate them using humour and encouragement. An app that could bring these various uses together was envisaged as more useful and functional than having to use a number of different apps that may not easily share information with each other.

While there is, as yet, little academic research on how different social groups use apps, market research reports have generated some insights. The Accenture seven-country study showed that 36 per cent of respondents across the included countries used health apps, with Singaporeans the most enthusiastic (44 per cent) and Australians the least (29 per cent). Across the sample who used apps, fitness and diet/nutrition apps were the most popular by far, followed by symptom trackers and health or condition trackers (Accenture Consulting 2016a). Among respondents to a survey of mobile phone users in the USA (Krebs and Duncan 2015), users of health-related apps were more likely to be younger, have higher incomes, be more educated, of Latino/Hispanic ethnicity and have a body mass index that was in the 'obese' category.

Gender has been identified as an important structuring factor in health and medical app use. One report showed that women install 40 per cent more apps of any type than men and buy 17 per cent more paid apps. However, men used health and fitness apps slightly more than women (Koetsier 2013). A Nielsen market report on the use of wearable devices in the USA found that, while men and women used wearable fitness activity bands in equal numbers, women were more likely to use diet and calorie counter apps (Nielsen 2014). Wearable devices have been taken up thus far by a very small proportion in the UK: market research suggests that less than 2 per cent have purchased a wearable fitness device and less than 1 per cent owned a smartwatch. Of those who had purchased a smartwatch, three-quarters were male, and more than half were under the age of 35 (Harris 2014).

Hundreds of apps are available for women who are pregnant or experiencing the early years of motherhood (Thomas and Lupton 2015). A survey I conducted in Australian women who were pregnant or had given birth in the past three years (Lupton and Pedersen 2016) found that pregnancy and parenting app use was common among the respondents. Almost three-quarters of respondents had used at least one pregnancy app, while half reported using at least one parenting app. The vast majority of respondents who had ever used a pregnancy app said that they found the apps useful or helpful, particularly for providing information, monitoring fetal development and changes in their own bodies, and providing reassurance. While fewer women used parenting apps, those who did also found them useful as sources of information, for helping to monitor their children's growth and development and to provide reassurance. When discussing the types of digital technologies which they would like to use, these respondents, like those in the Krebs and Duncan (2015) survey, were enthusiastic about apps that could offer many different functions simultaneously. They were also keen to use apps and other software that could connect them readily to healthcare professionals when they needed expert advice or to other mothers to arrange face-to-face meetings.

Personal health data and social disadvantage

There are profound implications for digital social inequalities related to the collection and use of big health and medical data. As I discussed in the previous chapter, these data are being used in a variety of ways to shape government policy related to health service delivery and contribute to medical and public health knowledge, as well as being exploited by commercial enterprises. Data-mining and data-brokering companies and advertisers have a vested interest in health and medical data. Some of these agencies use the data to construct detailed profiles or predictive analytics inferring future behaviour. The possibilities of these data profiles being used in discriminatory ways are clear, given that many of these conditions are stigmatised. Indeed, it has been contended by some commentators that the use of digital personal data in such ways is a civil rights issue (Gangadharan 2017).

In relation to health and medical data, existing inequities may be perpetuated by their misuse. Data brokers sell lists of people with conditions such as mental health illnesses, HIV/AIDS, Alzheimer's disease and cancer and who may have been the victims of sexual or domestic assault, as part of their commercial efforts to profit from personal data (Libert 2014; Pasquale 2014; World Privacy Forum 2013). Sensitive medical conditions can become identifiable by the examination of other data sets, such as purchasing habits (Rosenblat *et al.* 2014). This is made even easier by platforms such as retailers' customer loyalty programmes that encourage people to upload self-tracked health and fitness data in addition to purchasing habits. Major supermarkets in many countries in the Global North offer such reward programmes, which enable them to discern for all individual customers not only what kinds of food and beverages (including alcohol in some cases) they purchase but in how much exercise they engage. These data sets already generate detailed information on the customers' health-related lifestyle choices.

These data profiles and other sources of digital health data may have significant implications for people's life chances. They may be denied rights and services such as employment, credit or travel opportunities, for example (Crawford and Schultz 2014; Rosenblat *et al.* 2014). Personal data on health, fitness and medical conditions are used by some companies to assess customers' eligibility for health or life insurance. While these assessments may mean that conditions or risks can be identified early, there is also the prospect of certain types of patients being excluded from healthcare coverage once these analytics have decreed that they are susceptible. Particularly in the USA, such individuals are often those who lack sufficient access to healthcare in the first place because of their socioeconomic disadvantage. As part of commercial marketing and advertising using data harvesting and targeting, people who have been identified from their online activities such as searching and browsing as having a serious health condition or as unemployed may be excluded from favourable offers because they are not viewed as profitable (Libert 2014).

Concerns have been consequently raised by privacy and ethics organisations and legal scholars about invasions of personal privacy, and the implications for social justice and civil rights (Crawford and Schultz 2014; Nuffield Council on Bioethics 2015; Polonetsky and Tene 2013). People who are already marginalised, excluded from education and employment opportunities and access to digital technologies or knowledge about how to use these technologies, are far more vulnerable to data privacy breaches or further discrimination based on the information that they may contribute when interacting with digital technologies (Gangadharan 2017; Rosenblat *et al.* 2014). They often possess less knowledge about how to protect themselves from incursions on their personal data or are forced to use digital technologies in ways that offer them less data protection, for example, in public libraries rather than at home, or sharing devices with other people (Gangadharan 2017).

Exclusion from digital technology use can have other negative effects. Those people who are actively using digital media are highly visible in digital data sets. As I showed in the previous chapter, this extreme visibility brings with it potential risks. But lack of visibility can also be harmful. Certain social groups tend to be less subjected to dataveillance because they do not engage in the activities that tend to be routinely collected via interactions with digital technologies. These groups (for example, the very poor, the homeless, the elderly or people with disabilities who find it difficult to use digital technologies) tend to be already disadvantaged and marginalised. This disadvantage may be exacerbated if the needs of these groups are not identified in procedures and policy development that rely on digital data for decision making about funding and resource allocation (Lerman 2013).

★★★

The research reviewed in this chapter highlights the importance of considering the diversity of digital health use and the social determinants that structure this diversity. In the next chapter, I delve a little deeper into the reasons why people use (or do not use) digital health technologies. I review research that has identified the meanings and practices of these experiences from a phenomenological perspective to explore the lived experience of digital health.

6

THE LIVED EXPERIENCE OF DIGITAL HEALTH

The previous chapter outlined research investigating broad patterns in digital health technology use, with a particular focus on differences between social groups and geographical regions. The present chapter continues with examining digital health use, but moves into a different direction by discussing more in-depth research investigating people's lived experiences of digital health and implications for selfhood, embodiment and social relations. The discussion directs attention to how and why these technologies are used and actively incorporated into everyday life or otherwise resisted, rejected or ignored, and the sensory and emotional dimensions of these enactments and entanglements.

Social connection and emotion online

An important element of the ethos of contemporary online discussion forums and social media platforms is the expectation that users divulge details about themselves in collaborative efforts to establish social ties and a sense of community. The interactive affordances of online media, including the possibility of adopting an anonymous pseudonym on some platforms, promotes a culture of confession and sharing. Details about the self and the body that were once kept to the private sphere are now often broadcast online, often to potentially very large audiences (Banning 2016; John 2017). The affordances for social connections that online media offer are central to their emotional resonances and meanings.

A wealth of literature has demonstrated the value that patients have derived from being able to share their experiences on blogs and social media. The opportunity to engage with other people online can be immensely helpful and comforting. Many people go online because these technologies are so readily available and accessible any time of the day or night. People sometimes feel that they do not want to 'bother' healthcare providers with questions or concerns that may appear trivial, or find that access to face-to-face medical expertise is limited (Kraschnewski *et al.* 2014; Powell *et al.* 2011). As numerous studies have now shown, patients appreciate the greater access to information about their conditions and the reassurance, support, opportunity to express themselves, feeling part of a community and greater sense of control over their illness that they may gain from their participation in online forums and blogs (see, for example, Lee *et al.* 2014a; Mazanderani *et al.* 2013a, 2013b; McCosker and Darcy 2013; Powell *et al.* 2011; Ziebland and Wyke 2012). Online forums can also provide a place for people to express their grief at the serious illness or death of a loved one, thus providing them with an opportunity to talk about their feelings in ways that may be less socially accepted in face-to-face encounters (Chapple and Ziebland 2011; Gibson 2017).

Blogs and social media sites also help people who feel marginalised because of their health conditions, disability or their non-normative bodies to communicate with each other, find and give support and express their feelings. These media are used by people who identify as lesbian, bisexual, gay, transsexual or queer to find others to seek support or information, engage in activism or to develop friendships or sexual relationships (Fink and Miller 2014; O'Riordan and Phillips 2007; Pullen and Cooper 2010). Online forums and social media can be particularly helpful for people with illnesses that are stigmatised, such as HIV/AIDS or severe mental illness, providing opportunities to deal with feelings of social isolation and hopelessness (McDermott 2015; Mo and Coulson 2014; Naslund *et al.* 2014) or to discuss how medications affect them (Tucker and Goodings 2017).

My research with Sarah Pedersen on the ways in which pregnant women and mothers of young children used forums, social media and apps (Lupton 2016d; Lupton and Pedersen 2016; Pedersen and Lupton 2017) revealed that the women commonly went online to alleviate feelings of boredom, social isolation and distress. Immediate access to content was a priority for the majority of participants. The women referred to googling information constantly in an attempt to deal with worries or questions about pregnancy or their infants, and commented on the emotional relief they obtained when they could access advice from healthcare providers or other mothers online. They appreciated being able to connect to others at any time of the day or night. Our analysis of maternal feeling expressed on a popular parenting forum Mumsnet (Pedersen and Lupton 2017) showed that women expressed highly negative emotions about their experiences of motherhood. Contributors to the forum frequently noted that it was the only place they could express socially proscribed emotions such as anger, frustration, shame, guilt and sadness about motherhood and their children.

Social media affordances reinforce the emotional gratifications of interacting online. The ability to 'like', 'favourite', share, tag or comment on personal content provides an array of responses to other users. The practice of contributing to social media by posting updates or images or comments on other people's posts can be experienced as playful and pleasurable, as can observing the ways in which other users respond to one's posts and updates (Gerlitz and Helmond 2013; Grosser 2014). As observed in Chapter 4, the opportunity to engage as a 'good citizen' in sharing and pooling information that can benefit others is a major discourse on patient support platforms and online forums. Participants can gain satisfaction from contributing to scientific research, volunteering for clinical trials and the production of better understanding of their condition, as well as providing information and emotional support to other patients (Adams 2011; Harris *et al.* 2012; Mazanderani *et al.* 2013a; Tucker and Goodings 2017).

Not all people want to engage online, however. Studies of people living with cancer, for example, have discovered that some would rather avoid being confronted with a high level of detail about what may lie in store for them in terms of their treatment and prognosis, and therefore choose to avoid blogs, discussion groups and other online forums about cancer (Broom and Tovey 2008; Sandaunet 2008). People who are ill may also prefer not to represent this part of their lives to their social media friends and followers. Research involving interviews with Canadian teenagers hospitalised with chronic illness (Van Der Velden and El Emam 2013) identified that the participants were reluctant to reveal details of their illness on their Facebook accounts. These young people preferred to represent themselves as 'normal', healthy adolescents on Facebook, and used the platform as a way of escaping a focus on their illness. They were also reluctant to search for information about their conditions online or connect with other patients with their condition using digital media or with organisations related to their condition.

Another study interviewed people with diabetes and those attempting to lose weight and who were active users of online health forums and Facebook (Newman *et al.* 2011) The researchers found that, while participants were keen users of these platforms for support, advice, motivation and information-sharing purposes, they were confronted with constantly negotiating what type of details they should reveal. These participants were concerned about maintaining self-presentation in positive ways and were wary of boring other members with too much information about themselves. They thought carefully about what information about their health or weight loss they decided to share and with whom. These people wanted to present themselves as positive and helpful members of forums and also as actively managing their own health well. This meant that they did not necessarily want other members knowing about their struggles to engage in self-care (for diabetes) or their difficulties in achieving weight loss. Some topics, such as sexual health issues, may be considered simply too personal, sensitive or embarrassing to discuss on social media sites (Byron *et al.* 2013).

Nor do patients necessarily want access to all the medical information that their healthcare providers record about them. Interviews with British patients with a chronic illness (Winkelman *et al.* 2005) found that the information contained in the patients' electronic health records was limited in its usefulness. The patients observed that the doctors' accounts of their illness, as transcribed in the records, differed significantly from their own. This raises the question of clashing views of interpretation of their bodies from the patient compared with the health provider perspective and how these might be resolved. Some patients expressed the view that they did not necessarily want to be 'empowered' by being able to view all their information; they would rather not know about negative test findings or prognoses, for example, by reading it on the record before being able to discuss this information with their doctor.

It should also be acknowledged that a diversity of opinion is expressed by lay people who contribute to online health and medical sites. There may be disputes and disagreements with and outright hostility directed at other users. This is often the case, for example, on platforms or social media groups in which parents interact. Medical topics attracting strong opinions or emotions can provoke online arguments, as witnessed in discussions of childhood vaccination on a parenting forum (Skea *et al.* 2008). If participants hold different views from the majority of members of an online forum or Facebook health support group, they can find themselves shunned, castigated or asked to leave. Thus, for example, a study of a pro-anorexia online community found that participants were often challenged about their authenticity as 'pro-ana' advocates, labelled as 'wannarexics' or 'real' anorexics instead (Boero and Pascoe 2012).

People who are considered to lack the ability to engage in self-control and management of their health can be subjected to a high degree of moral opprobrium and abuse in online forums. This is a common experience of fat people (De Brún *et al.* 2014). It has also been encountered by people with cancer who openly admit that they smoke cigarettes (Luberto *et al.* 2016) and people with HIV/AIDS whose views differed from other members of online support groups (Mo and Coulson 2014). People from minority, marginalised or stigmatised social groups can find themselves discriminated against or simply not acknowledged on mainstream discussion forums and online support groups. As revealed in a study of Australian breast cancer information and support websites, women who were lesbian or from ethnic minority backgrounds were often not acknowledged or catered for (Gibson *et al.* 2016).

Online forums, therefore, work as important outlets for emotional expression and finding the support of likeminded others. However, they can also operate in highly normative ways, working to silence dissent and promote one set of opinions over others. Just as is the case with other avenues for the public discussion of health and illness matters, people who do not conform to accepted norms may find themselves marginalised. There is also the possibility that inaccurate, misleading or overly confronting information may be shared on these forums which may exacerbate rather than ameliorate health conditions and emotional wellbeing.

The emotional dimensions of digitised self-care

As in discourses attempting to represent the patient as a 'consumer' in earlier eras (Lupton 1997a, 1997b, 2012; Lupton *et al.* 1991), contemporary writings on patient engagement assume a rational, emotionally disengaged and 'empowered' subject who is motivated and equipped with the economic and cultural capital to engage in self-monitoring and self-care. In the discourse of the digitally engaged patient, 'empowerment' becomes a set of obligations (Veitch 2010). This perspective dominates in medical and popular representations of digitised patient self-care. Patients' resistance to the use of digital health devices for self-care is often explained by factors such as incompetence, indifference, ignorance or even technophobia (particularly in relation to older people). Yet even younger people, who are more experienced in the use of digital technologies more generally, may resent, challenge or simply ignore the tasks and responsibilities demanded of them by telemedicine. As Oudshoorn (2016: 767) has observed, while there are many 'heroic stories about the fusion of bodies and machines', very little literature on the entanglements of humans and medical technologies has paid attention to the vulnerabilities that such encounters may generate for people.

Taking on the ideals of the 'digitally engaged patient' is complex and can involve significant ambivalence for both patients and their healthcare professionals. Telemedical and telehealth devices have disciplinary and surveillant capabilities, making specific demands of patients and workers. Digital health technologies and the disciplinary regimes they configure as part of the practices of self-monitoring and self-care may be said both to empower and disempower patients. Researchers have commented on the 'invisible labour' required of patients in adapting self-care and other telecare technologies into their lives (Oudshoorn 2008, 2016; Piras and Miele 2017). Digital self-care technologies make specific demands of patients, requiring them to engage in self-monitoring practices at certain times of the day, for example, or beeping to remind them to take medication, or requesting them to rate and rank their healthcare providers on an evaluation website, or to upload their personal experiences of illness and medical treatment on patient support websites. Appropriating and incorporating any form of digital device into everyday life involves embodied practice and emotional responses. Users adopt ways of adjusting to wearing the devices, developing mundane embodied routines for attaching them, taking them off, ensuring that they are connected to the internet or other devices, responding to visual notifications and any haptic or auditory signals they send (such as buzzes or beeps) and ensuring that they are charged with power.

Medical technologies such as the insulin pump that are permanently implanted in bodies work to manage the body by monitoring it and also providing a substance that manages disease and maintains the user's health and bodily integrity. In a piece on 'hacking the feminist disabled body', Laura Forlano, a woman with diabetes who is also a feminist science and technologies studies academic, observes: 'At times, living with a chronic disease and disability such as diabetes can be a comedy of objects – a humorous negotiation between the human body and an entirely new set of actors [the apparatuses that are required to self-manage diabetes]' (Forlano 2016). Forlano acknowledges that her digital devices for managing diabetes are life-saving and health-giving. Having the insulin pump attached to her body provided her with reassurance and feelings of security and safety.

Kerry Sparling (2014), another woman with diabetes, wrote on her blog about how she has found that uploading her continuous blood glucose measurements to a cloud-based digital data archive meant that her husband and other family members could log in and check her data. The device is inserted under the user's skin on her stomach and the sensor within it constantly monitors blood glucose levels in body tissue fluid every few seconds and wirelessly transmits the data to a monitoring device worn or carried on the user's body. Sparling notes that if she were at home alone with her infant daughter or travelling, her family could check the data to ensure that she hadn't lapsed into a diabetic coma with no other adult present to help her.

As these women's accounts demonstrate, there are many possibilities for experiencing a sense of community and intimacy, reassurance and comfort from engaging with patient self-monitoring technologies. When patients think that they have achieved better knowledge of their bodies via self-monitoring devices they feel as if they are more in control and this leads to feelings of security and reassurance. However, if the data patients produce suggest that their health is suffering, or if these data conflict with their own subjective and phenomenological interpretation of their state of health and wellbeing, this can be unsettling and anxiety- or fear-provoking.

Many studies have demonstrated that the lived reality of tracking one's illness and engaging in self-care can simply be too confronting, tiring or depressing for people who are chronically or acutely ill. Self-monitoring and self-care for health and medical purposes become part of the burden of treatment with which patients are confronted. A Dutch study of people with diabetes (Hortensius *et al.* 2012) discovered that, while some of the interviewees described the self-monitoring technology they used as a 'friend', bestowing peace of mind, confidence, freedom and certainty, others represented it as a 'foe'. They disliked having to prick their finger constantly to elicit the blood for the test, and feeling ashamed, anxious, helpless or frustrated by glucose readings that were not in the appropriate range. Danish research (Huniche *et al.* 2013), investigating patients' experiences with self-monitoring their chronic obstructive pulmonary disease at home, found that the biometric readings these patients produced on their bodies, such as their oxygen saturation levels and lung function, were valued for their objectivity, their ability to uncover the mysteries of their bodies. The patients responded emotionally to the numerical data they produced, feeling encouraged, more secure or reassured when the numbers were in the acceptable range, but experiencing anxiety, depression or fear of physical deterioration when their data exceeded this range.

The dominant discourses idealising the engaged, self-responsible patient can lend a moralistic tenor to self-care practices. This was evident in an interview study with patients with multiple chronic conditions living in New York City (Ancker *et al.* 2015a, 2015b). Some patients did not wish to confront their biometric data, as it made them feel depressed, anxious, guilty or worried when 'bad numbers' appeared in their results. Spikes in blood glucose levels could happen for no apparent reason, and this was frustrating and demoralising for people who thought that they were managing their diabetes well. Personal biometric data were described by the patients in moralistic terms, as denoting that they had 'cheated' or somehow failed to maintain an appropriate health regimen if their data suggested this. Failing to engage consistently in self-tracking was also considered by the interviewees as evidence of being a 'bad patient' by failing to live up to healthcare providers' expectations of them, whereas those who were considered too thorough were also viewed negatively by healthcare providers, who described them as 'obsessive' or 'compulsive'. Some patients expressed their frustration or anger about being placed in a position where they had to focus on their disease continually, and would rather seek to forget that they were ill.

The pleasures and frustrations of self-tracking

For healthy people who are not dealing with illness or managing chronic conditions, self-tracking of elements of one's bodily functions and practices can be experienced as productive, empowering and playful. Via self-tracking initiatives, people are encouraged to generate information on themselves that can be used to optimise their lives and health status. Some self-trackers engage in competitive endeavours or see their self-tracking efforts as contributing to the aestheticisation and performance of parts of their lives. The opportunity to demonstrate to oneself, and perhaps also to others, that a self-tracker is becoming physically fitter, more productive, moving towards a weight-loss goal or beating a habit like smoking can be a powerful motivator. Many self-trackers who track their physical achievements and exploits using digital devices and then post their data to social media platforms or dedicated fitness tracking sites have identified their pleasure at being able to view and review the information about their activities, show them off to others and even compete against other users (Fotopoulou and O'Riordan 2017; Lupton 2016a: 201a, 2017b; Nafus and Sherman 2014; Ruckenstein 2014, 2015; Sharon and Zandbergen 2017; Smith and Vonthethoff 2017; Stragier *et al.* 2015; Sumartojo *et al.* 2016).

The acts of measuring and monitoring aspects of embodiment can significantly change the ways in which bodies are conceptualised and experienced, and also how people who engage in these activities are viewed by others. A wearable device such as a Fitbit can signal to others that the wearer is interested in his or her health and physical fitness as a symbolic object, whether or not the wearer is actually moving more or even pays any attention to the data the device generates. Alternatively, such a device or the presence of a fitness-monitoring app on a smartphone may be interpreted as evidence of obsessiveness, laziness or weakness, revealing the wearer's need to be disciplined and motivated by a technology rather than possessing internal willpower (Dennison *et al.* 2013) or that person's overenthusiastic interest in the numbers generated over other aspects of exercise (Copelton 2010).

For self-trackers, generating data about their body is an opportunity to acquire self-knowledge, engage in self-reflection and optimise their lives. Self-trackers often seek to make meaning from their data. The practice is not simply about collecting data but also attempting to engage with issues such as what should be done with these data, how they should be presented and interpreted and what the implications are for self-trackers' identity and future life prospects and success (Fotopoulou and O'Riordan 2017; Lupton 2017a; Lupton *et al.* 2017; Nafus and Sherman 2014; Smith and Vonthethoff 2017; Sumartojo *et al.* 2016). In so doing, self-trackers are engaging in voluntary self-surveillance. The process of meaning making may be facilitated by engaging in data-sharing practices. For those who participate in the communal mode of self-tracking (Lupton 2016a, 2017b), these data offer means of entering into exchanges of personal information for the mutual benefit of other users or the opportunity to contribute to aggregated big data sets that promise to reveal insights that may be of use to themselves and others (Barta and Neff 2016; Fotopoulou and O'Riordan 2017; Lomborg and Frandsen 2016; Lupton 2017b). When self-trackers engage in these practices, they are inviting the surveillance of others.

Mundane practices may be reconsidered as offering valuable contributions to accumulating metrics about heart rate or steps taken. Routine activities like strolling in the neighbourhood, walking or cycling to work or the shops or carrying out housework are reinterpreted as evidence of measurable bodily activity. Many people who use digital devices for monitoring their bodies find that the act of self-tracking and the data generated make them think about their bodies and their everyday physical activities differently.

A study of pedometer use in a USA-based walking group for adults aged over 50 is instructive (Copelton 2010). Pedometers are devices for measuring the number of steps taken. When this walking group was first formed, all participants were issued with a pedometer as a way of tracking their exercise patterns. However, resistance was identified among the members of the group to wearing the pedometers. It was contended by participants that these devices would interfere with sociability by introducing competitiveness and instituting a hierarchy of fitness into the group, and might place unwanted pressure on members to walk faster or longer. Wearing a pedometer upon one's body was viewed as an overt sign that one is monitoring oneself and thus placing emphasis on health or achievement over sociability. Hence these devices were quickly discarded.

A project involving young English men using smartphone apps to monitor their steps (Harries and Rettie 2016) came to similar conclusions concerning the ways in which monitoring walking using digital devices attracted new meanings. It was found that the participants' awareness that their physical activity was being tracked by the app resulted in them changing their habits. They tended to walk more in an attempt to increase their step metrics. Short walks that were part of their everyday movements received greater attention as opportunities to accumulate steps, transforming these walks into 'exercise'. Both this study and that undertaken by Copelton identified that moral meanings concerning responsible healthy citizenship and competitive and comparative impulses adhered to walking that was monitored and quantified, while non-tracked walking was invested with different meanings.

People often respond emotionally to their personal data when they view the visualisations that are produced from the data, such as graphs. A study of Finns using digital self-monitoring devices for physical activity and heart rate tracking (Pantzar and Ruckenstein 2015; Ruckenstein 2014) revealed that participants found the visualisations that were generated from their data meaningful and motivational, generating feelings of pride, accomplishment and satisfaction. The data visualisations were viewed as more credible and accurate by the participants than the 'subjective' assessments of their bodily sensations; indeed they expressed the desire for more data about their bodies to add to those already collected, so as to provide further insights.

My research investigating cycling self-tracking practices and meanings with Sarah Pink, Shanti Sumartojo and Christine Heyes Labond (Lupton *et al.* 2017; Sumartojo *et al.* 2016) discovered that people who monitored their cycling trips often invested emotionally in the data they generated. Quantified evidence that people were becoming fitter and faster when cycling proved to be highly motivating, lending confidence to people who had begun feeling unfit or incompetent at cycling. Several of the participants we talked to experienced much pleasure in reviewing their data and noting improvements in their speed or heart rate or noting that they had achieved 'personal bests' or trounced other users of the self-tracking platform they used for monitoring their rides. When data were lost due to a technical error or human forgetfulness (failing to charge up a device, for example) or if the details appeared inaccurate, people often reported feeling disappointed or frustrated.

As this study and others on self-tracking discussed here identify, digitised self-monitoring can have profound emotional resonances for those who take up these practices. Devoting time and attention to adopting a self-tracking practice and learning to make sense of the data it generates involves a continual assessment of how 'good' or 'valuable' these data are, what worth they have and how they should contribute to one's sense of self and embodiment. Like other self-care or self-monitoring practices, digitised self-tracking involves various forms of labour, including emotional, technical and sense-making work.

Spaces of digital health and surveillance

With the advent of mobile devices that can be carried or worn by users and insertible, implantable and ingestible sensors, not only has the clinic moved into the home, it has dispersed to every possible spatial and temporal location. Not only are medical and health-related data now mobile, but so are the bodies/devices that produce these data. As is the case with previous forms of telecare, many of the new digital health technologies are directed at repositioning healthcare, locating it within the domestic domain rather than the clinic and moving physical encounters of patients with healthcare providers to virtual encounters (Mort *et al.* 2009; Mort and Smith 2009; Oudshoorn 2011; 2012; Pols 2012). The home consequently becomes one node of a dispersed network of healthcare technologies in multiple sites and involving multiple actors who interpret the data supplied by telecare patients, diagnose and prescribe treatments and answer patients' queries.

With the use of digital health technologies like telemedicine and patient self-care devices, the 'medical gaze' is fragmented and distributed over different actors and locations (Nicolini 2007; Oudshoorn 2011, 2012; Pols 2012; Ruckenstein

2015). Medical care becomes simultaneously 'at a distance' (Oudshoorn 2008) and 'closer' than ever before by virtue of its surveillance capacities (Pols 2012). The spatial distance these technologies enact allows patients to avoid the direct medical gaze and disciplinary power that was the focus in Foucault's writings on the clinic (Chapter 1). However, this medical gaze becomes virtual and moves towards self-governance, as patients are expected to turn the gaze upon themselves and then report what they observe to their healthcare providers.

The techno–utopian ideals of the technologies used for these purposes are frequently challenged in the lived experiences of the patients who use them. As several sociologists of science and technology have discovered in their empirical work, while the assumed uses of telemedicine offer various defined possibilities, when they are actually put into use across a diverse range of contexts, the outcomes can be hard to predict. Merely providing the technologies to patients does not guarantee that they will be used as expected. Technologies like those used in patient self-care must be 'tamed' or 'tinkered with' to fit into patients' lives and operate usefully. They may end up being employed in ways that are very different from original expectations as users transform the technologies to make them meaningful (Nicolini 2007; Oudshoorn 2016; Pols 2012; Pols and Willems 2011).

People use various strategies to domesticate digital health technologies to render them more familiar and acceptable. In her analysis of the experiences of New Zealand patients using computerised self-dialysis technologies, Shaw (2015) used the term 'body-in-dialysis' to highlight the entanglements of digital machine and flesh that are configured when patients use their self-dialysis technologies at home. She observed that patients must carefully plan their daily and weekly routines around dialysis and ensure that a part of their homes is set up with all the equipment they need, including storage facilities for equipment such as boxes of fluid bags. Acknowledging a certain ambivalence about self-dialysis as both life-saving and overly dominating, patients personalised the dialysis machine, giving it human names and attributes such as personalities, describing the intimate, friendly relationships with their machines or alternatively noting the machine's tendency to 'misbehave' or act in controlling ways.

Some people find the obligation of self-surveillance in their homes to be frustrating and overwhelming. Thus, for example, research on Dutch heart patients using telemedicine devices such as a system to measure their body weight and blood pressure, a mobile phone capable of conducting and transmitting an electrocardiogram and a device to diagnose heart rhythm irregularities found that patients' bodies and home environments were disciplined by the routines expected of them. They were expected to conform to precise daily schedules of monitoring their bodies and sending data to their healthcare providers and to respond to messages and indicators sent to them at various times daily (Oudshoorn 2009, 2011, 2012). Oudshoorn (2011) discovered that some of the heart patients she studied who resisted using these technologies did so because they did not wish to have a constant reminder that they were ill and they resented the task of monitoring themselves constantly and having their homes transformed into a medical clinic. The surveillance offered by these technologies was thus positioned by these resistant users as restrictive of their autonomy, contributing to anxiety about their health or detracting from their preferred sense of selfhood and embodiment.

While some users experience self-monitoring or self-care technologies as restrictive and constraining of their autonomy, for others they afford the possibility to evade the medical gaze, to take control over their illness and their wayward body or to achieve independence. Some patients value these technologies as a way of avoiding a visit to the doctor when they would rather not see the doctor face to face, and thus establish a distance from medical surveillance (Andreassen *et al.* 2006). Patients may respond to the disciplinary and surveillance imperatives of self-care and self-monitoring by resisting or evading healthcare providers' directions and the obligations expected of them. Individuals may have other priorities and thus simply fail to use the devices provided them in the ways expected of them. Some patients 'play the system', experiment with their therapies or withdraw information from the healthcare providers if it does not conform to expectations (Nicolini 2007; Piras and Miele 2017).

However, there are limits to the extent to which people can resist or modify digital health technologies. Mol and Law (Mol 2009; Mol and Law 2004) conducted a study of Dutch people with diabetes who were required to monitor their blood glucose levels regularly throughout the day. They noted the complexities and difficulties of using self-monitoring technologies and in interpreting the data produced: 'in practice daily care turns around messy, material, smelly, bloody, frightening, or tedious activities that tend to be difficult to do (for professionals as well as patients)' (Mol 2009: 1756–1757). Mol points out that attempts to exercise control over the diabetic body, including the use of monitoring and self-care devices, are doomed to fail, simply because of the vagaries and erratic nature both of the body and the technologies designed to assist people to take control: '[t]echnology is never quite tamed. It doesn't offer control, and it changes along with the other elements of daily care practices' (Mol 2009: 1757).

Digital health technologies that are worn on or implanted in patients' bodies can continually announce their presence to the user, by rubbing against the skin, not fitting well and therefore feeling wrong, making disruptive noises or vibrating. Feminist technoscience critic Laura Forlano (2016) describes living with diabetes as involving continual decisions about what to eat, how to manage her insulin pump and continuous glucose monitor, how to dress in response to wearing the pump and the context of where she would be seen by others that day and how to respond to the readings that devices gave her about her body. She observes that the data flows that are generated by these devices are constantly disciplining as well as monitoring and therapeutically adjusting her body, provoking responses from her: 'As such, I am part of them, and they are part of me.'

Forlano (2016) recounts times when her sleep was disturbed by the continuous glucose monitor buzzing constantly during the night in response to a technical error. She contends that the constant adjustments, learning of technical knowledge and other responses required of her to manage her medical devices position her as a 'feminist hacker of my own cyborg body'. The perspective of the feminist hacker, she asserts, involves moving beyond techno-utopian discourses by drawing attention to the invisible labour, constant adjustments and responses and other embodied practices of using digital technologies.

As Forlano's narrative emphasises, people with chronic conditions like diabetes and kidney failure must engage in the constant invisible labour of negotiating and managing their devices and data. Sometimes these requirements can simply prove too demanding. The late health blogger and activist Jessie Gruman struggled with several chronic conditions as well as stomach cancer. She wrote in her blog (Gruman 2013) that she did not want to use apps that required time and effort to use, given that she was already facing a high load of self-care. Neither did she want to be 'nagged' by her smartphone or to collect detailed data that would simply be ignored by her doctor. In this blog piece, Gruman contended that:

> the things that apps do – remind us, nudge us, identify patterns for us, help us monitor symptoms, send data to our doctor for us – constitute tiny fragments of days that we spend gasping for breath in our chairs, lying on our couches in pain or forcing ourselves to slog through endless uncomfortable chores.

Digital health technologies potentially reconfigure the subject of surveillance and complicate the concept of the panoptic and medical gaze. Telemedicine disperses the spaces of medical care and also the medical gaze from well beyond the clinic into and beyond patients' homes. A patient self-care device worn on the body or positioned in a prominent place in the home can be a potent symbol of illness, marking out the user as unwell or unhealthy. The clinic and the normalising and assessing gaze of healthcare providers are incorporated into the everyday domestic spaces and practices of the lay person via these technologies.

The lack of personal contact in remote consultations or regimens of patient self-care can also present challenges to patients. I referred in the previous chapter to a survey conducted in seven countries which included asking people whether they preferred to use virtual consultations with doctors or face-to-face encounters. The survey found that, in each country, face-to-face encounters were preferred, as they were considered to offer higher-quality medical care (Accenture Consulting 2016a). Qualitative research has similarly shown that some people prefer to engage in physical rather than virtual encounters with healthcare providers, wanting what they view as a more personal interaction (Mort *et al.* 2009; Oudshoorn 2011).

Norwegian researchers (Andreassen 2011; Andreassen and Dyb 2010; Andreassen *et al.* 2006) found that patients may appreciate the opportunities that using telemedical technologies offer for communicating with healthcare professionals, particularly if they find it difficult to travel to seek face-to-face medical attention. However, trust remains an integral aspect of such use: without trust, communicating via technologies would not be effective. Indeed, trust may be even more important than in a face-to-face medical encounter, given the less personal nature of digital communication (Andreassen *et al.* 2006).

Several researchers have explored the use of digital health technologies by older people, including the use of monitoring digital devices such as motion detectors, tags or badges for people with dementia so that their movements might be kept track of without the need for physical restraints, sensors in beds and chairs which are able to monitor sleep patterns, weight and movement in individuals living in residential care, and 'smart floors' that can detect if a person has fallen. Some researchers have concluded that they may be regarded as enabling and empowering devices which are able to assist older people achieve better mobility, independence and feelings of security and allow them to achieve their goal of living at home longer (Brittain *et al.* 2010; Loe 2010; Long 2012). Others, however, warn against the possibilities of coercing older people to use these technologies and the detrimental possibilities of depriving them of face-to-face human contact if they are lonely and feeling isolated (Mort *et al.* 2013; Oudshoorn *et al.* 2016; Roberts *et al.* 2012).

Indeed, in a study on older people and telecare at home in the UK and Spain Mort and colleagues (2013) showed that their participants often expressed resentment about being required to use the technologies and even deliberately 'misused' them in order to provoke responses from caregivers or healthcare professionals that would involve a greater degree of human contact. Greenhalgh and colleagues (2013) talked to older British people with assisted living needs, and found that the digital technologies provided to them failed to meet their requirements. Their interviewees valued social relationships over technologies, and many felt socially isolated and lonely. At best, the digital devices that monitored their health and physical activity were viewed as useful sources of information; but they did not improve participants' wellbeing.

Some older people simply do not see a reason to use a particular digital health technology as it does not offer them any advantage or it clashes with their self-perceptions. Oudshoorn and colleagues (2016) conducted research on the design and development of a human interaction robot for use in caring for older people in their homes and Dutch older people's opinions about this idea. They point out that the prevailing discourse assumes homogeneity of this age group, with little recognition of their diversity (differences based on whether a person has a disability, health status, community links, gender, ethnicity and race, and so on). Oudshoorn and colleagues' findings demonstrate that the telecare technologies that have been designed for this group positioned them as 'a dependent and decrepit "other"' in need of and desiring assistance to achieve independence and self-responsibility for their health and wellbeing (Oudshoorn *et al.* 2016: 172). The Dutch people they spoke to were reluctant to position themselves in this way – or indeed, even to categorise themselves as 'old' – and therefore these robots held little attraction for them.

As these in-depth studies conducted in different sociocultural milieux demonstrate, the ways in which people take up – or challenge, resist or transform – digital health technologies take place as part of highly complex human–non-human assemblages. Designers, policy makers and healthcare providers may hold certain defined expectations about how these devices may be used, but these often do not recognise the shifting and heterogeneous lifeworlds which the devices enter. These devices have the potential to be lively – to be incorporated usefully into people's mundane practices and concepts of selfhood, embodiment and social relations and to allow them to enhance the capacities of their bodies and improve their health and wellbeing. However, if their affordances offer little of value to prospective users, or if such individuals fail to imagine how they can be incorporated into their lives or, indeed, view themselves as appropriate users, then this potential cannot be realised.

★★★

The research reviewed above has demonstrated the contingencies and compromises that are part of the use of digital health technologies by both patients and healthcare workers. Human actors respond to digital health technologies by shaping them to fit their domestic or work practices where they can. Technologies are thereby appropriated and domesticated as part of regular or everyday routines. However, humans may themselves be disciplined by the technologies at those points where the technologies are resistant to intervention or change. Furthermore, patients and lay people use digital health technologies in diverse and sometimes contradictory or ambivalent ways. It is not simply a matter of either taking up or rejecting these technologies: many people move between these two positions. Some technologies are embraced on some occasions, while others may be rejected or resisted. Their meanings and uses are not stable but rather are subject to change and contestation, depending on the context in which they are located and the other actors with which they interact. As I go on to demonstrate in the next chapter, these issues are also pertinent in the context of the work of healthcare professionals.

7

DIGITISED MEDICAL AND HEALTH WORK

In this chapter, I address the topics of how and why digital health technologies are taken up in healthcare workplaces and what the implications are for medical power and authority. A certain ambivalence is evident in the medical literature on lay people using some digital health technologies, and medical practitioners and public health workers also have varying attitudes to using technologies as part of their professional lives. Many people in healthcare and public health are encouraged or compelled to use these technologies, while some make the decision to take up their use voluntarily. In other cases, however, workers may be actively dissuaded from engaging from using digital technologies for professional purposes. These issues are discussed in the chapter. I end with some reflections on the contribution of digital health to the biomedicalisation of society and consider whether these technologies have contributed to the deprofessionalisation of medicine.

Digital technology use in health and medical work

Medical and health apps

A body of literature has developed that examines the ways in which people working in health and medical domains are using digital technologies for professional purposes. Numerous studies have shown that smartphone ownership and tablet computer use for medical education, finding medical information, taking clinical images of patients and clinical decision making are high among physicians, medical residents or interns and medical students in countries such as the USA (Nuss et al. 2014; Robinson and Burk 2013), the UK (Payne et al. 2012; Robinson et al. 2013), Australia (Kirk et al. 2014; Koehler et al. 2012), Malaysia (Wan et al. 2014), Ireland (O'Connor et al. 2014) and Canada (Boruff and Storie 2014).

Medical schools are beginning to employ mobile devices and apps for medical education, often using tablet computers (Husain 2011), including providing medical textbooks and curricula in digital formats (Nuss *et al.* 2014). Medical trainee programmes, including those for anatomy and surgery, now often use several other forms of digital resources, including wearable digital headsets or mini-cameras to record real-time surgical techniques from the perspective of the surgeon, and simulation tools such as virtual reality, digital games and robotics (Evans and Schenarts 2016; Park *et al.* 2017; Prentice 2013).

Apps have become commonly used in medical and allied healthcare work. In one study that surveyed US doctors (Huang 2014), more than two-thirds said that they used apps as part of their work. Medication interaction apps were most commonly used, followed by diagnosis apps. Another USA-based study (Franko and Tirell 2012) found that over half of respondents participating in graduate training programmes for physicians used apps in their clinical work, with drug guides and medical calculators the most popular. A British survey of medical students and junior doctors in a healthcare region (Payne *et al.* 2012) also found that over half of both students and junior doctors had medical-related apps on smartphones, with apps for medical education purposes the most popular. The use of apps on tablet computers by US physiotherapy students during their clinical training was investigated by Tilson and colleagues (2016). They noted that apps for medical information seeking, patient education, communicating with other healthcare professionals and documentation purposes were popular among these students.

Research suggests that nurses have been slower than doctors to adopt medical apps use for their work. A British five-hospital study asking both nurses and doctors about their app use (Mobasheri *et al.* 2015) revealed that almost all of both groups owned a smartphone. A high percentage of doctors (almost 90 per cent) and a substantially lower percentage of nurses (67 per cent) responded that they found medical apps to be useful for their clinical practice. In Australian research that involved introducing nurses working in a gynaecological ward to using smartphones and apps for work (Farrell 2016), the participants raised the issue of a lack of availability of Australian-based apps (for uses such as drug dosage calculation) and the screen of smartphones being too small to use effectively for patient education purposes. Several nurses felt that they had not received enough training on how to use smartphones and download and use apps appropriate for their clinical work. They were also concerned that if patients or supervisors saw them using their phone at work, this might reflect negatively on them, as it might be assumed by observers that they were using the phone for personal purposes.

The nurses in this study noted that using a smartphone while at a patient's bedside or engaging with patients' family members could be considered rude or unprofessional and therefore not consonant with ideals of quality nursing care, as the nurse's attention is diverted to the device. The nurses observed that doctors appeared far less concerned about these issues, and were using their phones at work much more frequently than were nursing staff members. These findings highlight the importance of accepted norms and understandings related to the work of different healthcare professionals, as well as power gradients between categories of healthcare professionals. Nurses are expected to be more engaged with their patients in face-to-face encounters than are doctors working in the hospital setting.

There are numerous intersections developing between devices and software introduced for medically related patient monitoring and self-care regimens and those offered on the market for individuals to use for fitness and health promotion purposes. Doctors commonly recommend health and medical apps to their patients, particularly for the management of smoking, body weight, physical fitness, mental health and chronic diseases (IMS Institute for Healthcare Informatics 2015). Physiotherapists and neurological disorder specialists are beginning to use such self-tracking technologies as medical devices in their practice to monitor and assess patients' mobility (MobiHealthNews 2014).

Social media

Many medical practitioners are wary about using social media for work purposes, particularly if this may expose them to the scrutiny of their patients or challenge patient confidentiality. A survey of Australian doctors (Brown *et al.* 2014) identified that, while most used social media privately, only a minority did so as part of their work. Few were even using email to communicate with patients and the majority expressed discomfort about the idea that patients might be seeking information about them online before consulting with them. The doctors were worried about public access to details about them and also had concerns about legal issues, such as patient confidentiality.

Studies have shown that doctors and other healthcare professionals are more open to using social media to access and share information with other healthcare professionals. Research involving oncologists and primary care physicians in the USA (McGowan *et al.* 2012) revealed that a quarter of the respondents used social media regularly to access medical information, with a far smaller percentage (14 per cent) contributing medical information to social media. However, more than half of the respondents considered that social media enabled them to care for patients more effectively and to improve the quality of care they delivered.

A systematic review of research published on the use of social media for communicating with other healthcare professionals (Rolls *et al.* 2016) revealed that many find these sites useful for networking, professional development and sharing information. The research showed that a culture of altruism, trust, collectivism and reciprocity underpinned the professionals' engagement. Those who used social media, discussion forums and other information-sharing platforms (such as wikis and listservs) appreciated the opportunity to engage in the community of knowledge established on such sites, particularly if they were closed groups designed only for the interaction of professionals working in a relevant medical field. The practices of conference tweeting, tweet chats and journal clubs on social media were also shown to be emergent uses by healthcare professionals.

As is the case with research on lay people's and patients' use of social media, studies on healthcare professionals' use of Twitter predominate over investigations of other social media platforms. Analysis of the presence of journals, professional organisations and specialists in ophthalmology on Facebook and Twitter (Micieli and Tsui 2015) found modest engagement; patient advocacy organisations were more active. A study of the use of social media in neurosurgery (Alotaibi *et al.* 2016) similarly identified that not many professional journals were using accounts to publicise research findings, but some neurosurgical private practices were active on Facebook and Twitter. Japanese medical institutions use Twitter to communicate medical knowledge and information about the services they offer, essentially using it as a forum for advertising (Sugawara *et al.* 2016). Medical professionals are beginning to use Twitter as part of professional conference participation, engaging in the practice of 'live tweeting' details of presentations (Djuricich and Zee-Cheng 2015; Matta *et al.* 2014; Mishori *et al.* 2014).

Researchers who examined the content of remarks made by Swedish physicians and medical students using Twitter (Brynolf *et al.* 2013) discovered that most conformed to what was considered to be 'professional' standards, with only some lapses that breached patient confidentiality. An ethnographic study of medical students who use Twitter (Chretien *et al.* 2015) revealed that the students were very careful about maintaining a professional demeanour in their interactions and found it a useful way to supplement their learning at medical school by sharing information and to feel part of a community of students. They used Twitter to access experts in the fields they were studying and to gain insights into patients' perspectives.

Healthcare providers have begun to use social media sites, online forums and their own blogs and websites to provide information about their services and about preventive health and medical treatments in general. These efforts are particularly evident in the context of the more privatised and commodified healthcare system in the USA. One study of US hospitals (Griffis *et al.* 2014) showed that nearly all had adopted at least one social media platform, with more than 90 per cent using Facebook, Yelp and FourSquare and 40 per cent using a Twitter account. In response to healthcare-rating platforms, individual doctors, hospitals and health systems in the USA are beginning to offer patients incentives, such as prize draws, to rate them on the platforms. The US government's Medicare programme offers bonuses to hospitals that are rated highly in patients' assessments.

With this new prominence given to patients' assessments of their healthcare providers using online platforms and apps, the public relations arms of healthcare organisations and businesses are finding ways to identify what types of discussions operate in social media. Various institutions and companies have set out to offer advice to them. The Mayo Clinic Social Media Network, for example, offers courses to healthcare and public relations professionals in healthcare and medical industry organisations to train them in how to access and analyse the content of patients' social media interactions as well as intervene in online discussions in ways that offer information and promote their services or products. The Symplur company provides the services of public relations professionals who are expert in healthcare-related social media analysis and promotion, as well as offering social media analytics via its website, such as the HealthCare Hashtag Project (2017) for monitoring Twitter activity related to health and medical topics.

After realising the reach and potential impact of these technologies, health promoters have experimented with using text messages, social media sites and apps to disseminate strategically information about preventive health, collect data about people's health-related behaviours and attempt to persuade members of target groups to change their behaviour in the interests of their health (for example, Balatsoukas *et al.* 2015; Jacobs *et al.* 2016; Kelleher and Moreno 2016; Korda and Itani 2013; Muessig *et al.* 2013; M Smith *et al.* 2015). Some people have begun to discuss the possibilities of incorporating self-tracking technologies into health promotion programmes. For example, Swan (2009, 2012, 2013) has written several articles in which she outlines the ways in which voluntary self-tracking efforts can be mobilised by health promotion and preventive medicine.

Few researchers have asked public health workers about their experiences of using social media in their work. One exception is a project based in Florida, USA, in which interviews were conducted with 15 stakeholders associated with the Rural South Public Health Training Center (Hart *et al.* 2016). The findings revealed that the participants used social media for professional development and networking, particularly with colleagues they already knew personally. No participants used Twitter for work-related purposes. Many expressed their difficulty in accessing social media sites in their workplaces, because the sites had been blocked by the state. Their attempts at communicating with their colleagues and the public were limited, therefore, to the quite static content offered on official state department websites.

A survey of public health researchers at Johns Hopkins University in the USA (Keller *et al.* 2014) showed that few used any of the major social media platforms for work purposes. Although the respondents were positive about the possibilities of using social media as part of their work, most were either not interested in trying it or actively opposed to professional engagement. Social media were viewed as avenues for promoting health information to the public, rather than as sources of information for public health research or as a means for career advancement. Another American survey of health education professionals revealed that only one-third of respondents were using social media in the workplace (Hanson *et al.* 2011).

An interview-based study I conducted with Mike Michael (Lupton and Michael 2017b) of Australian healthcare and public health professionals working in communicable disease was able to identify some of the benefits and constraints to using social media. The findings of this study highlighted the importance of context when considering how people use social media in the workplace. The benefits of social media use identified by these interviewees included connecting and establishing networks not only with peers but also people or groups outside the workplace, promoting openness and sharing of information and the publicising and development of research. The health workers' concerns included issues of privacy and the blurring of boundaries between personal and professional use, the risk of jeopardising their career through injudicious use of social media, lack of credibility, the quality of the content they posted, time pressures and becoming a target of attack.

The context of the communicable disease workplace in dealing with infectious diseases that are often stigmatised and involve political and personal sensitivities as well as discussion of intimate behaviours such as sexual activity meant the health workers needed to consider these issues carefully. Given the highly bureaucratic and conservative nature of the environments in which many of our participants worked, they confronted significant barriers to using social media, including experiencing difficulties accessing the internet from work.

For the most part, our participants did not conceptualise social media use as a channel by which members of disadvantaged or marginalised social groups could receive a voice, but instead as simply a newer and potentially more effective way to disseminate targeted messages developed by experts or to monitor disease trends and dissenting public opinion. The potential to use social media more radically to engage publics as active and equal contributors to health knowledges, and beyond this, to promote activist causes challenging health and social disparities, was not raised in the participants' accounts. Social media knowledge production and sharing were primarily viewed as affordances for professional peers rather than as elements of communication with publics. We found that, while many of the health workers in our study who were engaged in public health initiatives were considering the ethical and political issues related to their professional presentation on social media and the type of content they generated, few had begun to consider data privacy and security issues for the publics they targeted in health communication strategies using these media.

Doctors' views on lay people's use of digital health

It is evident that the medical profession has responded in diverse and often contradictory ways to the challenges to medical authority enacted by some forms of digital technologies. As I have outlined in earlier chapters, the concept of digital patient engagement has been extensively championed in many orthodox medical forums, including medical journals, conferences and books, by members of the medical profession such as Eric Topol. Topol, a US professor of genomics and a cardiologist, is one of the better-known public advocates of digital health in the medical profession. In two books, *The Creative Destruction of Medicine: How the Digital Revolution Will Create Better Health Care* (Topol 2012) and *The Patient Will See You Now: The Future of Medicine is in Your Hands* (Topol 2015), as well as numerous interviews, blog posts and academic articles, Topol has outlined his vision for using digital technologies to improve medical care. In these publications, Topol argues that medical professionals and their patients need to embrace these technologies not only to contribute to improvement of medical care and patient wellbeing but also to reduce healthcare costs.

However, medical discussions of digital patient engagement often demonstrate a degree of ambivalence. The medical and healthcare literature does not present a unified definition of 'patient engagement' or 'activation'. In some contexts, these terms are used principally to describe patients' adherence to medically prescribed treatments and their ability to manage their symptoms; in others, it is used to refer to health-related beliefs and behaviours on the part of lay people or the quality of the doctor–patient encounter; in yet others, it relates to organisational measures designed to improve health outcomes and reduce spending (Barello *et al.* 2012).

What *is* clear is that in medical forums some elements of patients taking more responsibility for their health management and seeking medical information to educate themselves are considered appropriate and beneficial. This approval is particularly evident when such practices conform to medical guidelines and increase the extent to which patients comply with advice from their healthcare providers (as in adhering to the drug or self-monitoring regimens they have been prescribed). However, other elements of lay people's use of digital health technologies are considered ill advised, too extreme or even dangerous in challenging medical authority. It would appear that there is a fine line between what doctors may consider to be appropriate information seeking by patients and what they consider to be excessive attempts by patients to use online sources or apps to discover, create or share information about health, illness and disease.

This ambivalence on the part of the medical profession has been apparent since the onset of health and medical websites, with much discussion of the power of 'Dr Google' to inform (or misinform) lay people. Indeed, ever since lay people began to use websites to seek information and share their own perspectives and knowledges about health and medical issues, as well as to engage in activism, some concern has been expressed in the medical literature about the challenge to medical authority offered by patients who have armed themselves with information obtained from the internet (Ahmad *et al.* 2006; Antheunis *et al.* 2013). Such arguments tend to be articulated by focusing on concerns such as the potential for health and medical information accessed in online forums or apps to be dangerously inaccurate or invalid (for example, Diaz *et al.* 2002; Wicks and Chiauzzi 2015; Yetisen *et al.* 2014), or the possibility that lay people may become overly anxious about their symptoms or dependent on digitally mediated medical advice. Self-diagnosis by lay people using apps and symptom-tracking software is frequently represented in the medical literature as pathological or disordered, itself a psychological medical condition (Loos 2013).

A strong degree of caution is also evident in the medical literature about the value of medical and health apps, particularly those that do not demonstrate significant contributions from medical experts or which provide medical information that is assessed to be inaccurate or misleading (for example, Wicks and Chiauzzi 2015; Yetisen *et al.* 2014). These types of digital media are quite controversial among the medical profession, who has expressed concern not only that wrong information is provided but that lay people may make wrong diagnoses, become overly anxious or, alternatively, be reassured by using these apps when in fact they have a serious medical condition (Semigran *et al.* 2015). Other potential problems that have been identified in the medical literature refer to the time and responsibility burden on doctors who are faced with negotiating patients' opinions on their diagnosis (Farmer *et al.* 2011; Ryan and Wilson 2008; Semigran *et al.* 2015; Wald *et al.* 2007). A new psychological condition has even been invented: namely, 'cyberchondria' or excessive anxiety about health states that could eventuate from obtaining information about diseases and conditions online (for example, Doherty-Torstrick *et al.* 2016; Fergus 2013; Loos 2013; Starcevic and Berle 2013).

In recent years, the medical profession has been further alarmed by the phenomenon of 'do-it-yourself surgery' and other lay medical treatments online. Facilitated by sites such as YouTube, 'how to' videos are available, directed at the general public, that demonstrate various medical procedures for lay people to conduct on themselves or others. These include procedures such as removing cysts, extracting bullets and stitching up wounds. YouTube videos about surgical procedures and other medical treatments that have been designed for medical students and practitioners can also be viewed by members of the public who may be interested in learning more about these practices (Vogel 2011). As I observed in earlier chapters, social media platforms have provided spaces for people who challenge medical authority by engaging in or supporting behaviours that have been medically deemed harmful or pathological, or by seeking information about and accessing controversial or unproven treatments. Here again, the medical profession has expressed disquiet about the potential dangers for patients of taking these avenues (Crooks *et al.* 2013).

The newer digital health technologies, as well as continuing to negotiate all of these issues, also raise other difficulties and complexities for doctors. In relation to patient-ranking sites, it has been argued that views expressed on healthcare-ranking sites might be unrepresentative, unfair or inaccurate and that healthcare providers may 'game' the system by giving positive ratings to their own service or denigrating a rival service (Greaves *et al.* 2013; Rozenblum and Bates 2013). Healthcare providers can become the butt of attacks on social media, including on patient opinion or ranking platforms, in which their identity may be revealed. This was an issue identified in an article published on the *Australian Family Physician* website (Bird 2014). The author gave examples of doctors finding what they considered to be unfair and inappropriate comments about their services made by patients online. She notes that 'most medical practitioners find adverse postings on these websites immensely upsetting and anxiety-provoking, especially as there is little that can be done to remove, or even respond to, these negative posts'. A number of ways for doctors to respond to such comments are suggested, including commencing defamation proceedings against the patient if the comments can be considered detracting to the medical practitioner's professional reputation.

Public health departments can also find themselves targeted by people and groups using social media as platforms for protest or challenges to policy. One study focused on the public's responses to the Chicago Department of Public Health's Twitter campaign concerning proposed policy to regulate e-cigarettes as tobacco products (Harris *et al.* 2014b). It was found that the Department was targeted for tweets from members of the public actively opposing the proposed policy. The

Department was represented as disseminating propaganda and making false statements. Many of these opposing tweeters were affiliated with the e-cigarette industry or advocacy groups, although a larger number were apparently private citizens. This research draws attention to the openness of debates that occur on social media, which facilitate the expression of opposing or counter views from a wider array of viewpoints that would previously not have received public expression.

Despite discourses attesting to the value of patient-generated data, concerns have been raised about how patients and healthcare providers will be trained to use self-tracking technologies and how the reams of data that lay people can now collect about their bodies should be used by healthcare providers (Malykhina 2013; Neff 2013; Ringquist 2013). Some doctors find that patients bringing the personal data they have collected about their bodies and health conditions to their consultations serves only to distract from what are considered more important elements to discuss. Doctors are concerned that these data may be inaccurate or misleading and that patients may become too focused on what their data tell them to the exclusion of other indicators of their health and wellbeing. They often feel more comfortable about data that they have collected themselves about the patient or with devices that they have recommended or provided to patients rather than those generated by patients themselves on their own initiative (Fiore-Gartland and Neff 2015).

Doctors and healthcare institutions are also concerned about the boundaries between patient and doctor breaking down and about confidentiality and patient privacy issues when social media are used as a medium for communication between doctors and patients. This issue has received extensive discussion in medical ethics journals and websites (for example, Chretien and Kind 2013; Lagu and Greysen 2010). Questions have been raised in these forums about whether or not medical professionals and other healthcare workers should become friends or followers of their patients on social media, and vice versa, whether healthcare workers should use search engines to discover information about their patients and what the implications are for the doctor–patient relationship. The privacy implications for both healthcare providers and patients of sharing personal details online have been discussed. The *British Medical Journal* has even published an opinion piece on its Careers webpage on the use of Snapchat by healthcare students and professionals (Patel *et al.* 2016). The authors warn of the ethical problems of using this platform to post images of themselves in medical settings and highlighting the possibility of patient confidentiality breaches and damaging the status of, and patient trust and faith in, the medical profession.

A position paper written by the US College of Physicians and the Federation of State Medical Boards and published online in 2013 in the *Annals of Internal Medicine* journal examines many of these concerns (Farnan *et al.* 2013). The authors note the benefits that the use of email, text messaging services and online media can provide medical professionals, namely professional education, sharing of information and networking, community education and outreach, ready communication with and follow-up of patients, and improved patient adherence to therapy and patient satisfaction. However, they also identify many potential risks and harms of such use. They recommend that training for medical professionals for maintaining professional standards and decorum online should be established at all levels, from medical school onwards. The authors nominate issues such as doctors discovering from online searches of social media (referred to as 'patient-targeted Googling') that their patients are not following their advice or engaging in risk-taking behaviours and recommend that doctors use their clinical judgement about whether to do this and if so, whether or not to reveal this knowledge to their patients.

In this position paper, doctors are also urged to consider carefully what online sources of medical information they recommend to their patients and to ensure that these are 'accurate' and 'objective'. It is recommended that if doctors use online media to interact with each other as professionals, they should ensure that these networks are secure, that only other professionals can gain access and that all clinical information that may be shared in their forums is anonymised. The authors suggest that doctors should not make personal contact with patients on social media because it will undermine the professionalism of their relationship and their authority and objectivity. Medical practitioners are further advised not to vent their frustrations about their colleagues, workplaces or patients online, as such opinions may undermine respect and trust in their profession. It is noted in the position paper that the recruitment of medical students, residency trainees and physicians may now involve online searches of their social media use and other online engagement, and that individuals should therefore be careful about the type of content they place online about themselves. It is concluded that: 'Being proactive by controlling posted content, using privacy settings, and limiting access to personal information is in the best interest of both the profession and the individual physician'.

As such statements suggest, the position of many medical authorities on the use of social and other digital media by doctors and patients tends to take a paternalistic and defensive stance. Serious ethical issues, such as whether doctors should monitor their patients' health-related behaviours by observing their social media content, are represented as subject to individual doctors' 'clinical judgements'. The interests of members of the medical profession and their right to privacy and confidentiality are privileged over those of patients. Many doctors are very ambivalent about how 'empowered' their patients should be and how open to public discussion or ranking their own practices should be made. There is little recognition of the value that patients and lay people receive from being able to access and share health and medical information readily online, including access to each other's experiences and evaluations of healthcare services and medical therapies. Rather, it appears that the medical profession wants better control over how lay people create content and interact with each other. The desire of the medical profession to protect its professional autonomy, control over medical knowledge and subsequent authority is overt in these kinds of statements.

Redefining and re-enacting healthcare practice

Critical social research has delved deeply into the profound issues concerning medical practice and training that are mediated by digital technologies. This research has shown that the use of these technologies can have profound implications for the embodied practices and professional identities of healthcare workers. If patients use apps to make a diagnosis of a medical condition or employ self-care technologies to monitor and care for their health, the interventions of healthcare professionals can be excluded, or at least, minimised. Suggestions that robots can take over in an expanding array of medical practices, including conducting surgery and providing bodily care to the ill, the elderly and people with disabilities, further call into question the nature of human engagement in healthcare. Even when healthcare professionals are directly involved in using digital health technologies with patients, their modes of practice are altered. The materialities of care, as enacted by healthcare workers' bodies, are often at stake in professional experiences of digitised caregiving.

As outlined in Chapter 1, the hands-on physical examination of patients is a central element of healthcare provision and diagnosis. Healthcare workers have been trained to rely on multisensory ways of knowing the bodies of their patients and using these knowledges to make judgements about their states of health. The accumulation of interactions with patients allows them to develop sensitivity to aspects of human bodies, noticing features that would be less discernible to people without such experience. The body, in this context, becomes a 'communicative apparatus' (Gardner and Williams 2015: 766). These knowledges and judgements may also include the healthcare workers' sensory responses to the environment of the patients. They combine to develop an intuitive response to patients that healthcare professionals have traditionally relied on as a key element of their work.

In their Dutch study of palliative care conducted by oncology nurses for patients with terminal cancer, van Hout et al. (2015) noted that when they had conducted at-home visits in person, the nurses were able to discern subtle indicators of their patients' wellbeing such as whether decorative items on display had been dusted, if the washing-up had been done and how easily the patients moved about. The nurses were using multisensory judgements in identifying these signs: not only how the patients or their home settings looked, but indicators such as smell and sound. Embodied practices such as making patients coffee, checking that chairs and beds are comfortable, adopting a pose that conveys both calm and full attention to the patient's needs, and so on, are elements of the material care offered by the nurses.

Digital health technologies that remove healthcare workers from the physical presence of their patients demand different ways of sensing the patient's physical state and emotional wellbeing. Telecare and telemedicine, for example, change the materialities of care in relation to embodiment. Healthcare workers can no longer use many of these forms of material and sensory care. As discussed in the previous chapter, telemedicine and other forms of digital healthcare also potentially alter the surveillance possibilities and capacities of the medical gaze. In the individual medical encounter, doctors practise a type of personalised surveillance over each of their patients, testing, measuring and investigating features of patients' bodies, constructing and maintaining health records, noting patients' adherence to their advice and so on. In their face-to-face encounters with their patients, they have opportunities to use their embodied senses to observe and monitor patients' states of health and wellbeing and their responses to therapies. In contrast, when digital self-care or self-tracking technologies are used, the direct gaze of the doctor or nurse becomes mediated. They must interpret patients' bodies using video or text-based encounters, rely on the judgements of any caregiver or healthcare worker who is physically present or review the metric information that digital devices generate on patients (Mort *et al.* 2003; Oudshoorn 2008; Roberts *et al.* 2012).

Critical social research has identified that when healthcare workers demonstrate resistance to using these technologies, such a response is multifaceted and complex. It is not simply a matter of inertia or an unwillingness to try new technologies on the part of these professionals, as some of the health informatics and other digital health literature within health services tend to imply. Healthcare professionals find it difficult at times working with digitised virtual bodies that are at a physical distance and mediated via technologies. While the data provided by digital sensors may offer certain capacities to enact patients' bodies, illnesses and healthcare, other forms of sensory knowledges gained from physical co-presence with fleshly human bodies are lost or diminished. Consequently, both patients and healthcare workers are required to use and conceptualise their bodies in different ways (Mort *et al.* 2009; Mort and Smith 2009; Oudshoorn 2008; Pols 2012; Roberts *et al.* 2012).

These elements were identified in Prentice's (2013) anthropological study of anatomy and surgery education. In observing the use of virtual reality simulators for surgical training, she noticed the difficulty of both building and using these simulators so that they work effectively to train surgeons. The simulator must help trainees develop a muscular gestalt or embodied knowledge that allows them to perform techniques safely and effectively on living human bodies. This involves complex visual and haptic sensations and feedback, with the simulator and trainee interrelating to enact the surgical body. The creators and users of virtual reality simulators find it very difficult to achieve the highly sophisticated, often tacit and mutually responsive sensations that contribute to the degree of muscular gestalt and intuitive experience required of capable surgeons.

In an ethnography of medical work in intensive care units, Carmel (2013) showed that healthcare professionals constantly sought to mediate the information conveyed to them about their patients from digital (and other) monitoring technologies. They used their own embodied experiential judgement to make sense of this information, often choosing to trust their intuitive perception of the patient over 'the numbers' provided to them by monitoring technologies. This is not say, however, that each form of judgement or knowledge (that of the intuitive body and that of the technology) is necessarily separate. As healthcare workers engage in the continuing experiential process of developing their skills in perceiving and making sense of patients' bodies, their interactions with the information delivered to them by technologies are part of this learning process. Experience and intuitive knowledge, therefore, are themselves inevitably technologically mediated.

I referred in the previous chapter to the invisible labour in which patients and other lay people are called on to engage as part of self-care and information-seeking and sharing practices. Invisible labour can also be part of medical and health work in response to digital technologies. In their study of clinicians using telemedical devices, Mort and Smith (2009) discovered that clinicians' work practices involve much invisible work. They observe that the clinicians' knowledge and actions were often acquired despite, rather than facilitated by, digitised information systems. Digital data, like any other kinds of data, must be interpreted, made sense of, located within existing knowledges and data sets and negotiated.

Little in-depth research has explored how people in the medical or public health domains are using and making senses of big data as part of their work. Mort and Smith (2009) remark upon the mythological status that information/data has obtained in healthcare discourses and policies, noting that knowledge and action in healthcare delivery are often achieved in spite of, rather than as a result of, information systems. They point out that the methods used to obtain data in the telemedicine setting structure what is recorded and what is not within stringent limits. The healthcare workers working in this system often struggle with and rework the information they gather or are provided with in their attempts to diagnose and treat patients, seeking to add greater contextual information to these data. Their medical judgement is based on interpreting multiple and often conflicting heterogeneous streams of incomplete data.

Sometimes health and medical digital data negotiations and sense making detract from, rather than complement, other forms of expert knowledges. The doctors interviewed by Greenhalgh et al. (2014) commented that using a centralised online appointment booking system interfered with the local and contextualised knowledges they had developed through their work. When doctors are confronted with patients bringing their personal data to the medical encounter, they must contend with incorporating this new source of information into their work of diagnosis, assessing patients' wellbeing and making recommendations for treatment. Doctors and other healthcare providers must learn how to incorporate patient-generated data into their practices, which may involve not only using these data but also resisting their use, as other sources of information may be considered more important for their work (Fiore-Gartland and Neff 2015).

Certain highly specific skills are also required in public health disease surveillance systems involving the manipulation of digital data. As described in Chapter 4, medical and health workers have attempted to exploit the capacities of the big data sets generated on social media, blogs, search engines and other digital media as well as electronic medical records to generate knowledges about people's attitudes and behaviours and to conduct surveillance of disease outbreaks across populations. In a Canadian study, French (2014) used interviews to investigate the working practices of medical and public health professionals involved with digital disease surveillance. This study identified the work involved with identifying, entering, manipulating and taming digital data and software, or what he refers to as the 'informatic practices' involved in the configuration of disease-surveillant assemblages. As French shows, the task of making diverse and complex forms of digital data sets and software successfully interact with each other to configure the desired end product – high-quality useable and useful data – can be time consuming and difficult. It also demands new capacities and knowledges from workers, requiring additional training or hands-on experience in often unanticipated ways. These included developing professional sensitivity to data privacy and security issues and awareness of the potential unintended consequences of bringing diverse data sets together for analysis. The affordances and limitations of the non-human actors with which health and medical workers must engage to enact digital disease surveillance systems are highlighted in this research.

In summary, digital health technologies raise questions about how medical and public health work, training, practice and knowledge should be defined and enacted, and even superseded. Just as patients are required to domesticate or 'tame' digital health technologies as part of incorporating them into their everyday lives (Pols 2012; Pols and Willems 2011), so too doctors, nurses and other healthcare workers are called on to work out how best to engage with the technologies to suit the demands, commitments and materialities of their working lives.

Digitised biomedicalisation

Sociologists have long drawn attention to the power relations and social structures shaping the delivery of healthcare and the health status of social groups in capitalist economies. As outlined in Chapter 1, the political economy perspective is the most dominant theoretical position critical researchers have employed to examine these topics. They have addressed issues such as how the medical profession has established and maintained its authority over medical knowledge and healthcare provision. Foucauldian theory is also influential in analyses of medical power, particularly in analyses of phenomena such as biopolitics, biopower and the medical gaze. Writers adopting both perspectives have contended that medical technologies have contributed to the expansion of medical authority and its capacity for the surveillance, monitoring, regulation and management of human bodies.

Digital health technologies can contribute to the biomedicalisation of everyday life. Once a technology is invented and can be applied to portraying, monitoring or measuring elements of human bodies and behaviours for health and medical-related reasons, this technology and its affordances become transformed (wholly or partially) into a health or medical device. Thus, for example, a geo-locational device for tracking and generating data on the routes taken by a runner, walker or cyclist may have been devised initially as a way for users to keep track of where their journeys have taken them and how much ground they have covered. If these data are imbricated into corporate wellness programmes or health insurance systems, these data and the device itself become transformed into health-monitoring technologies. The number of kilometres covered by users or the altitude they have scaled become signifiers of the extent of their physical activity, which itself is treated as a marker for bodily health and fitness. Three-dimensional (3D) printers have become devices for the fabrication of medical prosthetic or medical education materials. Online search engines can become medical and health information-locating devices. Social media sites are repurposed as forums for discussing illness experiences and sharing images of human bodies, health and fitness activities and surgical procedures.

These technologies promote the expansion of concerns about health, wellbeing and disease prevention into the realm of everyday life. When people's smartwatches are beeping or buzzing insistently throughout the day to remind them to move more, or when a notification appears on their smartphone reminding them to check their blood pressure or blood glucose levels, these are clearly instances of more intrusive nudges entering into people's consciousness and routines in ways that cannot easily be ignored. So too, employees who are nudged to participate in workplace wellness programmes involving digitised self-tracking, or school students in physical education classes whose physical activities and fitness levels are monitored by wearable devices, find themselves in situations where digital health technologies are almost inescapable.

When these aspects of digital technology use are highlighted, medicine does appear to have colonised even more aspects of people's lives and entered into institutions such as the family, the workplace and the school in new and more pervasive ways. Digitised biomedicalisation is also evident in the ways in which personal health and medical data are available for repurposing beyond their original use. As I showed in Chapter 4, the data that are generated from lay people's interactions online, such as their discussions of their health on social media platforms, have become drawn into other medical domains by virtue of their use by actors such as medical researchers and pharmaceutical and medical device companies. A multitude of types of personal information in digital form are now treated as relevant to manipulation and analysis for the purposes of configuring medical or public health knowledges. When medical workers and health promoters employ digital devices as part of their work, they and the target groups they seek to influence are imbricated within and form part of a complex digital knowledge economy and a system that can be employed for mass surveillance of people's personal data.

The deprofessionalisation of medicine?

Writers addressing the topics of medicalisation and medical dominance have considered for several decades the issue of whether patient consumerism and patient engagement, developments in medical technology and changes in the regulation and provision of healthcare have contributed to a 'deprofessionalisation' of medicine. This argument rests on the assumption that a profession is underpinned by its members' claims to authority, autonomy, knowledge and ability to exert power over other groups, who are dependent on and trusting in their special expertise (Freidson 1988; Starr 1982). Deprofessionalisation involves a decline in these characteristics.

Some elements of digital health do appear to contribute to medical depro-fessionalisation, particularly those that provide the capacity for elements such as diagnosis, self-monitoring and self-care to lay people. Indeed, as early as the 1980s, some sociologists had begun to suggest that computer software and digital medi-cal technologies and the technicians who developed and used them were begin-ning to erode doctors' authority and control over diagnosis, as well as challenge their status by routinising and thereby demystifying medical expertise (Ritzer and Walczak 1988).

The contribution of digital health to contemporary biomedicalisation raises some interesting questions about medical power. The expansion of health and medical imperatives into everyday life in many ways supports and facilitates the authority of the medical profession and medical knowledge. However, the use of some types of digital health technologies can be a way for lay people to challenge medical authority and seek alternatives. Many examples of these possibilities have been described in previous chapters, including patient self-care technologies that allow people to reduce their visits to their doctors' surgeries (and thereby at least partly evade the direct surveillance of the doctor), patient support platforms, online discussion forums or social media groups that help patients share information about their condition without the intervention of medical practitioners and critique forms of medical interventions, apps designed for self-diagnosis or platforms and apps that encourage patients to give their opinion of healthcare providers and pub-licly rank and rate their quality. Patients worldwide can go online to seek informa-tion about or access alternative forms of healthcare, including those that contravene traditional medical knowledge and authority. Using digital media, patients or their advocates are able to group together more easily to work on activist programmes to challenge medical authority.

Diverse perspectives are offered in online forums and social media, from those that support medical authority to those that challenge or resist it. As outlined in Chapter 3, social media sites are used by many groups seeking to challenge medical knowledges, definitions and expertise. A more controversial use of online media for patient activism is the pressure that activists seek to place on health authorities or the medical profession to offer novel therapeutic treatments that have not yet undergone rigorous clinical testing and validation. Orthodox medical authority is contested in these media, with contributors challenging medical advice that they should not access these therapies, to the extent that people are willing to invest additional time and money and take significant risks in their efforts to gain better access to them.

Some patient activism attempts negotiated on social media platforms have man-aged to be successful in gaining access to drugs or surgical treatments (Mazanderani et al. 2013b). One example of such success is a patient-led movement for multiple sclerosis that used Facebook, YouTube and other online media to gain access to a radical surgical procedure, despite mainstream medical advice that it was inef-fective (Slezak 2011). Patients who had undergone the procedure, offered by an Italian surgeon, posted videos on YouTube and accounts on Facebook and multiple sclerosis patient forums of their recovery. The forums worked to provide information to assist individual patients with the condition to find access to the treatment. Some neurologists who continued to oppose this treatment were singled out for high levels of criticism on these forums, charged with attempting to maintain their power, their relationship with drug companies and their income stream over patients' interests.

Patients have also been able to access more readily information and novel therapies via the internet, sometimes bypassing referrals from their usual doctors and going directly to these services. Untested treatments that may not be offered or that are even outlawed in some countries can be publicised on the internet, facilitating access by patients to these therapies if they choose to travel to places where they are offered. What has been described as 'medical tourism', or travelling to foreign countries to undergo medical procedures that are publicised as either less expensive or more innovative than those offered in a patient's home country, has also profited from the expansion of the internet and social media (Lunt *et al.* 2010).

The case of experimental stem cell therapies is an example of such activities. In many cases the efficacy of these therapies is still unknown and they remain controversial among the biomedicine establishment. Stem cell therapies are subsequently not available in some countries. However, many websites established by clinics offer them through 'direct-to-consumer' marketing. Such websites rarely provide details of the risks of these treatments, focusing instead on their imputed benefits and providing case studies of satisfied patients. On these sites and online forums for patients, 'communities of hope' have been established, in which healthcare providers and patients have advocated for better access to stem cell therapies and shared information about travelling abroad to seek them (Petersen and Seear 2011; Petersen *et al.* 2016).

It should be noted, however, for the large part, medical authority and expertise still tend to be privileged in digital media representations and policy related to digital health. As noted in Chapter 2, Google has changed its search returns for health and medical information so that authoritative medical sources are placed at the top. While there is a high degree of diversity of opinion publicised on online media and far more opportunities for patients to share their experiences than ever before, dominant medical views still tend to receive prominence over alternative perspectives offered from outside medicine, including those of patient activists and support groups (Mager 2009; McDaniel *et al.* 2012; Oudshoorn and Somers 2006). For example, a study of two Wikipedia articles on schizophrenia and its causes (Wyatt *et al.* 2016) found that the edits made by medical doctors tended to be accepted as more valid and 'scientific' compared with some of those made by people with schizophrenia, which tend to be viewed as anecdotal and biased. The guidelines by which Wikipedia entries are created and edited insist on contributors using references (hyperlinked) to authoritative texts: here again, scientific journals are privileged over lay sources of knowledge.

The authority of the medical profession, government-funded health promotion agencies and medical industries, and their access to greater resources are reflected in the design and reach of websites, platforms and apps. Groups and organisations that have access to greater resources can pay for technical expertise and for their online content to achieve greater visibility. Those websites and platforms funded by large medical organisations and drug or health insurance companies are able to develop much more sophisticated websites and attract more users, which in turn results in their site ranking more highly on search engines than a patient support or activist group's website because of search engine optimisation strategies that influence page-ranking algorithms.

Patients are rarely encouraged to participate in the design of websites (Oudshoorn and Somers 2006) or in the design, analysis and writing phases of research studies using their data (Harris *et al.* 2012). When lay people are uploading their experiences to patient support or healthcare rating and evaluation websites, they must conform to the organisational demands of these platforms, which typically do not offer full scope for criticism of healthcare providers. Therefore, the sites themselves monitor and discipline patients who are providing data as part of official forms of monitoring healthcare quality and patient satisfaction (Adams 2011; Hart *et al.* 2004).

As I suggested earlier in this chapter, the medical literature and public health professions still retain a paternalistic and pedagogical orientation towards patients and lay people. Patients and lay people continue to be represented as requiring appropriate, 'accurate' medical information and advice in making decisions about their health and wellbeing. Members of the medical and public health profession continue to position themselves, and be positioned by others, as possessing ultimate authority and expertise. While personal health and medical data have taken on various forms of biovalue, this does not necessarily mean that the views of patients are privileged over those of members of the medical profession.

Patients themselves demonstrate ambivalence about challenges to medical authority in digital media. Particularly in the case of contested illnesses or the quest for a diagnosis and the formal recognition of an illness, people interacting in online forums or social media often demonstrate a paradoxical willingness and desire to challenge medical authority as well as wanting a medical diagnosis and treatment (Barker 2008; Lian and Nettleton 2015). Most people still invest great faith and trust in the expertise of medical authorities and continue to want better access to their advice (Lee *et al.* 2014a; Powell *et al.* 2011).

A study involving interviews with Australians (Willis *et al.* 2016) identified that many people continued to adhere to the idea of medical authority and wanted to be able to trust their doctors. However, they also felt it was expected of them to be actively seeking out information beyond that offered by their healthcare providers. Using Google to find this information was a very common practice. Doctors were positioned as the arbiters of information accessed on the internet, helping people to make sense of it and providing advice on which source of information was most authoritative and valid. While people tended to consult internet sources to make decisions about issues such as what health insurance scheme to use or whether they needed to seek medical advice, they relied on their doctors to know the best specialists to consult or to make a good decision about a healthcare service. The study showed that sources of online information that were trusted tended to be medically informed or from government agencies.

Our research with Australian pregnant women and mothers of very young children (Lupton 2016d; Lupton and Pedersen 2016) revealed similar findings. The participants in a survey and focus group study I conducted were constantly seeking information online about pregnancy, childbirth and the care of infants and young children. They placed high value on being able to access information at any time of the day or night, connect with other mothers going through similar experiences and juggle accessing online information and support with demanding childcare tasks. However, these women also expressed their desire for greater access to the expertise of healthcare professionals, with many noting that they would like better and more immediate online contact with these experts.

It would appear, therefore, that biomedicalisation and medical authority continue as dominant trends in the context of emerging digital health technologies. Despite some misgivings and concern expressed by the medical profession relating to the explosion of access of lay people to sources of information and opportunities for them to share their experiences with each other, it still holds a key role in the generation and application of knowledges about the human body, health and illness.

★★★

This chapter has identified a set of issues and topics concerning the use of digital health technologies for health and medical work. The implications for medical power, knowledge and status and for patient 'empowerment' are complex, as there are many competing interests and imperatives operating. The research I have discussed here raises several key points concerning the contribution of digital technologies to the biomedicalisation of society, the ways in which these technologies work both to support and undermine the status and authority of the medical profession, the potential offered by social media for medical and health professionals to communicate with each other and with members of the public and the significant implications of digital technologies for the nature of medical care and health surveillance practices.

CONCLUDING COMMENTS

In this book, I have identified several key features of contemporary digital health technologies uncovered from a critical perspective. These are by no means exhaustive, but they do refer to many of the major meanings, practices and political dimensions that I and others have identified in our research and scholarship. In this concluding chapter, I summarise each of these features. The discussion ends with my suggestions about directions for further research in critical digital health studies.

Key features of contemporary digital health

Social differences in digital health use and access

As in most other areas of social life, different social groups use digital health technologies in different ways. Factors such as access to technologies, education level and literacy, income, gender, age, ethnicity or race, health status and whether or not individuals are living with a disability or chronic illness can all influence the ways in which digital health technologies are adopted. While digital technologies can alleviate existing sociodemographic inequalities in some ways, there are other ways in which they may also exacerbate disadvantage.

The dominance of the ideals of healthism and the responsible citizen

Those who invent, promote and use digital health technologies assume that the achievement and maintenance of good health should be prioritised over other aspects of life. The ideal of the responsible healthy citizen is continually emphasised and promulgated in digital health. Indeed, most digital health strategies and discourses render health states even more individualised, and draw attention away from the social determinants of health to a greater degree than ever before.

The datafication of human embodiment, medicine and public health

Engagements and encounters with digital technologies generate continual flows of detailed information about people's bodily functions, health conditions or concerns and personal preferences and activities, as well as about medical and health workers, health services and corporate actors in medical and public health domains. The watching capabilities of digital health technologies involve diverse forms of dataveillance across the spectrum. These include voluntary self-surveillance, intimate or social surveillance by members of the public on each other, synoptic and sousveillance the public conducts on medical and public health workers and officials, the panoptic surveillance of populations and traditional medical surveillance of patients. The use of digital technologies blurs the spatial boundaries between public and private surveillance, bringing public surveillance into the domestic sphere.

New ways of practising and conceptualising embodiment

With these reams of digital data, new conceptualisations, performances and enactments of human bodies are configured. Lay people can use devices and software that provide information about their bodies and health status in the kind of detail that in previous times could only be gathered by healthcare professionals using clinical technologies. For their part, medical and health workers as well as government and corporate entities have access to far greater and more detailed information about patients and populations. Metrics have become privileged over other forms of knowledge in health and medicine. Digitised data are commonly portrayed as more neutral, scientific and insightful than other forms of knowledges.

The intersections of corporate, state and personal interests

Digital health is a site at which diverse interests intersect. Many digital health technologies can readily transverse domains, from the personal and everyday, to the corporate to government – and back again. Many devices and software are readily incorporated into a broader digital ecosystem of interoperable technologies. Personal digital health data have acquired significant biovalue well beyond that offered to the people from whom they are generated. These data can be exploited and compromised in a multitude of ways, both legally and illicitly, both openly and covertly. Data sets created in one domain can be reused in other domains. Power differentials remain, however. Wealthy corporations have more resources to create and disseminate technologies and influence digital content than do patient organisations and ordinary citizens. Digital developers and the internet empires have greater access to and opportunities to exploit medical and health digital data sets than do other actors and agencies.

Transformations in health and medical care

Health and medical work is changed in significant ways by the use of digital technologies. Professionals must recalibrate the ways in which they gather information on and relate to patients and the public, involving the enactments of new forms of care and knowledge production. Some digital health practices allow patients and other lay people to become more expert in their medical knowledge and understanding of their bodies and health and illness states, and share these knowledges and understandings with each other. But these practices also allow patients to challenge medical authority and publicly comment on, monitor and assess the services and fees of medical and other healthcare providers. They can use online sources to find information about complementary and alternative therapies and access less expensive or controversial treatments that their doctors may not be willing or able to provide.

The importance of materiality to the experience of digital health technologies

Objects, space and place play integral roles in configuring the embodied engagements of people with these technologies. These non-human actors contribute to the affective atmospheres in which digital health practices take place. Digital devices and software, as well as the data they generate, often demand novel sensory and sense-making responses from lay people and healthcare professionals alike. The design and affordances of digital health technologies shape the ways in which they can be used. They mobilise and promote certain types of enactments on the part of users, and close off other possibilities. While people can 'tame' or domesticate technologies to some extent, often in unexpected ways, there are limits to how they can do so.

Bolstering of medical authority and expertise

Digital health extends the concept of health and medical data and practices well beyond the signs and symptoms of health states. The aegis of medicine and public health is consequently expanded into more and more social domains and social institutions, contributing to the biomedicalisation of everyday life. There remain significant limits to the contribution that patients and lay people in general are able to make to medical knowledge, the authority they are able to develop and the benefits they are able to accrue in using digital health technologies. Dominant medical discourses and practices, for the most part, continue to be supported and promoted in digital health. The standard paternalistic approach to patient engagement and health education and promotion continues to pervade digital health. Medical and public health knowledges remain privileged over lay experiential knowledges. Doctors and public health professionals continue to portray patients and lay people as requiring their advice and sometimes their encouragement to behave as ideal engaged patients and healthy citizens. Many patients themselves continue to want to seek and rely on medical expertise.

As I have shown in this book, participation in digital health can offer many benefits to lay people and to health and medical professionals. These include opportunities to access and share health and medical information better and to give and receive emotional support, develop medical and health communities and networks, find medical expertise and alternative therapies, develop a sense of control over their health and generate new medical and public health knowledges at both the individual and communal levels. However, digital health technologies may also contribute to social inequalities and socioeconomic disadvantage. People who do not conform to the ideal of the healthy citizen may be marginalised or stigmatised. The emotional dimensions and vulnerabilities that may be associated with using digital health technologies are also frequently ignored or not acknowledged. Digital health discourses and practices tend to draw attention away from the social determinants of ill health and from state responsibilities for providing social support and funding to improve the health of the disadvantaged.

Directions for further research in critical digital health studies

I have covered many aspects of digital health in this book. Given the rapid proliferation of digital technologies relating to health and medicine, however, many more elements require continuing or further investigation from a critical and in-depth perspective. While the topic of the public's use of digital health technologies has received attention from social researchers, particularly those contributing to the valuable literature on telemedicine, there are many elements that have remained under-researched. As yet little critical social research has addressed the role played by digital technologies such as apps, gaming devices, YouTube videos, social media or wearable technologies in medical or public health domains. Detailed research that investigates the ways in which these technologies are incorporated into everyday life is called for. Analysis of how digital technologies are used for medical education and training, public health surveillance, health promotion and the sharing of information as part of professional networks by healthcare and public health workers has received scant attention from critical scholars.

Thinking through the ways in which digital technologies are used for health and medical-related purposes involves the recognition of the complexities of the affordances of contemporary interlinked technological devices and software. It also requires awareness of the multiplicity of ways in which people can use these technologies and distribute their content across them. We have very little information about the working practices and ideas of the commercial interests involved in the development, production and marketing of digital health technologies, of the technology developers, coders, designers and those who commission them to build software and hardware.

Further examination of the ways in which digital devices, software and the data they generate work to delimit and prescribe concepts of health and wellbeing is another area that needs more attention. This should include identifying how digital health and medical data are manipulated algorithmically and used by the developers and other actors and agencies. This perspective highlights the position of digital technology users not as atomised individuals, but as actors who are part of the social, cultural and geographical contexts in which they are located as well as networks of software and hardware devices and a global digital knowledge economy.

Much remains to be investigated in relation to the meanings and politics of personal health and medical data. For example, what types of subjects, bodies and relations (both to other humans and to objects) do digital media technologies and data enact? How do the various forms of digital data produced by the varieties of digital health technologies interact with each other? How do people make sense of and use these data? What are the pleasures, gratifications, motivations, resistances and frictions that are inherent to personal data engagement and living with and co-evolving with our digital data assemblages? Future investigations in critical digital health studies may involve investigating alternatives to the dominant commercialised social media platforms that can provide better options for data security and privacy and for people and communities to own and control their personal data.

Another intriguing direction for research is that which pursues investigation into the embodied and affective dimensions of digital technology use. Building on the studies I have reviewed in the book, more research is needed that can explore the ways in which people's appropriation of digital technologies involves affective attachments to the devices and software they use, the online networks and communities they establish and the digital data these generate. Investigations are needed that can devote attention to how the human senses interact with digital devices, what kinds of knowledges are configured and which kinds are lost as part of these enactments of technologies.

We know little, as yet, about the details of how digital mediation transforms care. This inquiry should include examination of the ways in which the doctor–patient encounter operates when it is conducted via remote consulting and patient-monitoring technologies, or the relationships engendered when people who are in caregiving roles for family members use digital devices and rely on digital data for their caregiving practices. When detailed information about people is systematically gathered across a time period, this information often becomes the basis of decision making about how to engage in care. This reliance on digital data rather than the sensory knowledges generated in face-to-face encounters has significant implications for caregiving. Here again, the key questions concern how knowledges about human embodiment are configured and how people make sense of and incorporate data into their lives.

The movement of digital health technologies into new arenas, such as healthy communities and cities initiatives, school physical and health education and parenting and family life, also requires further research. As the Internet of Things develops and smart objects start to exchange digital data on human bodies with each other, a new and different level of digital data generation is occurring. The implications of this for the ways in which biometric information is produced and used have yet to be fully realised or understood. In a context in which cities are becoming increasingly programmable with computer software and monitored using sensor-based technologies, even the concept of the 'healthy city' is open to reinterpretation via the lens of digitisation. When people's homes can monitor their body movements and sleep patterns, the concept of 'the home' is digitised. When special-interest groups are configured and interact via digital technologies such as social media, the very notion of 'community' has become digitised. When citizens use self-monitoring and self-care technologies and are continually surveilled by the digital technologies with which they routinely interact and the sensor-embedded environments in which they move about, their bodies and behaviours are digitised. The notion that people can be tracked every minute of the day, and the data sent to healthcare providers, caregivers, health promoters, their workplaces and health insurers, and that they may be rewarded or punished with financial incentives or penalties, is no longer a product of speculative design but has become a reality for some people.

Finally, what are the radical possibilities that digital health technologies may afford? Thus far, initiatives encouraging the use of digital health tend to focus on using these data for improving individuals' health by encouraging self-optimisation and self-responsibility that ascribe to normative categories of health and fitness. They demonstrate a highly conservative and neoliberal orientation towards personal responsibility for health and support of datafication and dataveillance of ordinary citizens as a means of achieving this. There are possibilities for individuals and social groups to take up digital health technologies in alternative ways to those envisaged by their developers or advocates. Collaborative and participatory design efforts are also a way forward. Rather than technology designers and developers envisioning what devices and software might suit the needs of their target markets, working with members of those groups in the design and development phases could help them to transcend the limitations of their own culture-bound assumptions. This approach need not merely be directed at better design of digital health technologies to make them more useful and useable, but also offers possibilities for marginalised and disenfranchised groups to contribute to design ideas for social change.

Members of the public could also engage in 'citizen hacking' activities, working to confound and disrupt the intended uses of already-existing technologies, or to uncover and challenge top-down, exploitative and hidden modes of dataveillance of citizens. A more radical vision might extend the ideals of crowdsourcing, data sharing and open data to agitate for social change, draw attention to the social determinants of illness and disease and work towards the alleviation of socioeconomic disadvantage. Building on pre-existing initiatives using crowdsourcing and citizen sensing to generate environmental data, another possibility is the strategic communal use of dataveillance techniques on the part of marginalised social groups to monitor and record elements of their disadvantage and then publicise these data to agitate for social change. The potential for such resistant and activist uses of digital health technologies has barely been explored.

As a final comment, I again emphasise the importance of taking a critical approach to understanding and uncovering both the advantages and possibilities of digital health technologies, and their potential harms and ethical implications. It is all too easy to hail novel technologies as effecting better ways of achieving objectives such as delivering better healthcare, reducing government spending on healthcare budgets and encouraging and facilitating citizens to engage in self-care and personal health promotion. While good intentions may be enshrined in these claims, they have unintended or perverse outcomes. As I have contended throughout this book that the realities of introducing new digital technologies into the domain of health and medicine are far more complex, messy and fraught with contradiction and ambivalence than is often recognised in initial enthusiasm for their use. Continuing attention to the cultural imaginaries, social relations, moral imperatives and political dimensions of digital health, and the details of the spaces, places and lifeworlds in which people take up (or resist, tinker with or reinvent) these technologies is vital. It is my hope that this volume has gone some way to revealing these complexities as part of a new agenda in critical digital health studies.

REFERENCES

3D Babies (2014) About us. Accessed 30 October 2014. Available from www.3d-babies.com/about/.

Ablon, L., Libicki, M. and Golay, A. (2015) *Markets for Cybercrime Tools and Stolen Data*. Santa Monica, CA: RAND Corporation.

Accenture Consulting. (2015) Losing Patience: Why Healthcare Providers Need to Up Their Mobile Game. Accessed 28 October 2015. Available from www.accenture.com/t20160516T051341__w__/us-en/_acnmedia/Accenture/Conversion-Assets/DotCom/Documents/Global/PDF/Dualpub_24/Accenture-Losing-Patience.pdf.

Accenture Consulting. (2016a) Accenture 2016 Consumer Survey on Patient Engagement. Accessed 13 July 2016. Available from www.accenture.com/t00010101T000000__w__/au-en/_acnmedia/Accenture/Conversion-Assets/DotCom/Documents/Local/au-en/PDF/1/Accenture-Patients-Want-A-Heavy-Dose-of-Digital-Research-Global-Report.pdf.

Accenture Consulting. (2016b) Australian Patients Anticipate the Onset of Digital Medicine. Accessed 13 July 2016. Available from www.accenture.com/t00010101T000000__w__/au-en/_acnmedia/Accenture/Conversion-Assets/DotCom/Documents/Local/au-en/PDF/1/Accenture-Digital-Health-Consumer-Survey-Research-Brief-Australia.pdf#zoom=50.

Ackerman, L. (2013) Mobile Health and Fitness Applications and Information Privacy. San Diego, CA: Privacy Rights Clearing House.

Adams, S. (2011) Sourcing the crowd for health services improvement: the reflexive patient and 'share-your-experience' websites. *Social Science & Medicine*, 72 (7), 1069–1076.

Ahmad, F., Hudak, P., Bercovitz, K., Hollenberg, E. and Levinson, W. (2006) Are physicians ready for patients with internet-based health information? *Journal of Medical Internet Research* (3). Accessed 27 February 2016. Available from www.jmir.org/2006/3/e22/.

Ahmed, O.H., Lee, H. and Struik, L. (2016) A picture tells a thousand words: a content analysis of concussion-related images online. *Physical Therapy in Sport*, 21, 82–86.

Ahrens, J. (2013) Between 'me-time' and household duty: male and female home internet use. *Media International Australia*, 146, 60–68.

Ali, M., Khan, S.U. and Vasilakos, A.V. (2015) Security in cloud computing: opportunities and challenges. *Information Sciences*, 305, 357–383.

Alliance Health Networks. (2016) Accessed 2 July 2016. Available from www.alliancehealthnetworks.com/.

Alnemer, A.K., Alhuzaim, M.W., Alnemer, A.A., Alharbi, B.B., Bawazir, S.A., Barayyan, R.O. and Balaraj, K.F. (2015) Are health-related tweets evidence based? Review and analysis of health-related tweets on Twitter. *Journal of Medical Internet Research* (10). Accessed 17 June 2016. Available from www.jmir.org/2015/10/e246/.

Alotaibi, N.M., Badhiwala, J.H., Nassiri, F., Guha, D., Ibrahim, G.M., Shamji, M.F. and Lozano, A.M. (2016) The current use of social media in neurosurgery. *World Neurosurgery*, 88, 619–624.

Amoore, L. (2011) Data derivatives: on the emergence of a security risk calculus for our times. *Theory, Culture & Society*, 28 (6), 24–43.

Amoore, L. and Hall, A. (2009) Taking people apart: digitised dissection and the body at the border. *Environment and Planning D: Society and Space*, 27 (3), 444–464.

Amoore, L. and Piotukh, V. (2015) Life beyond big data: governing with little analytics. *Economy and Society*, 44 (3), 341–366.

Ancker, J., Witteman, H., Hafeez, B., Provencher, T., Van de Graaf, M. and Wei, E. (2015a) "You get reminded you're a sick person": personal data tracking and patients with multiple chronic conditions. *Journal of Medical Internet Research* (8). Accessed 30 August 2015. Available from www.jmir.org/2015/8/e202/?trendmd-shared=0.

Ancker, J., Witteman, H., Hafeez, B., Provencher, T., Van de Graaf, M. and Wei, E. (2015b) The invisible work of personal health information management among people with multiple chronic conditions: qualitative interview study among patients and providers. *Journal of Medical Internet Research* (6). Accessed 30 August 2015. Available from www.jmir.org/2015/6/e137/?trendmd-shared=0.

Andalibi, N., Ozturk, P. and Forte, A. (2015) Depression-related imagery on Instagram. *Proceedings of the 18th ACM Conference Companion on Computer Supported Cooperative Work & Social Computing* (CSCW '15). Vancouver: ACM Press, 231–234.

Anderson, B. (2009) Affective atmospheres. *Emotion, Space and Society*, 2 (2), 77–81.

Anderson, M. (2015) Technology Device Ownership: 2015. Accessed 25 April 2016. Available from www.pewinternet.org/files/2015/10/PI_2015-10-29_device-ownership_FINAL.pdf.

Andreassen, H. (2011) What does an e-mail address add? Doing health and technology at home. *Social Science & Medicine*, 72 (4), 521–528.

Andreassen, H. and Dyb, K. (2010) Differences and inequalities in health: empirical reflections on telemedicine and politics. *Information, Communication & Society*, 13 (7), 956–975.

Andreassen, H., Trondsen, M., Kummervold, P.E., Gammon, D. and Hjortdahl, P. (2006) Patients who use e-mediated communication with their doctor: new constructions of trust in the patient–doctor relationship. *Qualitative Health Research*, 16 (2), 238–248.

Andrejevic, M. (2013) *Infoglut: How Too Much Information is Changing the Way We Think and Know*. New York: Routledge.

Andrejevic, M. (2014) The big data divide. *International Journal of Communication*, 8, 1673–1689.

Andrejevic, M. and Burdon, M. (2015) Defining the sensor society. *Television & New Media*, 16 (1), 19–36.

Andrews, G., Chen, S. and Myers, S. (2014) The 'taking place' of health and wellbeing: towards non representational theory. *Social Science & Medicine*, 108, 210–222.

Anonymous. (2013) Chicago starts posting photos of dead bodies online. *RT.com*. Accessed 30 May 2016. Available from www.rt.com/usa/chicago-dead-bodies-photo-008/.

Anonymous. (2015) Fury as pathologist builds up half a million Instagram followers by posting gruesome pictures of dead bodies and foetuses without relatives' permission. *Daily Mail*. Accessed 30 May 2016. Available from www.dailymail.co.uk/news/article-3283933/I-t-believe-detached-humanity-Outrage-pathologist-half-million-Instagram-followers-posts-gruesome-pictures-dead-bodies-fetuses-online-without-relatives-permission.html.

Antheunis, M.L., Tates, K. and Nieboer, T.E. (2013) Patients' and health professionals' use of social media in health care: motives, barriers and expectations. *Patient Education and Counseling*, 92 (3), 426–431.

Anuta, J. (2014) Hudson's Yards to be first 'quantified community'. Crain's New York. Accessed 16 June 2014. Available at www.crainsnewyork.com/article/20140414/REAL_ESTATE/140419932/hudson-yards-to-be-first-quantified-community#.

Apple. (2016) Apple advances health apps with CareKit. Accessed 29 March 2016. Available from www.apple.com/pr/library/2016/03/21Apple-Advances-Health-Apps-with-CareKit.html.

Appleby, J. (2013) Walmart to open health screening kiosks. Accessed 27 March 2013. Available from www.healthcareitnews.com/news/walmart-open-health-screening-kiosks?page=0.

Armstrong, D. (1983) *Political Anatomy of the Body: Medical Knowledge in Britain in the Twentieth Century*. Cambridge: Cambridge University Press.

Armstrong, D. (1995) The rise of surveillance medicine. *Sociology of Health & Illness*, 17 (3), 393–404.

Baer, H.A., Singer, M. and Johnsen, J.H. (1986) Toward a critical medical anthropology. *Social Science & Medicine*, 23 (2), 95–98.

Balatsoukas, P., Kennedy, M.C., Buchan, I., Powell, J. and Ainsworth, J. (2015) The role of social network technologies in online health promotion: a narrative review of theoretical and empirical factors influencing intervention effectiveness. *Journal of Medical Internet Research* (6). Accessed 6 July 2016. Available from www.jmir.org/2015/6/e141/.

Ball, D.E., Tisocki, K. and Herxheimer, A. (2006) Advertising and disclosure of funding on patient organisation websites: a cross-sectional survey. *BMC Public Health* (1). Accessed 29 April 2013. Available from www.biomedcentral.com/1471–2458/6/201.

Banning, M.E. (2016) Shared entanglements – Web 2.0, info-liberalism & digital sharing. *Information, Communication & Society*, 19 (4), 489–503.

Barello, S., Graffigna, G. and Vegni, E. (2012) Patient engagement as an emerging challenge for healthcare services: mapping the literature. *Nursing Research and Practice*. Accessed 16 March 2013. Available from www.ncbi.nlm.nih.gov/pmc/articles/PMC3504449/.

Barker, K.K. (2008) Electronic support groups, patient-consumers, and medicalization: the case of contested illness. *Journal of Health and Social Behavior*, 49 (1), 20–36.

Barr, A. (2014) Google's new moonshot project: the human body. *The Wall Street Journal*. Accessed 29 July 2014. Available from http://online.wsj.com/articles/google-to-collect-data-to-define-healthy-human-1406246214.

Barta, K. and Neff, G. (2016) Technologies for sharing: lessons from Quantified Self about the political economy of platforms. *Information, Communication & Society*, 19 (4), 518–531.

Basch, C.H., Basch, C.E., Hillyer, G.C. and Reeves, R. (2015) YouTube videos related to skin cancer: a missed opportunity for cancer prevention and control. *JMIR Cancer* (1). Accessed 10 July 2016. Available from http://cancer.jmir.org/2015/1/e1/?trendmd-shared=1.

Baum, F. (2008) The Commission on the Social Determinants of Health: reinventing health promotion for the twenty-first century? *Critical Public Health*, 18 (4), 457–466.

Baum, F. and Fisher, M. (2014) Why behavioural health promotion endures despite its failure to reduce health inequities. *Sociology of Health & Illness*, 36 (2), 213–225.

Baum, F., Newman, L. and Biedrzycki, K. (2014) Vicious cycles: digital technologies and determinants of health in Australia. *Health Promotion International*, 29 (2), 349–360.

Beard, L., Wilson, K., Morra, D. and Keelan, J. (2009) A survey of health-related activities on Second Life. *Journal of Medical Internet Research* (2). Accessed 11 November 2013. Available from www.jmir.org/2009/2/e17/.

Beck, F., Richard, J.-B., Nguyen-Thanh, V., Montagni, I., Parizot, I. and Renahy, E. (2014) Use of the internet as a health information resource among French young adults: results from a nationally representative survey. *Journal of Medical Internet Research* (5). Accessed 30 January 2016. Available from www.jmir.org/2014/5/e128/.

Beck, M. (2016) How telemedicine is transforming health care. *The Wall Street Journal*. Accessed 2 July 2016. Available from www.wsj.com/articles/how-telemedicine-is-transforming-health-care-1466993402#.

Beer, D. (2017) *Metric Power*. Houndmills: Palgrave Macmillan.

Beer, D. and Burrows, R. (2010) Consumption, prosumption and participatory web cultures: an introduction. *Journal of Consumer Culture*, 10 (1), 3–12.

Bell, S.L., Wheeler, B.W. and Phoenix, C. (2017) Using geonarratives to explore the diverse temporalities of therapeutic landscapes: perspectives from 'green' and 'blue' settings. *Annals of the American Association of Geographers*, 107 (1), 93–108.

Bender, J.L., Jimenez-Marroquin, M.-C. and Jadad, A.R. (2011) Seeking support on Facebook: a content analysis of breast cancer groups. *Journal of Medical Internet Research* (1). Accessed 30 January 2016. Available from www.jmir.org/2011/1/e16/.

Bennett, C.J. (2011) In defence of privacy: the concept and the regime. *Surveillance & Society*, 8 (4), 485–496.

Berman, B. (1989) The computer metaphor: bureaucratizing the mind. *Science as Culture*, 1 (7), 7–42.

Better Information Means Better Care (2014) Accessed 13 June 2014. Available from www.nhs.uk/NHSEngland/thenhs/records/healthrecords/Pages/care-data.aspx.

Beykikhoshk, A., Arandjelović, O., Phung, D., Venkatesh, S. and Caelli, T. (2015) Using Twitter to learn about the autism community. *Social Network Analysis and Mining*, 5 (1), 1–17.

Bidmon, S. and Terlutter, R. (2015) Gender differences in searching for health information on the internet and the virtual patient–physician relationship in Germany: exploratory results on how men and women differ and why. *Journal of Medical Internet Research* (6). Accessed 25 April 2016. Available from www.ncbi.nlm.nih.gov/pmc/articles/PMC4526954/?report=classic.

Bird, S. (2014) Patients' use of social media: e-ratings of doctors. *Australian Family Physician*. Accessed 21 June 2016. Available from www.racgp.org.au/afp/2014/december/patients%E2%80%99-use-of-social-media-e-rating-of-doctors/.

Bleich, S.N., Jarlenski, M.P., Bell, C.N. and LaVeist, T.A. (2012) Health inequalities: trends, progress, and policy. *Annual Review of Public Health*, 33, 7–40.

Boero, N. and Pascoe, C.J. (2012) Pro-anorexia communities and online interaction: bringing the pro-ana body online. *Body & Society*, 18 (2), 27–57.

Boiten, E. (2014) FoI reveals cynical logic that compromises NHS data privacy. *The Conversation*. Accessed 13 June 2014. Available from https://theconversation.com/foi-reveals-cynical-logic-that-compromises-nhs-data-privacy-24750.

Borrelli, B. and Ritterband, L.M. (2015) Special issue on eHealth and mHealth: challenges and future directions for assessment, treatment, and dissemination. *Health Psychology*, 34 (S), 1205–1208.

Boruff, J. and Storie, D. (2014) Mobile devices in medicine: a survey of how medical students, residents, and faculty use smartphones and other mobile devices to find information. *Journal of the Medical Library Association*, 102 (1), 22–30.

boyd, d. (2012) Networked privacy. *Surveillance & Society*, 10 (3/4), 348–350.

Brainform. (2015) Brainform. Accessed 17 August 2015. Available from www.brainform. co.nz/.

Braveman, P., Egerter, S. and Williams, D.R. (2011) The social determinants of health: coming of age. *Annual Review of Public Health*, 32, 381–398.

Brittain, K., Corner, L., Robinson, L. and Bond, J. (2010) Ageing in place and technologies of place: the lived experience of people with dementia in changing social, physical and technological environments. *Sociology of Health & Illness*, 32 (2), 272–287.

Broom, A. and Tovey, P. (2008) The role of the internet in cancer patients' engagement with complementary and alternative treatments. *Health:*, 12 (2), 139–155.

Brown, J., Ryan, C. and Harris, A. (2014) How doctors view and use social media: a national survey. *Journal of Medical Internet Research* (12). Accessed 23 June 2016. Available from www.jmir.org/2014/12/e267/.

Brown, R. and Gregg, M. (2012) The pedagogy of regret: Facebook, binge drinking and young women. *Continuum*, 26 (3), 357–369.

Brynolf, A., Johansson, S., Appelgren, E., Lynoe, N. and Edstedt Bonamy, A.-K. (2013) Virtual colleagues, virtually colleagues – physicians' use of Twitter: a population-based observational study. *BMJ Open* (7). Accessed 23 June 2016. Available from http://bmjopen.bmj. com/content/3/7/e002988.abstractN2.

Bujnowska-Fedak, M.M. (2015) Trends in the use of the internet for health purposes in Poland. *BMC Public Health*. Accessed 5 January 2016. Available from http://bmcpubli-chealth.biomedcentral.com/articles/10.1186/s12889-015-1473-3.

Buntin, M.B., Burke, M.F., Hoaglin, M.C. and Blumenthal, D. (2011) The benefits of health information technology: a review of the recent literature shows predominantly positive results. *Health Affairs*, 30 (3), 464–471.

Burri, R.V. (2013) Visual power in action: digital images and the shaping of medical practices. *Science as Culture*, 22 (3), 367–387.

Buse, C.E. (2010) E-scaping the ageing body? Computer technologies and embodiment in later life. *Ageing & Society*, 30 (6), 987–1009.

Byron, P., Albury, K. and Evers, C. (2013) "It would be weird to have that on Facebook": young people's use of social media and the risk of sharing sexual health information. *Reproductive Health Matters*, 21 (41), 35–44.

Calbucci, M. (2013) XBox One, Kinect 2.0 and the future of health technology. *Mobi Health News*. Accessed 10 October 2013. Available from http://mobihealthnews.com/22628/ xbox-one-kinect-2-0-and-the-future-of-health-technology/?goback=%2Egde_80236_ member_5793497035143401472#%21.

Campbell, D. (2016) NHS to offer free devices and apps to help people manage illnesses. *The Guardian*. Accessed 7 July 2016. Available from www.theguardian.com/society/2016/ jun/17/nhs-to-offer-free-devices-and-apps-to-help-people-manage-illnesses.

Captain, S. (2016) Can crowdsourcing help make life easier for people with disabilities? *FastCompany*. Accessed 9 May 2016. Available from www.fastcompany.com/3059158/ crowdsourced-knowledge-is-helping-people-with-disabilities-navigate-life?utm_ content=bufferc534d&utm_medium=social&utm_source=twitter.com&utm_ campaign=buffer.

Carmel, S. (2013) The craft of intensive care medicine. *Sociology of Health & Illness*, 35 (5), 731–745.

Caron, J. and Light, J. (2015) 'My world has expanded even though I'm stuck at home': experiences of individuals with amyotrophic lateral sclerosis who use augmentative and alternative communication and social media. *American Journal of Speech-Language Pathology*, 24 (4), 680–695.

Cartwright, L. (1995) *Screening the Body: Tracing Medicine's Visual Culture*. Minneapolis, MN: University of Minnesota Press.

Center for Innovative Public Health Research. (2014) Self-harm websites and teens who visit them. Accessed 4 May 2016. Available from http://innovativepublichealth.org/blog/self-harm-websites-and-teens-who-visit-them/.

Chamberlain, K. and O'Neill, D. (1998) Understanding social class differences in health: a qualitative analysis of smokers' health beliefs. *Psychology and Health*, 13 (6), 1105–1119.

Chapple, A. and Ziebland, S. (2011) How the internet is changing the experience of bereavement by suicide: a qualitative study in the UK. *Health:*, 15 (2), 173–187.

Chemaly, S. (2014) #FreeTheNipple: Facebook changes breastfeeding mothers photo policy. *Huffpost Parents*. Accessed 4 May 2016. Available from www.huffingtonpost.com/soraya-chemaly/freethenipple-facebook-changes_b_5473467.html.

Cheney-Lippold, J. (2011) A new algorithmic identity: soft biopolitics and the modulation of control. *Theory, Culture & Society*, 28 (6), 164–181.

Choi, G.N. and DiNitto, M.D. (2013) The digital divide among low-income homebound older adults: internet use patterns, eHealth literacy, and attitudes toward computer/internet use. *Journal of Medical Internet Research* (5). Accessed 22 November 2013. Available from www.jmir.org/2013/5/e93/.

Chretien, K.C. and Kind, T. (2013) Social media and clinical care: ethical, professional, and social implications. *Circulation*, 127 (13), 1413–1421.

Chretien, K.C., Tuck, M.G., Simon, M., Singh, L.O. and Kind, T. (2015) A digital ethnography of medical students who use Twitter for professional development. *Journal of General Internal Medicine*, 30 (11), 1673–1680.

Christie, M. and Verran, H. (2014) The Touch Pad body: a generative transcultural digital device interrupting received ideas and practices in Aboriginal health. *Societies* (2). Accessed 11 July 2014. Available from www.mdpi.com/2075–4698/4/2/256.

Cimini, N. (2010) Struggles online over the meaning of 'Down's syndrome': a 'dialogic' interpretation. *Health:*, 14 (4), 398–414.

Citron, D.K. (2009) Law's expressive value in combating cyber gender harassment. *Michigan Law Review*, 108 (3), 373–415.

Clarke, A. and Shim, J. (2011) Medicalization and biomedicalization revisited: technoscience and transformations of health, illness and American medicine. In A.B. Pescosolido, K.J. Martin, D.J. McLeod and A. Rogers (eds) *Handbook of the Sociology of Health, Illness, and Healing: A Blueprint for the 21st Century*. New York: Springer New York, 173–199.

Clarke, A., Shim, J., Mamo, L., Fosket, J.R. and Fishman, J. (2010) Biomedicalization: a theoretical and substantive introduction. In A. Clarke, L. Mamo, J.R. Fosket, J. Fishman and J. Shim (eds) *Biomedicalization: Technoscience, Health, and Illness in the U.S.* Durham, NC: Duke University Press, 1–44.

Classen, C. (1999) Other ways to wisdom: learning through the senses across cultures. *International Review of Education*, 45 (3/4), 269–280.

Classen, D.C. and Bates, D.W. (2011) Finding the meaning in meaningful use. *New England Journal of Medicine*, 365 (9), 855–858.

Comstock, J. (2015) IMS: 1 in 10 health apps connects to a device, 1 in 50 connects to healthcare providers. *Mobi Health News*. Accessed 18 September 2015. Available from http://mobihealth news.com/46863/ims-1-in-10-health-apps-connects-to-a-device-1-in-50-connects-to-healthcare-providers/.

Conrad, C.C. and Hilchey, K.G. (2011) A review of citizen science and community-based environmental monitoring: issues and opportunities. *Environmental Monitoring and Assessment*, 176 (1–4), 273–291.

Conrad, P. (1992) Medicalization and social control. *Annual Review of Sociology*, 18, 209–232.

Conrad, P. (2007) *The Medicalization of Society: On the Transformation of Human Conditions into Treatable Disorders.* Baltimore, MD: The Johns Hopkins University Press.

Conradson, D. (2005) Landscape, care and the relational self: therapeutic encounters in rural England. *Health & Place*, 11 (4), 337–348.

Consumer eHealth Program. (2016) *Consumer eHealth Program.* Accessed 10 July 2016. Available from www.healthit.gov/policy-researchers-implementers/consumer-ehealth-program.

Consumer Electronics Association. (2015) Guiding principles on the privacy and security of personal wellness data. Accessed 26 May 2016. Available from www.cta.tech/CorporateSite/media/gla/CEA-Guiding-Principles-on-the-Privacy-and-Security-of-Personal-Wellness-Data-102215.pdf.

Coole, D.H. and Frost, S. (2010) *New Materialisms: Ontology, Agency, and Politics.* Durham, NC: Duke University Press.

Cooper, C. (2011) Fat lib: how fat activism expands the obesity debate. In E. Rich, L. Monaghan and L. Aphramor (eds) *Debating Obesity: Critical Perspectives.* Houndmills: Palgrave Macmillan, 164–191.

Cooper, M. (2012) The pharmacology of distributed experiment – user-generated drug innovation. *Body & Society*, 18 (3–4), 18–43.

Copelton, D. (2010) Output that counts: pedometers, sociability and the contested terrain of older adult fitness walking. *Sociology of Health & Illness*, 32 (2), 304–318.

Cozza, M. (2011) Bridging gender gaps, networking in computer science. *Gender, Technology and Development*, 15 (2), 319–337.

Crawford, K. and Schultz, J. (2014) Big data and due process: toward a framework to redress predictive privacy harms. *Boston College Law Review*, 55 (1), 93–128.

Crawford, R. (1977) You are dangerous to your health: the ideology and politics of victim blaming. *International Journal of Health Services*, 7(4), 663–680.

Crawford, R. (1980) Healthism and the medicalization of everyday life. *International Journal of Health Care Services*, 10 (3), 365–388.

Crawshaw, P. (2013) Public health policy and the behavioural turn: the case of social marketing. *Critical Social Policy*, 33 (4), 616–637.

Crooks, V.A., Turner, L., Cohen, I.G., Bristeir, J., Snyder, J., Casey, V. and Whitmore, R. (2013) Ethical and legal implications of the risks of medical tourism for patients: a qualitative study of Canadian health and safety representatives' perspectives. *BMJ Open* (2). Accessed 24 April 2016. Available from http://bmjopen.bmj.com/content/3/2/e002302.

CSIRO. (2016) Cutting hospital waiting times. Accessed 15 July 2016. Available from www.csiro.au/en/Research/BF/Areas/Digital-health/Waiting-times.

Daniels, J. (2013) Race and racism in internet studies: a review and critique. *New Media & Society*, 15 (5), 695–719.

Davidson, J. and Milligan, C. (2004) Embodying emotion sensing space: introducing emotional geographies. *Social & Cultural Geography*, 5 (4), 523–532.

Davies, S. (2010) *Global Politics of Health.* Cambridge: Polity.

de Almeida, A.N., Delicado, A., de Almeida Alves, N. and Carvalho, T. (2015) Internet, children and space: revisiting generational attributes and boundaries. *New Media & Society*, 17 (9), 1436–1453.

De Brún, A., McCarthy, M., McKenzie, K. and McGloin, A. (2014) Weight stigma and narrative resistance evident in online discussions of obesity. *Appetite*, 72, 73–81.

De Choudhury, M. (2015). Anorexia on Tumblr: a characterization study. *Proceedings of the 5th International Conference on Digital Health* (DH '15), Florence: ACM Press, 43–50.

De Choudhury, M., Morris, M.R. and White, R.W. (2014). Seeking and sharing health information online: comparing search engines and social media. *Proceedings of the 32nd Annual ACM Conference on Human Factors in Computing Systems* (CHI '14), Toronto: ACM Press, 1365–1367.

De la Torre-Díez, I., Díaz-Pernas, F.J. and Antón-Rodríguez, M. (2012) A content analysis of chronic diseases social groups on Facebook and Twitter. *Telemedicine Journal and e-Health*, 18 (6), 404–408.

De Vogli, R. (2011) Neoliberal globalisation and health in a time of economic crisis. *Social Theory & Health*, 9 (4), 311–325.

Del Casino, V.J. and Brooks, C.F. (2015) Talking about bodies online: Viagra, YouTube, and the politics of public(ized) sexualities. *Gender, Place & Culture*, 22 (4), 474–493.

Dennison, L., Morrison, L., Conway, G. and Yardley, L. (2013) Opportunities and challenges for smartphone applications in supporting health behavior change: qualitative study. *Journal of Medical Internet Research* (4). Accessed 8 April 2014. Available from www.jmir. org/2013/4/e86/.

Dentzer, S. (2013) Rx for the 'blockbuster drug' of patient engagement. *Health Affairs*, 32 (2), 202.

Deterding, S., Dixon, D., Khaled, R. and Nacke, L. (2011). From game design elements to gamefulness: defining gamification. *Proceedings of the 15th International Academic MindTrek Conference: Envisioning Future Media Environments (MindTrek '11)*. Tampere: ACM Press, 9–15.

Diaz, J.A., Griffith, R.A., Ng, J.J., Reinert, S.E., Friedmann, P.D. and Moulton, A.W. (2002) Patients' use of the internet for medical information. *Journal of General and Internal Medicine*, 17 (3), 180–185.

Dickins, M., Thomas, S.L., King, B., Lewis, S. and Holland, K. (2011) The role of the fatosphere in fat adults' responses to obesity stigma: a model of empowerment without a focus on weight loss. *Qualitative Health Research*, 21 (12), 1679–1691.

Digital Exclusion Heatmap. (2016) Accessed 18 June 2016. Available from https://doteveryone.org.uk/resources/heatmap/.

Djuricich, A.M. and Zee-Cheng, J.E. (2015) Live tweeting in medicine: 'tweeting the meeting'. *International Review of Psychiatry*, 27 (2), 133–139.

Dobransky, K. and Hargittai, E. (2012) Inquiring minds acquiring wellness: uses of online and offline sources for health information. *Health Communication*, 27 (4), 331–343.

Dobransky, K. and Hargittai, E. (2016) Unrealized potential: exploring the digital disability divide. *Poetics*, 58, 18–28.

Doherty-Torstrick, E.R., Walton, K.E. and Fallon, B.A. (2016) Cyberchondria: parsing health anxiety from online behavior. *Psychosomatics*, 57 (4), 390–400.

Donker, T., Petrie, K., Proudfoot, J., Clarke, J., Birch, M.-R. and Christensen, H. (2013) Smartphones for smarter delivery of mental health programs: a systematic review. *Journal of Medical Internet Research*, 15 (11). Accessed 5 February 2017. Available from www.jmir.org/2013/11/e247?utm_source=TrendMD&utm_medium=cpc&utm_campaign=JMIR_TrendMD_0.

Doyle, A. (2011) Revisiting the synopticon: reconsidering Mathiesen's 'The Viewer Society' in the age of Web 2.0. *Theoretical Criminology*, 15 (3), 283–299.

Draper, J. (2014) Embodied practice: rediscovering the 'heart' of nursing. *Journal of Advanced Nursing*, 70 (10), 2235–2244.

Duden, B. (1993) *Disembodying Women: Perspectives on Pregnancy and the Unborn.* Translated by L. Hoinacki. Cambridge, MA: Harvard University Press.

Duff, C. (2016) Atmospheres of recovery: assemblages of health. *Environment and Planning A*, 48 (1), 58–74.

Duggan, M. (2015) Mobile Messaging and Social Media 2015. Accessed 29 April 2016. Available from www.pewinternet.org/files/2015/08/Social-Media-Update-2015-FINAL2.pdf.

Dunbar-Hester, C. (2010) Beyond "Dudecore"? Challenging gendered and 'raced' technologies through media activism. *Journal of Broadcasting & Electronic Media*, 54 (1), 121–135.

Ebeling, M. (2016) *Healthcare and Big Data: Digital Specters and Phantom Objects.* Houndmills: Palgrave Macmillan.

eBizMBA. (2017a) Top 15 most popular health websites February 2017. *eBizMBA.* Accessed 12 February 2017. Available from www.ebizmba.com/articles/health-websites.

eBizMBA. (2017b) Top 15 most popular social networking sites February 2017. *eBizMBA.* Accessed 12 February 2017. Available from www.ebizmba.com/articles/social-networking-websites.

Eckert, S. (2017) Fighting for recognition: online abuse of women bloggers in Germany, Switzerland, the United Kingdom, and the United States. *New Media & Society*, online ahead of print.

Ellcessor, E. (2016) Cyborg hoaxes: disability, deception, and critical studies of digital media. *New Media & Society*, online ahead of print.

Ellis, K. and Goggin, G. (2014) Disability and social media. In J. Hunsinger and T. Senft (eds) *The Social Media Handbook.* New York: Routledge, 126–143.

Ellis, K., Goggin, G. and Kent, M. (2015) Disability's digital frictions: activism, technology, and politics. *The Fibreculture Journal* (26). Accessed 12 February 2017. Available from http://twentysix.fibreculturejournal.org/fcj-188-disabilitys-digital-frictions-activism-technology-and-politics/.

Elmer, G. (2003) A diagram of panoptic surveillance. *New Media & Society*, 5 (2), 231–247.

European Commission. (2016) Draft Code of Conduct on Privacy for Mobile Health Applications. Accessed 5 February 2017. Available from www.ehealthnews.eu/images/stories/pdf/code-of-conduct-final-draft.pdf.

Evans, B. (2014) Who responds to the responders? *Dose of Digital.* Accessed 2 June 2014. Available from www.doseofdigital.com/2014/04/responding-responders/#more-7900.

Evans, C. and Schenarts, K. (2016) Evolving educational techniques in surgical training. *Surgical Clinics of North America*, 96 (1), 71–88.

Eveleth, R. (2014) How self-tracking apps exclude women. *The Atlantic.* Accessed 16 December 2014. Available from www.theatlantic.com/technology/archive/2014/12/how-self-tracking-apps-exclude-women/383673/.

Farman, J. (2013) *Mobile Interface Theory: Embodied Space and Locative Media.* London: Routledge.

Farmer, S.E.J., Bernardotto, M. and Singh, V. (2011) How good is internet self-diagnosis of ENT symptoms using Boots WebMD symptom checker? *Clinical Otolaryngology*, 36 (5), 517–518.

Farnan, J.M., Sulmasy, L.S., Worster, B.K., Chaudhry, H.J., Rhyne, J.A. and Arora, V.M. (2013) Online medical professionalism: patient and public relationships: policy statement from the American College of Physicians and the Federation of State Medical Boards. *Annals of Internal Medicine* (8). Accessed 4 April 2016. Available from http://annals.org/article.aspx?articleid=1675927&cm_mid=2431409&cm_crmid=%7B388a30e3-915e-de11-91d2-0015600f6010%7D&cm_medium=email.

Farrell, M. (2016) Use of iPhones by nurses in an acute care setting to improve communication and decision-making processes: qualitative analysis of nurses' perspectives on iPhone use. *JMIR mHealth and uHealth* (2). Accessed 17 July 2016. Available from http://mhealth. jmir.org/2016/2/e43/.

Fergus, T. (2013) Cyberchondria and intolerance of uncertainty: examining when individuals experience health anxiety in response to internet searches for medical information. *Cyberpsychology, Behavior and Social Networking*, 16 (10), 735–739.

Ferreday, D. (2003) Unspeakable bodies: erasure, embodiment and the pro-ana community. *International Journal of Cultural Studies*, 6 (3), 277–295.

Fink, M. and Miller, Q. (2014) Trans media moments: Tumblr, 2011–2013. *Television & New Media*, 15 (7), 611–626.

Fiore-Gartland, B. and Neff, G. (2015) Communication, mediation, and the expectations of data: data valences across health and wellness communities. *International Journal of Communication*, 9, 1466–1484.

Fitzpatrick, K. and Tinning, R. (2013) Health education's fascist tendencies: a cautionary exposition. *Critical Public Health*, 24 (2), 132–142.

Fleishman, G. (2016) Apple, Facebook, Google, and Microsoft pursue strong security, but differing notions of privacy. *Macworld*. Accessed 21 April 2016. Available from www.macworld.stfi.re/article/3057196/privacy/apple-facebook-google-and-microsoft-pursue-strong-security-but-differing-notions-of-privacy.html?sf=kgpnrg.

Floridi, L. (2005) The ontological interpretation of informational privacy. *Ethics and Information Technology*, 7 (4), 185–200.

Fogg, B.J. (2002) Persuasive technology: using computers to change what we think and do. *Ubiquity*, 2002 (December), 89–120.

Fogg, B.J. (2009). A behavior model for persuasive design. Paper read at Persuasive '09, Claremont, CA.

Forlano, L. (2016) Hacking the feminist disabled body. *Journal of Peer Production* (8). Accessed 28 April 2016. Available from http://peerproduction.net/issues/issue-8-feminism-and-unhacking/peer-reviewed-papers/hacking-the-feminist-disabled-body/.

Fotopoulou, A. and O'Riordan, K. (2017) Training to self-care: fitness tracking, biopedagogy and the healthy consumer. *Health Sociology Review*, 26 (1), 54–68.

Foucault, M. (1975) *The Birth of the Clinic: An Archaeology of Medical Perception*. New York: Vintage Books.

Foucault, M. (1979) *The History of Sexuality: An Introduction*. London: Penguin.

Foucault, M. (1984) The politics of health in the eighteenth century. In Rabinow, P. (ed) *The Foucault Reader*. New York: Pantheon Books, 273–289.

Foucault, M. (1988) Technologies of the self. In L. Martin, H. Gutman and P. Hutton (eds) *Technologies of the Self: A Seminar with Michel Foucault*. London: Tavistock, 16–49.

Foucault, M. (1991) Governmentality. In G. Burchell, C. Gordon and P. Miller (eds) *The Foucault Effect: Studies in Governmentality*. Hemel Hempstead: Harvester Wheatsheaf, 87–104.

Foucault, M. (1995) *Discipline and Punish: The Birth of the Prison*. Translated by A. Sheridan. 2nd ed. New York: Vintage Books.

Foucault, M. (2008) *The Birth of Biopolitics: Lectures at the Collège de France, 1978–79*. Translated by G. Burchell. Houndmills: Palgrave Macmillan.

Fox, D.M. and Lawrence, C. (1988) *Photographing Medicine: Images and Power in Britain and America since 1840*. New York: Greenwood Press.

Fox, S. and Boyles, J.L. (2012) Disability in the Digital Age. *Pew Resarch Internet Project*. Accessed 6 August 2011. Available from www.pewinternet.org/Presentations/2012/Aug/Disability-in-the-Digital Age.aspx.

Fox, S. and Duggan, M. (2012) Mobile Health 2012. *Pew Research Center*. Accessed 21 December 2012. Available from www.pewinternet.org/Reports/2012/Mobile- Health. aspx.

Fox, S. and Duggan, M. (2013a) Health Online. *Pew Research Center.* Accessed 12 December 2013. Available from www.pewinternet.org/2013/01/15/health-online-2013/.

Fox, S. and Duggan, M. (2013b) The Diagnosis Difference. *Pew Research Center.* Accessed 26 November 2013. Available from http://pewinternet.org/Reports/2013/The-Diagnosis-Difference/Summary-of-Findings.aspx.

Fox, S. and Duggan, M. (2013c) Tracking for Health. *Pew Research Center.* Accessed 25 April 2016. Available from www.pewinternet.org/files/old-media//Files/Reports/2013/PIP_TrackingforHealth%20with%20appendix.pdf.

Fox, S., Duggan, M. and Purcell, K. (2013) Family Caregivers are Wired for Health. *Pew Research Center.* Accessed 25 April 2016. Available from www.pewinternet.org/files/old-media//Files/Reports/2013/PewResearch_FamilyCaregivers.pdf.

Franko, O.I. and Tirrell, T.F. (2012) Smartphone app use among medical providers in ACGME training programs. *Journal of Medical Systems*, 36 (5), 3135–3139.

Freidson, E. (1970) *Professional Dominance: The Social Structure of Medical Care.* New Brunswick, NJ: Transaction Publishers.

Freidson, E. (1988) *Profession of Medicine: A Study of the Sociology of Applied Knowledge.* Chicago, IL: University of Chicago Press.

French, M. (2014) Gaps in the gaze: informatic practice and the work of public health surveillance. *Surveillance & Society*, 12 (2), 226–242.

Fuchs, C. (2011) Web 2.0, prosumption, and surveillance. *Surveillance & Society*, 8 (3), 288–309.

Fuchs, C. (2014) *Social Media: A Critical Introduction.* London: Sage.

Fuchs, C. and Dyer-Witheford, N. (2013) Karl Marx @ Internet Studies. *New Media & Society*, 15 (5), 782–796.

Gabarron, E., Serrano, A.J., Wynn, R. and Lau, Y.S.A. (2014) Tweet content related to sexually transmitted diseases: no joking matter. *Journal of Medical Internet Research* (10). Accessed 17 June 2016. Available from www.jmir.org/2014/10/e228/.

Gabrys, J. (2014) Programming environments: environmentality and citizen sensing in the smart city. *Environment and Planning D: Society and Space*, 32 (1), 30–48.

Gangadharan, S.P. (2017) The downside of digital inclusion: expectations and experiences of privacy and surveillance among marginal internet users. *New Media & Society*, 19 (4), 597–615.

Gardner, J. and Williams, C. (2015) Corporal diagnostic work and diagnostic spaces: clinicians' use of space and bodies during diagnosis. *Sociology of Health & Illness*, 37 (5), 765–781.

Gauthier, T.P. and Spence, E. (2015) Instagram and clinical infectious diseases. *Clinical Infectious Diseases*, 61 (1), 135–136.

Gehl, R. (2014) *Reverse Engineering Social Media: Revealing the Underside of Our Technology-Laden World.* Philadelphia, PA: Temple University Press.

Gerlitz, C. and Helmond, A. (2013) The like economy: social buttons and the data-intensive web. *New Media & Society*, 15 (8), 1348–1365.

Gesler, W.M. (1992) Therapeutic landscapes: medical issues in light of the new cultural geography. *Social Science & Medicine*, 34 (7), 735–746.

Ghanbarzadeh, R., Ghapanchi, H.A., Blumenstein, M. and Talaei-Khoei, A. (2014) A decade of research on the use of three-dimensional virtual worlds in health care: a systematic literature review. *Journal of Medical Internet Research* (2). Accessed 18 February 2014. Available from www.jmir.org/2014/2/e47/.

Ghobarah, H.A., Huth, P. and Russett, B. (2004) Comparative public health: the political economy of human misery and well-being. *International Studies Quarterly*, 48 (1), 73–94.

Gibbons, M.C., Fleisher, L., Slamon, R.E., Bass, S., Kandadai, V. and Beck, J.R. (2011) Exploring the potential of Web 2.0 to address health disparities. *Journal of Health Communication*, 16 (S1), 77–89.

Gibson, A., Lee, C. and Crabb, S. (2016) Representations of women on Australian breast cancer websites: cultural 'inclusivity' and marginalisation. *Journal of Sociology*, 52 (2), 433–452.

Gibson, M. (2017) YouTube and bereavement vlogging: emotional exchange between strangers. *Journal of Sociology*, 52 (4), 631–645.

Giles, D.C. (2014) 'DSM-V is taking away our identity': the reaction of the online community to the proposed changes in the diagnosis of Asperger's disorder. *Health:*, 18 (2), 179–195.

Gillespie, T., Boczkowski, P.J. and Foot, K.A. (2014) Introduction. In T. Gillespie, P. Boczkowski and K. Foot (eds) *Media Technologies: Essays on Communication, Materiality, and Society*. Cambridge, MA: MIT Press, 1–19.

Gilliom, J. and Monahan, T. (2012) *SuperVision: An Introduction to the Surveillance Society*. Chicago, IL: University of Chicago Press.

Ging, D. and Garvey, S. (2017) 'Written in these scars are the stories I can't explain': a content analysis of pro-ana and thinspiration image sharing on Instagram. *New Media & Society*, online ahead of print.

Ginsburg, F. (2012) Disability in the digital age. In H. Horst and D. Miller (eds) *Digital Anthropology*. London: Berg, 101–126.

Goggin, G. (2015) Disability and mobile internet. *First Monday*, 20 (9). Accessed 15 February 2017. Available from http://128.248.156.56/ojs/index.php/fm/article/view/6171.

Goldstein, G. (2000) Healthy cities: overview of a WHO international program. *Reviews on Environmental Health*, 15 (1–2), 207–214.

Goodwin, D. (2010) Sensing the way: embodied dimensions of diagnostic work. In M. Büscher, D. Goodwin and J. Mesman (eds) *Ethnographies of Diagnostic Work: Dimensions of Transformative Practice*. London: Palgrave Macmillan, 73–92.

Google. (2015) A remedy for your health-related questions: health info in the knowledge graph. Accessed 7 September 2015. Available from http://googleblog.blogspot.com.au/2015/02/health-info-knowledge-graph.html.

Greaves, F., Ramirez-Cano, D., Millett, C., Darzi, A. and Donaldson, L. (2013) Harnessing the cloud of patient experience: using social media to detect poor quality healthcare. *BMJ Quality & Safety*, 22 (3), 251–255.

Greene, J. and Hibbard, J.H. (2012) Why does patient activation matter? An examination of the relationships between patient activation and health-related outcomes. *Journal of General Internal Medicine*, 27 (5), 520–526.

Greengard, S. (2015) *The Internet of Things*. Cambridge, MA: MIT Press.

Greenhalgh, T., Procter, R., Wherton, J., Sugarhood, P. and Shaw, S. (2012) The organising vision for telehealth and telecare: discourse analysis. *BMJ Open* (4). Accessed 5 March 2014. Available from http://bmjopen.bmj.com/content/2/4/e001574.long.

Greenhalgh, T., Stones, R. and Swinglehurst, D. (2014) Choose and book: a sociological analysis of 'resistance' to an expert system. *Social Science & Medicine*, 104, 210–219.

Greenhalgh, T., Wherton, J., Sugarhood, P., Hinder, S., Procter, R. and Stones, R. (2013) What matters to older people with assisted living needs? A phenomenological analysis of the use and non-use of telehealth and telecare. *Social Science & Medicine*, 93, 86–94.

Gregg, M. (2015) Inside the data spectacle. *Television & New Media*, 16 (1), 37–51.

Griffis, M.H., Kilaru, S.A., Werner, M.R., Asch, A.D., Hershey, C.J., Hill, S., Ha, P.Y., Sellers, A., Mahoney, K. and Merchant, M.R. (2014) Use of social media across US hospitals: descriptive analysis of adoption and utilization. *Journal of Medical Internet Research* (11). Accessed 11 July 2016. Available from www.jmir.org/2014/11/e264/.

Grogan, S., Flett, K., Clark-Carter, D., Gough, B., Davey, R., Richardson, D. and Rajaratnam, G. (2011) Women smokers' experiences of an age-appearance anti-smoking intervention: a qualitative study. *British Journal of Health Psychology*, 16 (4), 675–689.

Grosser, B. (2014) What do metrics want? How quantification prescribes social interaction on Facebook. *Computational Culture.* Accessed 16 November 2014. Available from http://computationalculture.net/article/what-do-metrics-want.

Gruman, J. (2013) What patients want from mobile apps. Accessed 9 April 2013. Available from www.kevinmd.com/blog/2013/04/patients-mobile-apps.html.

Grunewald, S. (2014) Would you like a 3D printed replica of your own brain? *3D Printing Industry.* Accessed 23 October 2014. Available from http://3dprintingindustry.com/2014/10/21/3d-printed-replica-brain/.

Guidry, J.P., Carlyle, K., Messner, M. and Jin, Y. (2015) On pins and needles: how vaccines are portrayed on Pinterest. *Vaccine,* 33 (39), 5051–5056.

Haggerty, K. and Ericson, R. (2000) The surveillant assemblage. *British Journal of Sociology,* 51 (4), 605–622.

Halford, S. and Savage, M. (2010) Reconceptualizing digital social inequality. *Information, Communication & Society,* 13 (7), 937–955.

Hallinan, B. and Striphas, T. (2016) Recommended for you: the Netflix Prize and the production of algorithmic culture. *New Media & Society,* 18 (1), 117–137.

Hanson, C., West, J., Neiger, B., Thackeray, R., Barnes, M. and McIntyre, E. (2011) Use and acceptance of social media among health educators. *American Journal of Health Education,* 42 (4), 197–204.

Haraway, D. (1985) Manifesto for cyborgs: science, technology, and socialist feminism in the 1980s. *Socialist Review,* 80, 65–108.

Haraway, D. (1995) Foreword: cyborgs and symbionts: living together in the new world order. In C.H. Gray (ed) *The Cyborg Handbook.* New York: Routledge, xi–xx.

Harbers, H., Mol, A. and Stollmeyer, A. (2002) Food matters: arguments for an ethnography of daily care. *Theory, Culture & Society,* 19 (5–6), 207–226.

Harries, T. and Rettie, R. (2016) Walking as a social practice: dispersed walking and the organisation of everyday practices. *Sociology of Health & Illness,* 38 (6), 874–883.

Harris, A. (2011) In a moment of mismatch: overseas doctors' adjustments in new hospital environments. *Sociology of Health & Illness,* 33 (2), 308–320.

Harris, A. (2016) Listening-touch, affect and the crafting of medical bodies through percussion. *Body & Society,* 22 (1), 31–61.

Harris, A., Kelly, S.E. and Wyatt, S. (2014a) Autobiologies on YouTube: narratives of direct-to-consumer genetic testing. *New Genetics and Society,* 33 (1), 60–78.

Harris, A., Wyatt, S. and Kelly, S.E. (2012) The gift of spit (and the obligation to return it). *Information, Communication & Society,* 16 (2), 236–257.

Harris, D. (2012) Better medicine, brought to you by big data. *Gigaom.* Accessed 8 April 2013. Available from http://gigaom.com/2012/07/15/better-medicine-brought-to-you-by-big-data/.

Harris, J. (2014) Fewer than 1% of Britons own a smartwatch. *Digital Spy.* Accessed 21 March 2014. Available from http://ht.ly/uO4wK.

Harris, K.J., Moreland-Russell, S., Choucair, B., Mansour, R., Staub, M. and Simmons, K. (2014b) Tweeting for and against public health policy: response to the Chicago Department of Public Health's electronic cigarette Twitter campaign. *Journal of Medical Internet Research* (10). Accessed 23 June 2016. Available from www.jmir.org/2014/10/e238/.

Hart, A., Henwood, F. and Wyatt, S. (2004) The role of the internet in patient–practitioner relationships: findings from a qualitative research study. *Journal of Medical Internet Research* (3). Accessed 30 March 2014. Available from www.jmir.org/2004/3/e36/.

Hart, M., Stetten, N. and Castaneda, G. (2016) Considerations for public health organizations attempting to implement a social media presence: a qualitative study. *JMIR Public*

Health Surveillance (1). Accessed 23 June 2016. Available from http://publichealth.jmir. org/2016/1/e6/.

Harvey, P. and Knox, H. (2014) Objects and materials: an introduction. In P. Harvey, E.C. Casella, G. Evans, H. Knox, C. McLean, E.B. Silva, N. Thoburn and K. Woodward (eds) *Objects and Materials: A Routledge Companion*. London: Routledge, 1–17.

Hawn, C. (2009) Take two aspirin and tweet me in the morning: how Twitter, Facebook, and other social media are reshaping health care. *Health Affairs*, 28 (2), 361–368.

Healthcare Hashtag Project. (2017) *Healthcare Hashtag Project*. Accessed 15 February 2017. Available from www.symplur.com/healthcare-hashtags/.

HealthUnlocked. (2016) *HealthUnlocked*. Accessed 6 July 2016. Available from www.healt-hunlocked.com/.

Heilman, J.M. and West, A. (2015) Wikipedia and medicine: quantifying readership, editors, and the significance of natural language. *Journal of Medical Internet Research* (3). Accessed 1 April 2016. Available from www.jmir.org/2015/3/e62/?trendmd-shared=0.

Hier, S.P. (2004) Risky spaces and dangerous faces: urban surveillance, social disorder and CCTV. *Social & Legal Studies*, 13 (4), 541–554.

Hilts, A., Parsons, C. and Knockel, J. (2016) Every Step You Fake: A Comparative Analysis of Fitness Tracker Privacy and Security. Accessed 8 April 2016. Available from https:// openeffect.ca/reports/Every_Step_You_Fake.pdf.

Hone, T., Palladino, R. and Filippidis, F.T. (2016) Association of searching for health-related information online with self-rated health in the European Union. *The European Journal of Public Health*, 26 (5), 748–753.

Hortensius, J., Kars, M., Wierenga, W., Kleefstra, N., Bilo, H. and van der Bijl, J. (2012) Perspectives of patients with type 1 or insulin-treated type 2 diabetes on self-monitoring of blood glucose: a qualitative study. *BMC Public Health* (1). Accessed 5 May 2013. Available from www.biomedcentral.com/1471-2458/12/167.

Howes, D. (2010) *Sensual Relations: Engaging the Senses in Culture and Social Theory*. Ann Arbor, MI: University of Michigan Press.

Howes, D. (2015) Anthropology of the senses. In J.D. Wright (ed) *International Encyclopedia of the Social & Behavioral Sciences*. Amsterdam: Elsevier, 615–620.

Howes, D. and Classen, C. (2013) *Ways of Sensing: Understanding the Senses in Society*. London: Routledge.

Huang, G. (2014) Doctors going mobile, but still skeptical of connected health. *Xconomy*. Accessed 14 April 2014. Available from www.xconomy.com/boston/2014/04/08/doc-tors-going-mobile-but-still-skeptical-of-connected-health/.

Hughes, L.S., Phillips, R.L., DeVoe, J.E. and Bazemore, A.W. (2016) Community vital signs: taking the pulse of the community while caring for patients. *The Journal of the American Board of Family Medicine*, 29 (3), 419–422.

Humer, C. and Finkle, J. (2014) Your medical record is worth more to hackers than your credit card. *Reuters US*. Accessed 26 July 2015. Available from www.reuters.com/article/ 2014/09/24/us-cybersecurity-hospitals-idUSKCN0HJ21I20140924.

Humphreys, S. and Vered, K.O. (2014) Reflecting on gender and digital networked media. *Television & New Media*, 15 (1), 3–13.

Huniche, L., Dinesen, B., Nielsen, C., Grann, O. and Toft, E. (2013) Patients' use of self-monitored readings for managing everyday life with COPD: a qualitative study. *Telemedicine and e-Health*, 19 (5), 396–402.

Husain, I. (2011) Brown Medical School will require medical students to use iPad medical textbooks via Inkling. *iMedicalApps*. Accessed 5 March 2014. Available from www.imedi-calapps.com/2011/06/brown-medical-school-require-medical-students-ipad-medical-textbooks-inkling/.

Husain, I. (2012) Three free healthcare apps physicians should prescribe to their patients. *IMedicalApps*. Accessed 15 March 2013. Available from www.imedicalapps.com/2012/04/free-healthcare-apps-physicians-prescribe-patients/.

Husain, I. (2016) Google's new filtered medical search results welcome news to physicians. *iMedicalApps*. Accessed 7 July 2016. Available from www.imedicalapps.com/2016/06/google-medical-search-results-physicians/.

Hutton, F., Griffin, C., Lyons, A., Niland, P. and McCreanor, T. (2016) 'Tragic girls' and 'crack whores': alcohol, femininity and Facebook. *Feminism & Psychology*, 26 (1), 73–93.

IBM. (2016) *IBM Watson Health*. Accessed 6 April 2016. Available from www.ibm.com/smarterplanet/us/en/ibmwatson/health/.

IMS Institute for Healthcare Informatics. (2015) *Patient Adoption of mHealth: Use, Evidence and Remaining Barriers to Mainstream Acceptance*. Parsipanny, NJ: IMS Institute for Healthcare Informatics.

Ingold, T. (2000) *The Perception of the Environment: Essays on Livelihood, Dwelling and Skill*. London: Routledge.

iOS8 Preview: Health. (2014) Accessed 22 June 2014. Available from www.apple.com/ios/ios8/health/.

Ipsos MORI. (2016) The One-Way Mirror: Public Attitudes to Commercial Access to Health Data. Accessed 13 July 2016. Available from https://wellcome.ac.uk/sites/default/files/public-attitudes-to-commercial-access-to-health-data-wellcome-mar16.pdf.

Jacobs, M.A., Cha, S., Villanti, A.C. and Graham, A.L. (2016) Using Tumblr to reach and engage young adult smokers: a proof of concept in context. *American Journal of Health Behavior*, 40 (1), 48–54.

Jawbone. (2016) *UP by Jawbone*. Accessed 6 September 2015. Available from https://jawbone.com/up.

John, N. (2017) *The Age of Sharing*. Cambridge: Polity.

Joiner, R., Gavin, J., Brosnan, M., Cromby, J., Gregory, H., Guiller, J., Maras, P. and Moon, A. (2012) Gender, internet experience, internet identification, and internet anxiety: a ten-year followup. *Cyberpsychology, Behavior and Social Networking*, 15 (7), 370–372.

Jones, R., Pykett, J. and Whitehead, M. (2010) Big society's little nudges: the changing politics of health care in an age of austerity. *Political Insight*, 1 (3), 85–87.

Kaiser Health News. (2016) Office chatter: your doctor will see you in this telemedicine kiosk. *Kaiser Health News*. Accessed 22 June 2016. Available from http://khn.org/news/office-chatter-your-doctor-will-see-you-in-this-telemedicine-kiosk/amp/.

Kamel Boulos, M. and Al-Shorbaji, N. (2014) On the Internet of Things, smart cities and the WHO Healthy Cities. *International Journal of Health Geographics* (1). Accessed 26 June 2014. Available from www.ij-healthgeographics.com/content/13/1/10.

Kamel Boulos, M., Hetherington, L. and Wheeler, S. (2007) Second life: an overview of the potential of 3-D virtual worlds in medical and health education. *Health Information & Libraries Journal*, 24 (4), 233–245.

Kamel Boulos, M., Resch, B., Crowley, D., Breslin, J., Sohn, G., Burtner, R., Pike, W., Jezierski, E. and Chuang, K.-Y.S. (2011) Crowdsourcing, citizen sensing and sensor web technologies for public and environmental health surveillance and crisis management: trends, OGC standards and application examples. *International Journal of Health Geographics* (1). Accessed 26 June 2104. Available from //www.ij-healthgeographics.com/content/10/1/67.

Kamel Boulos, M. and Yang, S. (2013) Exergames for health and fitness: the roles of GPS and geosocial apps. *International Journal of Health Geographics* (1). Accessed 26 June 2014. Available from //www.ij-healthgeographics.com/content/12/1/18.

Kelleher, E. and Moreno, M.A. (2016) #Mentalhealthresources: a pilot intervention targeting adolescents posting depression references on Tumblr. *Journal of Adolescent Health*, 58 (2), S72.

Keller, B., Labrique, A., Jain, M.K., Pekosz, A. and Levine, O. (2014) Mind the gap: social media engagement by public health researchers. *Journal of Medical Internet Research* (1). Accessed 11 July 2016. Available from //www.jmir.org/2014/1/e8/.

Kennedy, H., Elgesem, D. and Miguel, C. (2015) On fairness: user perspectives on social media data mining. *Convergence*, online ahead of print.

Kent, M. and Ellis, K. (2015) People with disability and new disaster communications: access and the social media mash-up. *Disability & Society*, 30 (3), 419–431.

Kirk, M., Hunter-Smith, S.R., Biomed, M., Smith, K. and Hunter-Smith, D.J. (2014) The role of smartphones in the recording and dissemination of medical images. *Journal of Mobile Technology in Medicine*, 3 (2), 40–45.

Kish, L. and Topol, E. (2015) Unpatients – why patients should own their medical data. *Nature Biotechnology* (33). Accessed 12 September 2015. Available from //www.nature.com/nbt/journal/v33/n9/full/nbt.3340.html.

Kitchin, R. (2014a) *The Data Revolution: Big Data, Open Data, Data Infrastructures and Their Consequences*. London: Sage.

Kitchin, R. (2014b) The real-time city? Big data and smart urbanism. *GeoJournal*, 79 (1), 1–14.

Kitchin, R. and Dodge, M. (2011) *Code/Space: Software and Everyday Life*. Cambridge, MA: MIT Press.

Kivits, J. (2013) E-health and renewed sociological approaches to health and illness. In K. Orton-Johnson and N. Prior (eds) *Digital Sociology: Critical Perspectives*. Houndmills: Palgrave Macmillan, 213–226.

Knowthenet (2015) Today's children will feature in almost 1,000 online photos by the time they reach age five. Knowthenet. Accessed 20 February 2016. Available from www.knowthenet.org.uk/articles/today%E2%80%99s-children-will-feature-almost-1000-online-photos-time-they-reach-age-five.

Koehler, N., Yao, K., Vujovic, O. and McMenamin, C. (2012) Medical students' use of and attitudes towards medical applications. *Journal of Mobile Technology in Medicine*, 1 (4), 16–21.

Koetsier, J. (2013) Battle of the mobile sexes: women install 40% more apps, spend 87% more than men. *Venturebeat*. Accessed 16 December 2014. Available from http://venturebeat.com/2013/04/26/battle-of-the-mobile-sexes-women-install-40-more-apps-spend-87-more-than-men/.

Kontos, E., Blake, D.K., Chou, S.W.-Y. and Prestin, A. (2014) Predictors of eHealth usage: insights on the digital divide from the Health Information National Trends Survey 2012. *Journal of Medical Internet Research* (7). Accessed 17 July 2014. Available from www.jmir.org/2014/7/e172/.

Korda, H. and Itani, Z. (2013) Harnessing social media for health promotion and behavior change. *Health Promotion Practice*, 14 (1), 15–23.

Kraschnewski, L.J., Chuang, H.C., Poole, S.E., Peyton, T., Blubaugh, I., Pauli, J., Feher, A. and Reddy, M. (2014) Paging "Dr. Google": does technology fill the gap created by the prenatal care visit structure? Qualitative focus group study with pregnant women. *Journal of Medical Internet Research* (6). Accessed 17 July 2014. Available from www.jmir.org/2014/6/e147/.

Krassenstein, E. (2014a) 3D printing aids in the complex brain surgery of a baby in Brazil. *3D Print.com*. Accessed 28 October 2014. Available from http://3dprint.com/13515/3d-printing-brain-surgery/.

Krassenstein, E. (2014b) After more than 20 years, man finally gets diagnosis after 3D printing his own CT scans. *3D Print.com*. Accessed 30 October 2014. Available from http://3dprint.com/21369/hyoid-bone-syndrom-3d-print/.

Krebs, P. and Duncan, D. (2015) Health app use among US mobile phone users: a national survey. *Journal of Medical Internet Research* (4). Accessed 17 April 2016. Available from http://mhealth.jmir.org/2015/4/e101/.

Labanyi, J. (2010) Doing things: emotion, affect, and materiality. *Journal of Spanish Cultural Studies*, 11 (3/4), 223–233.

Lagu, T. and Greysen, S.R. (2010) Physician, monitor thyself: professionalism and accountability in the use of social media. *The Journal of Clinical Ethics*, 22 (2), 187–190.

Lanzing, M. (2016) The transparent self. *Ethics and Information Technology*, 15 (2), 254–268.

Lash, S. (2007) Power after hegemony: cultural studies in mutation? *Theory, Culture & Society*, 24 (3), 55–78.

Latour, B. (2005) *Reassembling the Social: An Introduction to Actor-Network-Theory*. Oxford: Clarendon.

Law, J. and Hassard, J. (1999) *Actor Network Theory and After*. Oxford: Blackwell.

Law, J. and Singleton, V. (2005) Object lessons. *Organization*, 12 (3), 331–355.

Lazer, D., Kennedy, R., King, G. and Vespignani, A. (2014) The parable of Google flu: traps in big data analysis. *Science*, 343 (6176), 1203–1205.

Leder, D. (1990) *The Absent Body*. Chicago, IL: University of Chicago Press.

Lee, K., Hoti, K., Hughes, D.J. and Emmerton, L. (2014a) Dr Google and the consumer: a qualitative study exploring the navigational needs and online health information-seeking behaviors of consumers with chronic health conditions. *Journal of Medical Internet Research* (12). Accessed 25 May 2016. Available from www.jmir.org/2014/12/e262/.

Lee, L.J., DeCamp, M., Dredze, M., Chisolm, S.M. and Berger, D.Z. (2014b) What are health-related users tweeting? A qualitative content analysis of health-related users and their messages on Twitter. *Journal of Medical Internet Research* (10). Accessed 17 June 2016. Available from www.jmir.org/2014/10/e237/.

Lerman, J. (2013) Big data and its exclusions. *Stanford Law Review Online*. Accessed 13 December 2013. Available from www.stanfordlawreview.org/online/privacy-and-big-data/big-data-and-its-exclusions.

Levina, M. (2010) Googling your genes: personal genomics and the discourse of citizen bioscience in the network age. *Journal of Science Communication*, 9 (1), 1–8.

Levy, K. (2015) Intimate surveillance. *Idaho Law Review*. Accessed 31 October 2015. Available from www.uidaho.edu/law/law-review/articles.

Li, I., Dey, A. and Forlizzi, J. (2010). A stage-based model of personal informatics systems. *Proceedings of the SIGCHI Conference on Human Factors in Computing Systems* (CHI '10). Atlanta: ACM Press, 557–566.

Li, J. (2015) A privacy preservation model for health-related social networking sites. *Journal of Medical Internet Research* (7). Accessed 11 July 2015. Available from www.jmir.org/2015/7/e168/.

Lian, O.S. and Nettleton, S. (2015) "United we stand": framing myalgic encephalomyelitis in a virtual symbolic community. *Qualitative Health Research*, 25 (10), 1383–1394.

Libert, T. (2014) Health privacy online: patients at risk. In S. Pena Gangadharan, V. Eubanks, and S. Barocas (eds) *Data and Discrimination: Collected Essays*: Open Technology Institute, 11–15.

Lock, M. and Nguyen, V.-K. (2010) *An Anthropology of Biomedicine*. Malden, MA: Wiley Blackwell.

Loe, M. (2010) Doing it my way: old women, technology and wellbeing. *Sociology of Health & Illness*, 32 (2), 319–334.

Lomborg, S. and Frandsen, K. (2016) Self-tracking as communication. *Information, Communication & Society*, 19 (7), 1015–1017.

Long, S.O. (2012) Bodies, technologies, and aging in Japan: thinking about old people and their silver products. *Journal of Cross-Cultural Gerontology*, 27 (2), 119–137.

Longhurst, R. (2009) YouTube: a new space for birth? *Feminist Review*, 93, 46–63.

Loos, A. (2013) Cyberchondria: too much information for the health anxious patient? *Journal of Consumer Health On the Internet*, 17 (4), 439–445.

Low, K.E.Y. (2013) Olfactive frames of remembering: theorizing self, senses and society. *The Sociological Review*, 61 (4), 688–708.

Luberto, C.M., Hyland, K.A., Streck, J.M., Temel, B. and Park, E.R. (2016) Stigmatic and sympathetic attitudes toward cancer patients who smoke: a qualitative analysis of an online discussion board forum. *Nicotine & Tobacco Research*, 18 (12), 2194–2201.

Lunt, N., Hardey, M. and Mannion, R. (2010) Nip, tuck and click: medical tourism and the emergence of web-based health information. *The Open Medical Informatics Journal* (1). Accessed 24 April 2016. Available from http://benthamopen.com/FULLTEXT/TOMINFOJ-4-1.

Lupton, D. (1994) *Moral Threats and Dangerous Desires: AIDS in the News Media*. Bristol: Taylor & Francis.

Lupton, D. (1995a) *The Imperative of Health: Public Health and the Regulated Body*. London: Sage.

Lupton, D. (1995b) The embodied computer/user. *Body & Society*, 1 (3–4), 97–112.

Lupton, D. (1996) *Food, the Body and the Self*. London: Sage.

Lupton, D. (1997a) Consumerism, reflexivity and the medical encounter. *Social Science & Medicine*, 45 (3), 373–381.

Lupton, D. (1997b) Foucault and the medicalisation critique. In A. Petersen and R. Bunton (eds) *Foucault, Health and Medicine*. London: Routledge, 94–110.

Lupton, D. (1998) *The Emotional Self: A Sociocultural Exploration*. London: Sage.

Lupton, D. (2012) *Medicine as Culture: Illness, Disease and the Body*. 3rd ed. London: Sage.

Lupton, D. (2013a) *Fat*. London: Routledge.

Lupton, D. (2013b) *The Social Worlds of the Unborn*. Houndmills: Palgrave Macmillan.

Lupton, D. (2013c) *Risk*. 2nd ed. London: Routledge.

Lupton, D. (2014) Apps as artefacts: towards a critical perspective on mobile health and medical apps. *Societies*, 4 (4), 606–622.

Lupton, D. (2015a) *Digital Sociology*. London: Routledge.

Lupton, D. (2015b) Data assemblages, sentient schools and digitised health and physical education (response to Gard). *Sport, Education and Society*, 20 (1), 122–132.

Lupton, D. (2015c) Quantified sex: a critical analysis of sexual and reproductive self-tracking using apps. *Culture, Health & Sexuality*, 17 (4), 440–453.

Lupton, D. (2015d) Donna Haraway: the digital cyborg assemblage and the new digital health technologies. In F. Collyer (ed) *The Palgrave Handbook of Social Theory in Health, Illness and Medicine*. Houndmills: Palgrave Macmillan, 567–581.

Lupton, D. (2016a) *The Quantified Self: A Sociology of Self-Tracking*. Cambridge: Polity Press.

Lupton, D. (2016b) Digital companion species and eating data: implications for theorising digital data–human assemblages. *Big Data & Society* (1). Accessed 7 January 2016. Available from http://bds.sagepub.com/spbds/3/1/2053951715619947.full.pdf.

Lupton, D. (2016c) Towards critical digital health studies: reflections on two decades of research in health and the way forward. *Health:*, 20 (1), 49–61.

Lupton, D. (2016d) The use and value of digital media information for pregnancy and early motherhood: a focus group study. *BMC Pregnancy and Childbirth*, 16 (171). Accessed 5 December 2016. Available from http://bmcpregnancychildbirth.biomedcentral.com/articles/10.1186/s12884-016-0971-3.

Lupton, D. (2017a) Personal data practices in the age of lively data. In J. Daniels, K. Gregory and T. McMillan Cottom (eds) *Digital Sociologies*. Bristol: Policy Press, 339–354.

Lupton, D. (2017b) Lively data, social fitness and biovalue: the intersections of health self-tracking and social media. In J. Burgess, A. Marwick and T. Poell (eds) *The Sage Handbook on Social Media*. London: Sage, in press.

Lupton, D., Donaldson, C. and Lloyd, P. (1991) Caveat emptor or blissful ignorance? Patients and the consumerist ethos. *Social Science & Medicine*, 33 (5), 559–568.

Lupton, D. and Jutel, A. (2015) 'It's like having a physician in your pocket!' A critical analysis of self-diagnosis smartphone apps. *Social Science & Medicine*, 133, 128–135.

Lupton, D. and Michael, M. (2015) Big data seductions and ambivalences. *Discover Society*. Accessed 5 October 2015. Available from http://discoversociety.org/2015/07/30/big-data-seductions-and-ambivalences/.

Lupton, D. and Michael, M. (2017a) 'Depends on who's got the data': public understandings of personal digital dataveillance. *Surveillance & Society*, in press.

Lupton, D. and Michael, M. (2017b) 'For me, the biggest benefit is being ahead of the game': the use of social media in health work. *Social Media + Society*, 3 (2). Accessed 9 May 2017. Available at http://journals.sagepub.com/doi/full/10.1177/2056305117702541.

Lupton, D. and Pedersen, S. (2016) An Australian survey of women's use of pregnancy and parenting apps. *Women and Birth*, 29 (4), 368–375.

Lupton, D., Pink, S., Labond, C.H. and Sumartojo, S. (2017) Personal data contexts, data sense and self-tracking cycling. *International Journal of Communication*, in press.

Lupton, D. and Thomas, G.M. (2015) Playing pregnancy: the ludification and gamification of expectant motherhood in smartphone apps. *M/C Journal* (5). Accessed 22 October 2015. Available from http://journal.media-culture.org.au/index.php/mcjournal/article/viewArticle/1012.

Lupton, D. and Williamson, B. (2017) The datafied child: the dataveillance of children and implications for their rights. *New Media & Society*, online ahead of print.

Lyon, D. (2002) Everyday surveillance: personal data and social classifications. *Information, Communication & Society*, 5 (2), 242–257.

Lyon, D. (2010) Surveillance, power and everyday life. In P. Kalantzis-Cope and K. Gherab-Martin (eds) *Emerging Digital Spaces in Contemporary Society*. Houndsmills, Basingstoke: Palgrave Macmillan, 107–120.

Lyon, D. and Bauman, Z. (2013) *Liquid Surveillance: A Conversation*. Oxford: Wiley.

Lyons, A.C. and Chamberlain, K. (2006) *Health Psychology: A Critical Introduction*. Cambridge: Cambridge University Press.

Maathuis, I.J.H. and Oudshoorn, N. (2015) Technologies of compliance? Telecare technologies and self-management of COPD patients. *ea Journal*, 7, 63–86.

McCarthy, M. (2013) Experts warn on data security in health and fitness apps. *British Medical Journal*. Accessed 27 February 2014. Available from www.bmj.com/content/347/bmj.f5600.

McCosker, A. and Darcy, R. (2013) Living with cancer: affective labour, self-expression and the utility of blogs. *Information, Communication & Society*, 16 (8), 1266–1285.

McDaniel, B., Coyne, S. and Holmes, E. (2012) New mothers and media use: associations between blogging, social networking, and maternal well-being. *Maternal and Child Health Journal*, 16 (7), 1509–1517.

McDermott, E. (2015) Asking for help online: lesbian, gay, bisexual and trans youth, self-harm and articulating the 'failed' self. *Health:*. 19 (6), 561–577.

McGowan, S.B., Wasko, M., Vartabedian, S.B., Miller, S.R., Freiherr, D.D. and Abdolrasulnia, M. (2012) Understanding the factors that influence the adoption and meaningful use of social media by physicians to share medical information. *Journal of Medical Internet Research* (5). Accessed 23 June 2016. Available from www.jmir.org/2012/5/e117/.

McGregor, S. (2001) Neoliberalism and health care. *International Journal of Consumer Studies*, 25 (2), 82–89.

McIver, J.D., Hawkins, B.J., Chunara, R., Chatterjee, K.A., Bhandari, A., Fitzgerald, P.T., Jain, H.S. and Brownstein, S.J. (2015) Characterizing sleep issues using Twitter. *Journal of Medical Internet Research* (6). Accessed 17 June 2016. Available from www.jmir.org/2015/6/e140/.

Madden, M. and Rainie, L. (2015) Americans' Attitudes about Privacy, Security and Surveillance. *Pew Research Center*. Accessed 21 May 2015. Available from www.pewinternet.org/files/2015/05/Privacy-and-Security-Attitudes-5.19.15_FINAL.pdf.

Mager, A. (2009) Mediated health: sociotechnical practices of providing and using online health information. *New Media & Society*, 11 (7), 1123–1142.

Malykhina, E. (2013) Home is where the health is: Obamacare positions 'telehealth' tech as a remedy for chronic hospital readmissions. *Scientific American*. Accessed 12 April 2013. Available from www.scientificamerican.com/article.cfm?id=affordable-care-act-technology.

Mandel, E. (2015) Sleep deprived? Blame your commute. *Jawbone*. Accessed 6 September 2015. Available from https://jawbone.com/blog/sleep-deprived-inactive-must-commuter/.

Mann, S. and Ferenbok, J. (2013) New media and the power politics of sousveillance in a surveillance-dominated world. *Surveillance & Society*, 11 (1/2), 18–34.

Marcus, G. (2006) Assemblage. *Theory, Culture & Society*, 23 (2–3), 101–106.

Marketwire. (2013) PatientsLikeMe unveils new tool to match patients with clinical trials worldwide. Accessed 20 March 2013. Available from www.marketwire.com/press-release/patientslikeme-unveils-new-tool-to-match-patients-with-clinical-trials-worldwide-1767363.htm.

Marmot, M. and Allen, J.J. (2014) Social determinants of health equity. *American Journal of Public Health*, 104 (S4), S517–S519.

Marres, N. (2012) *Material Participation: Technology, the Environment and Everyday Publics*. New York: Palgrave Macmillan.

Marres, N. and Lezaun, J. (2011) Materials and devices of the public: an introduction. *Economy and Society*, 40 (4), 489–509.

Marres, N. and Weltevrede, E. (2013) Scraping the social? Issues in live social research. *Journal of Cultural Economy*, 6 (3), 313–335.

Marwick, A. (2012) The public domain: social surveillance in everyday life. *Surveillance & Society*, 9 (4), 378–393.

Marwick, A. and boyd, d. (2014) Networked privacy: how teenagers negotiate context in social media. *New Media & Society*, 16 (7), 1051–1076.

Marwick, A.E. (2013) *Status Update: Celebrity, Publicity, and Branding in the Social Media Age*. New Haven, CT: Yale University Press.

Måseide, P. (1991) Possibly abusive, often benign, and always necessary. On power and domination in medical practice. *Sociology of Health & Illness*, 13 (4), 545–561.

Maslen, S. (2015) Researching the senses as knowledge: a case study of learning to hear medically. *The Senses and Society*, 10 (1), 52–70.

Matta, R., Doiron, C. and Leveridge, M.J. (2014) The dramatic increase in social media in urology. *The Journal of Urology*, 192 (2), 494–498.

Mazanderani, F., Locock, L. and Powell, J. (2013a) Biographical value: towards a conceptualisation of the commodification of illness narratives in contemporary healthcare. *Sociology of Health & Illness*, 35 (6), 891–905.

Mazanderani, F., O'Neill, B. and Powell, J. (2013b) 'People power' or 'pester power'? YouTube as a forum for the generation of evidence and patient advocacy. *Patient Education and Counseling*, 93 (3), 420.

Measuring the Information Society. (2013). Geneva: International Telecommunication Union. Accessed 15 March 2015. Available from www.itu.int/en/ITU-D/Statistics/Documents/publications/mis2013/MIS2013_without_Annex_4.pdf.

MerckEngage. (2016) Accessed 13 July 2016. Available from www.merckengage.com.

Merleau-Ponty, M. (1962) *Phenomenology of Perception*. Translated by C. Smith. London: Routledge & Kegan Paul.

Merleau-Ponty, M. (1968) *The Visible and the Invisible*. Translated by A. Lingus. Evanston, IL: Northwestern University Press.

Micieli, J.A. and Tsui, E. (2015) Ophthalmology on social networking sites: an observational study of Facebook, Twitter, and LinkedIn. *Clinical Ophthalmology*, 9, 285–290.

Mielewczyk, F. and Willig, C. (2007) Old clothes and an older look: the case for a radical makeover in health behaviour research. *Theory & Psychology*, 17 (6), 811–837.

Millington, B. (2014a) Smartphone apps and the mobile privatization of health and fitness. *Critical Studies in Media Communication*, 31 (5), 479–493.

Millington, B. (2014b) Amusing ourselves to life: fitness consumerism and the birth of bio-games. *Journal of Sport & Social Issues*, 38 (6), 491–508.

Mishori, R., Levy, B. and Donvan, B. (2014) Twitter use at a family medicine conference. *Family Medicine*, 46 (8), 608–614.

Misra, S. (2016) UK's NHS to spend nearly $6 billion to go digital, including remote care and health apps. *iMedicalApps*. Accessed 7 July 2016. Available from www.imedicalapps.com/2016/02/nhs-digital-health-plan/.

Mitchell, R. and Waldby, C. (2006) *Tissue Economies: Blood, Organs, and Cell Lines in Late Capitalism*. Durham, NC: Duke University Press.

Mittelstadt, B.D. and Floridi, L. (2016) The ethics of big data: current and foreseeable issues in biomedical contexts. *Science and Engineering Ethics*, 22 (2), 303–341.

Mo, P.K.H. and Coulson, N.S. (2014) Are online support groups always beneficial? A qualitative exploration of the empowering and disempowering processes of participation within HIV/AIDS-related online support groups. *International Journal of Nursing Studies*, 51 (7), 983–993.

Mobasheri, M.H., King, D., Johnston, M., Gautama, S., Purkayastha, S. and Darzi, A. (2015) The ownership and clinical use of smartphones by doctors and nurses in the UK: a multicentre survey study. *BMJ Innovations*, 1 (4). Accessed 11 February 2017. Available from http://innovations.bmj.com/content/1/4/174.

MobiHealthNews. (2014) Indepth: how activity trackers are finding their way into the clinic. *MobiHealthNews*. Accessed 2 August 2014. Available from http://mobihealthnews.com/35373/in-depth-how-activity-trackers-are-finding-their-way-into-the-clinic/.

Mol, A. (2002) *The Body Multiple: Ontology in Medical Practice*. Durham, NC: Duke University Press.

Mol, A. (2008) *The Logic of Care: Health and the Problem of Patient Choice*. London: Routledge.

Mol, A. (2009) Living with diabetes: care beyond choice and control. *Lancet*, 373 (9677), 1756–1757.

Mol, A. and Law, J. (2004) Embodied action, enacted bodies: the example of hypoglycaemia. *Body & Society*, 10 (2–3), 43–62.

Monash University. (2014) 3D printed anatomy for medical training. *Monash University Medicine, Nursing and Health Sciences*. Accessed 24 October 2014. Available from www.med.monash.edu.au/sobs/news/2014/3d-printed-anatomy.html.

Moody, M. (2014) How patient specific 3D printed organ replicas help patients reach informed decisions. *3D Print.com*. Accessed 24 October 2014. Available from http://3dprint.com/9159/3d-printed-organ-replicas/.

Mooney, G. (2012) Neoliberalism is bad for our health. *International Journal of Health Services*, 42 (3), 383–481.

Moore, P. and Robinson, A. (2016) The quantified self: what counts in the neoliberal workplace. *New Media & Society*, 18 (11), 2774–2791.

Moores, S. (2012) *Media, Place and Mobility*. Houndmills: Palgrave Macmillan.

Morden, A., Jinks, C. and Ong, B.N. (2012) Rethinking 'risk' and self-management for chronic illness. *Social Theory & Health*, 10 (4), 78–99.

Morrison, A. (2011) "Suffused by feeling and affect": the intimate public of personal mommy blogging. *Biography*, 34 (1), 37–55.

Mort, M., Finch, T. and May, C. (2009) Making and unmaking telepatients: identity and governance in new health technologies. *Science, Technology & Human Values*, 34 (1), 9–33.

Mort, M., May, C. and Williams, T. (2003) Remote doctors and absent patients: acting at a distance in telemedicine? *Science, Technology, & Human Values*, 28 (2), 274–295.

Mort, M., Roberts, C. and Callén, B. (2013) Ageing with telecare: care or coercion in austerity? *Sociology of Health & Illness*, 35 (6), 799–812.

Mort, M. and Smith, A. (2009) Beyond information: intimate relations in sociotechnical practice. *Sociology*, 43 (2), 215–231.

Mostert, M., Bredenoord, A.L., Biesaart, M.C. and van Delden, J.J. (2016) Big data in medical research and EU data protection law: challenges to the consent or anonymise approach. *European Journal of Human Genetics*, 24, 956–960.

Muessig, K.E., Pike, E.C., Fowler, B., LeGrand, S., Parsons, J.T., Bull, S.S., Wilson, P.A., Wohl, D.A. and Hightow-Weidman, L.B. (2013) Putting prevention in their pockets: developing mobile phone-based HIV interventions for black men who have sex with men. *AIDS Patient Care and STDs*, 27 (4), 211–222.

Müller, M. (2015) Assemblages and actor-networks: rethinking socio-material power, politics and space. *Geography Compass*, 9 (1), 27–41.

Murray, M. (2015) Introducting critical health psychology. In M. Murray (ed) *Critical Health Psychology*. Houndmills: Palgrave Macmillan, 1–16.

Murthy, D. (2013) *Twitter: Social Communication in the Twitter Age*. Oxford: Wiley.

Nafus, D. and Sherman, J. (2014) This one does not go up to 11: the Quantified Self movement as an alternative big data practice. *International Journal of Communication*, 8, 1785–1794.

Nahar, P., Kannuri, N.K., Mikkilineni, S., Murthy, G.V.S. and Phillimore, P. (2017) mHealth and the management of chronic conditions in rural areas: a note of caution from southern India. *Anthropology & Medicine*, 24 (1), 1–16.

Naslund, J.A., Grande, S.W., Aschbrenner, K.A. and Elwyn, G. (2014) Naturally occurring peer support through social media: the experiences of individuals with severe mental illness using YouTube. *PloS One* (10). Accessed 24 April 2016. Available from http://journals.plos.org/plosone/article?id=10.1371/journal.pone.0110171.

Neff, G. (2013) Why big data won't cure us. *Big Data*, 1 (3), 117–123.

Nelkin, D. and Tancredi, L.R. (1994) *Dangerous Diagnostics: The Social Power of Biological Information*. Chicago, IL: University of Chicago Press.

New Scientist. (2016) Revealed: Google AI has access to huge haul of NHS patient data. *New Scientist*. Accessed 4 July 2016. Available from www.newscientist.com/article/2086454-revealed-google-ai-has-access-to-huge-haul-of-nhs-patient-data/?platform=hootsuite.

Newman, M.W., Lauterbach, D., Munson, S.A., Resnick, P. and Morris, M.E. (2011) It's not that I don't have problems, I'm just not putting them on Facebook: challenges and opportunities in using online social networks for health. *Proceedings of the ACM 2011 Conference on Computer Supported Cooperative Work* (CSCS '11). Hangzou: ACM Press, 341–350.

NHS Choices. (2016) Accessed 6 July 2016. Available from www.nhs.uk/pages/home.aspx.

Nicolini, D. (2007) Stretching out and expanding work practices in time and space: the case of telemedicine. *Human Relations*, 60 (6), 889–920.

Nielsen. (2015) So many apps, so much more time for entertainment. *Nielsen Newswire*. Accessed 15 June 2015. Available from www.nielsen.com/us/en/insights/news/2015/so-many-apps-so-much-more-time-for-entertainment.html.

Nielsen, C. (2014) Hacking health: how consumers use smartphones and wearable tech to track their health. Accessed 10 May 2014. Available from www.nielsen.com/us/en/newswire/2014/hacking-health-how-consumers-use-smartphones-and-wearable-tech-to-track-their-health.html.

Nissenbaum, H. (2011) A contextual approach to privacy online. *Daedalus*, Fall, 32–48.

Nuffield Council on Bioethics. (2015) *The Collection, Linking and Use of Data in Biomedical Research and Health Care: Ethical Issues.* No place of publication provided: Nuffield Council on Bioethics.

Nuss, M., Hill, J., Cervero, R., Gaines, J. and Middendorf, B. (2014) Real-time use of the iPad by third-year medical students for clinical decision support and learning: a mixed methods study. *Journal of Community Hospital Internal Medicine Perspectives*, 4 (4). Accessed 2 February 2017. Available at www.tandfonline.com/doi/full/10.3402/jchimp.v4.25184.

O'Connor, P., Byrne, D., Butt, M., Offiah, G., Lydon, S., Mc Inerney, K., Stewart, B. and Kerin, M. (2014) Interns and their smartphones: use for clinical practice. *Postgraduate Medical Journal*, 90 (1060), 75–79.

O'Mara, B., Gill, G.K., Babacan, H. and Donahoo, D. (2012) Digital technology, diabetes and culturally and linguistically diverse communities: a case study with elderly women from the Vietnamese community. *Health Education Journal*, 71 (4), 491–504.

O'Neill, B., Ziebland, S., Valderas, J. and Lupiáñez-Villanueva, F. (2014) User-generated online health content: a survey of internet users in the United Kingdom. *Journal of Medical Internet Resesarch* (4). Accessed 16 May 2016. Available from www.jmir.org/2014/4/e118/.

O'Riordan, K. and Phillips, D.J., eds. (2007) *Queer Online: Media Technology & Sexuality.* New York: Peter Lang.

Oh, H.J., Lauckner, C., Boehmer, J., Fewins-Bliss, R. and Li, K. (2013) Facebooking for health: an examination into the solicitation and effects of health-related social support on social networking sites. *Computers in Human Behavior*, 29 (5), 2072–2080.

Öhman, M., Almqvist, J., Meckbach, J. and Quennerstedt, M. (2014) Competing for ideal bodies: a study of exergames used as teaching aids in schools. *Critical Public Health*, 24 (2), 196–209.

Olphert, W. and Damodaran, L. (2013) Older people and digital disengagement: a fourth digital divide? *Gerontology*, 59 (6), 564–570.

Oudshoorn, N. (2008) Diagnosis at a distance: the invisible work of patients and healthcare professionals in cardiac telemonitoring technology. *Sociology of Health & Illness*, 30 (2), 272–288.

Oudshoorn, N. (2009) Physical and digital proximity: emerging ways of health care in face-to-face and telemonitoring of heart-failure patients. *Sociology of Health & Illness*, 31 (3), 390.

Oudshoorn, N. (2011) *Telecare Technologies and the Transformation of Healthcare.* Houndmills: Palgrave Macmillan.

Oudshoorn, N. (2012) How places matter: telecare technologies and the changing spatial dimensions of healthcare. *Social Studies of Science*, 42 (1), 121–142.

Oudshoorn, N. (2016) The vulnerability of cyborgs: the case of ICD shocks. *Science, Technology & Human Values*, 41(5), 767–792.

Oudshoorn, N., Neven, L. and Stienstra, M. (2016) How diversity gets lost: age and gender in design practices of information and communication technologies. *Journal of Women & Aging*, 28 (2), 170–185.

Oudshoorn, N., Rommes, E. and Stienstra, M. (2004) Configuring the user as everybody: gender and design cultures in information and communication technologies. *Science, Technology & Human Values*, 29 (1), 30–63.

Oudshoorn, N. and Somers, A. (2006) Constructing the digital patient: patient organizations and the development of health websites. *Information, Communication & Society*, 9 (5), 657–675.

Paasonen, S. (2011) Revisiting cyberfeminism. *Communications*, 36 (3), 335–352.

Pantzar, M. and Ruckenstein, M. (2015) The heart of everyday analytics: emotional, material and practical extensions in self-tracking market. *Consumption Markets & Culture*, 18 (1), 92–109.

Park, M.S., Brock, A., Mortimer, V., Taussky, P., Couldwell, W.T. and Quigley, E. (2017) GoPro Hero cameras for creation of a three-dimensional, educational, neurointerventional video. *Journal of Digital Imaging*, online ahead of print.

Pasquale, F. (2014) The dark market for personal data. *The New York Times*. Accessed 8 April 2015. Available from www.nytimes.com/2014/10/17/opinion/the-dark-market-for-personal-data.html.

Pasquale, F. (2015) *The Black Box Society: The Secret Algorithms that Control Money and Information*. Boston, MA: Harvard University Press.

Patel, S., Bewley, S. and Hodson, N. (2016) Snapchat is not for sharing. *BMJ Careers*. Accessed 18 June 2016. Available from http://careers.bmj.com/careers/advice/Snapchat_is_not_for_sharing.

Patient Opinion. (2016) Accessed 26 March 2013. Available from www.patientopinion.org.uk/.

PatientsLikeMe. (2016) Accessed 20 March 2013. Available from www.patientslikeme.com/.

Patterson, H. (2013) Contextual expectations of privacy in self-generated health information flows. *Social Science Research Network*. Accessed 10 April 2016. Available from http://papers.ssrn.com/sol3/papers.cfm?abstract_id=2242144.

Payne, K.F.B., Wharrad, H. and Watts, K. (2012) Smartphone and medical related app use among medical students and junior doctors in the United Kingdom (UK): a regional survey. *BMC Medical Informatics and Decision Making* (1). Accessed 1 March 2014. Available from www.biomedcentral.com/1472–6947/12/121.

Pedersen, S. and Lupton, D. (2017) 'What are you feeling right now?' Communities of maternal feeling on Mumsnet. *Emotion, Space and Society*, online ahead of print.

Petersen, A. and Lupton, D. (1996) *The New Public Health: Health and Self in the Age of Risk*. London: Sage.

Petersen, A., MacGregor, C. and Munsie, M. (2016) Stem cell miracles or Russian roulette? Patients' use of digital media to campaign for access to clinically unproven treatments. *Health, Risk & Society*, 17 (7–8), 592–604.

Petersen, A. and Seear, K. (2011) Technologies of hope: techniques of the online advertising of stem cell treatments. *New Genetics and Society*, 30 (4), 329–346.

Piller, C. (2015) Verily, I swear. Google Life Sciences debuts a new name. *Stat*. Accessed 3 April 2016. Available from www.statnews.com/2015/12/07/verily-google-life-sciences-name/.

Pink, S. (2015) Approaching media through the senses: between experience and representation. *Media International Australia, Incorporating Culture & Policy*, 154, 5–14.

Pink, S., Mackley, K.L., Mitchell, V., Wilson, G. and Bhamra, T. (2016a) Refiguring digital interventions for energy demand reduction: designing for life in the digital-material home. In S. Pink, E. Ardevol and D. Lanzeni (eds) *Digital Materialities: Design and Anthropology*. London: Bloomsbury, 79–97.

Pink, S., Sinanan, J., Hjorth, L. and Horst, H. (2016b) Tactile digital ethnography: researching mobile media through the hand. *Mobile Media & Communication*, 4, 237–251.

Piras, E.M. and Miele, F. (2017) Clinical self-tracking and monitoring technologies: negotiations in the ICT-mediated patient–provider relationship. *Health Sociology Review*, 26 (1), 38–53.

Pollak, J.P., Gay, G., Byrne, S., Wagner, E., Retelny, D. and Humphreys, L. (2010) It's time to eat! Using mobile games to promote healthy eating. *IEEE Pervasive Computing*, 9 (3), 21–27.

Polonetsky, J. and Tene, O. (2013) Privacy and big data: making ends meet. *Stanford Law Review Online*. Accessed 4 September 2013. Available from www.stanfordlawreview.org/online/privacy-and-big-data/privacy-and-big-data.

Pols, J. (2012) *Care at a Distance: On the Closeness of Technology*. Amsterdam: Amsterdam University Press.

Pols, J. and Willems, D. (2011) Innovation and evaluation: taming and unleashing telecare technology. *Sociology of Health & Illness*, 33 (3), 484–498.

Poushter, J. (2016) Smartphone Ownership and Internet Usage Continues to Climb in Emerging Economies. Accessed 12 July 2016. Available from www.pewglobal.org/files/2016/02/pew_research_center_global_technology_report_final_february_22__2016.pdf.

Powell, J., Inglis, N., Ronnie, J. and Large, S. (2011) The characteristics and motivations of online health information seekers: cross-sectional survey and qualitative interview study. *Journal of Medical Internet Research* (1). Accessed 25 March 2016. Available from www.jmir.org/2011/1/e20/.

Prentice, R. (2013) *Bodies in Formation: an Ethnography of Anatomy and Surgery Education*. Durham, NC: Duke University Press.

Pullen, C. and Cooper, M., eds. (2010) *LGBT Identity and Online New Media*. New York: Routledge.

Purdam, K. (2014) Citizen social science and citizen data? Methodological and ethical challenges for social research. *Current Sociology*, 62 (3), 374–392.

Puska, P. (2007) Health in all policies. *The European Journal of Public Health*, 17 (4), 328–328.

Pykett, J., Jones, R., Welsh, M. and Whitehead, M. (2014) The art of choosing and the politics of social marketing. *Policy Studies*, 35 (2), 97–114.

Pykett, J., Jones, R. and Whitehead, M. (2013) *Changing Behaviours: On the Rise of the Psychological State*. Cheltenham: Edward Elgar Publishing.

Rainie, L. (2015) Americans Conflicted About Sharing Personal Information with Companies. Accessed 15 January 2016. Available from www.pewresearch.org/fact-tank/2015/12/30/americans-conflicted-about-sharing-personal-information-with-companies/.

Rainie, L. and Duggan, M. (2016) Privacy and information sharing. Accessed 30 January 2016. Available from www.pewinternet.org/files/2016/01/PI_2016.01.14_Privacy-and-Info-Sharing_FINAL.pdf.

Rasberry, L. (2014) Wikipedia: what it is and why it matters for healthcare. *British Medial Journal*, 348. Accessed 28 May 2016. Available from www.bmj.com/content/348/bmj.g2478.

Read, J. (2008) Schizophrenia, drug companies and the internet. *Social Science & Medicine*, 66 (1), 99–109.

Reddy, E. (2015) Using Twitter data to study the world's health. *Twitter blog*. Accessed 4 July 2016. Available from https://blog.twitter.com/2015/twitter-data-public-health.

Regalado, A. (2016) 23andMe sells data for drug search. *MIT Technology Review*. Accessed 2 July 2016. Available from www.technologyreview.com/s/601506/23andme-sells-data-for-drug-search/.

Rennie, E., Hogan, E., Gregory, R. and Crouch, A. (2016) *Internet on the Outstation: The Digital Divide and Remote Aboriginal Communities*. Amsterdam: Institute of Network Cultures.

ResearchKit. (2015) Accessed 14 March 2015. Available from www.apple.com/research-kit/.

Richardson, R. (2006) Human dissection and organ donation: a historical and social background. *Mortality*, 11 (2), 151–165.

Ringquist, L. (2013) Re-admissions: is telehealth the answer? Accessed 14 April 2013. Available from www.bhmpc.com/2013/04/re-admissions-is-telehealth-the-answer/.

Ritzer, G. (2014) Prosumption: evolution, revolution, or eternal return of the same? *Journal of Consumer Culture*, 14 (1), 3–24.

Ritzer, G. and Walczak, D. (1988) Rationalization and the deprofessionalization of physicians. *Social Forces*, 67 (1), 1–22.

Roberge, J. and Melançon, L. (2015) Being the King Kong of algorithmic culture is a tough job after all: Google's regimes of justification and the meanings of Glass. *Convergence*, online ahead of print.

Roberts, C., Mort, M. and Milligan, C. (2012) Calling for care: 'disembodied' work, teleoperators and older people living at home. *Sociology*, 46 (3), 490–506.

Robillard, J.M., Johnson, T.W., Hennessey, C., Beattie, B.L. and Illes, J. (2013) Aging 2.0: health information about dementia on Twitter. *PLoS One* (7). Accessed 10 July 2016. Available from http://journals.plos.org/plosone/article?id=10.1371/journal.pone.0069861.

Robinson, L., Cotten, S.R., Ono, H., Quan-Haase, A., Mesch, G., Chen, W., Schulz, J., Hale, T.M. and Stern, M.J. (2015) Digital inequalities and why they matter. *Information, Communication & Society*, 18 (5), 569–582.

Robinson, R. (2014) The power of the hashtag. *PharmaVoice* (May 2014). Accessed 4 May 2014. Available from www.pharmavoice.com/content/digitaledition.html?pg=24.

Robinson, R.L. and Burk, M.S. (2013) Tablet computer use by medical students in the United States. *Journal of Medical Systems*, 37 (4). Accessed 16 February 2017. Available from http://link.springer.com/article/10.1007/s10916-013-9959-y.

Robinson, T., Cronin, T., Ibrahim, H., Jinks, M., Molitor, T., Newman, J. and Shapiro, J. (2013) Smartphone use and acceptability among clinical medical students: a questionnaire-based study. *Journal of Medical Systems*, 37 (3), 9936.

Rogers, R. (2013) *Digital Methods*. Cambridge, MA: The MIT Press.

Rolls, K., Hansen, M., Jackson, D. and Elliott, D. (2016) How health care professionals use social media to create virtual communities: an integrative review. *Journal of Medical Internet Research* (6). Accessed 22 June 2016. Available from www.jmir.org/2016/6/e166/.

Rose, N. (2007) *The Politics of Life Itself: Biomedicine, Power, and Subjectivity in the Twenty-First Century*. Princeton, NJ: Princeton University Press.

Rose, N. (2008) The value of life: somatic ethics and the spirit of biocapital. *Daedalus*, 137 (1), 36–48.

Rosenblat, A., Wikelius, K., boyd, d., Gangadharan, S.P. and Yu, C. (2014) Data & civil rights: health primer. *Data & Society Research Institute*. Accessed 16 December 2014. Available from www.datacivilrights.org/pubs/2014-1030/Health.pdf.

Rosenzweig, P. (2012) Whither privacy? *Surveillance & Society*, 10 (3/4), 344–347.

Rowlands, I.J., Loxton, D., Dobson, A. and Mishra, G.D. (2015) Seeking health information online: association with young Australian women's physical, mental, and reproductive health. *Journal of Medical Internet Research* (5). Accessed 25 April 2016. Available from www.ncbi.nlm.nih.gov/pmc/articles/PMC4468597/.

Rozenblum, R. and Bates, D.W. (2013) Patient-centred healthcare, social media and the internet: the perfect storm? *BMJ Quality & Safety*, 22 (3), 183–186.

Ruckenstein, M. (2014) Visualized and interacted life: personal analytics and engagements with data doubles. *Societies*, 4 (1), 68–84.

Ruckenstein, M. (2015) Uncovering everyday rhythms and patterns: food tracking and new forms of visibility and temporality in health care. In L. Botin, C. Nohr and P. Bertelsen (eds) *Techno-Anthropology in Health Informatics.* Amsterdam: IOS Press, 28–40.

Ruppert, E., Law, J. and Savage, M. (2013) Reassembling social science methods: the challenge of digital devices. *Theory, Culture & Society*, 30 (4), 22–46.

Ryan, A. and Wilson, S. (2008) Internet healthcare: do self-diagnosis sites do more harm than good? *Expert Opinion on Drug Safety*, 7 (3), 227.

Sadah, A.S., Shahbazi, M., Wiley, T.M. and Hristidis, V. (2016) Demographic-based content analysis of web-based health-related social media. *Journal of Medical Internet Research* (6). Accessed 17 June 2016. Available from www.jmir.org/2016/6/e148/.

Salander, P. and Moynihan, C. (2010) Facilitating patients' hope work through relationship: a critique of the discourse of autonomy. In R. Harris, N. Wathen and S. Wyatt (eds) *Configuring Health Consumers: Health Work and the Imperative of Personal Responsibility.* Houndmills: Palgrave Macmillan, 113–125.

Salathé, M., Mabry, P.L., Vespignani, A., Bengtsson, L., Bodnar, T.J., Brewer, D.D., Brownstein, J.S., Buckee, C., Campbell, E.M., Cattuto, C. and Khandelwal, S. (2012) Digital epidemiology. *PLoS Computational Biology* (7). Accessed 28 March 2014. Available from www. ploscompbiol.org/article/info%3Adoi%2F10.1371%2Fjournal.pcbi.1002616.

Sandaunet, A.G. (2008) The challenge of fitting in: non-participation and withdrawal from an online self-help group for breast cancer patients. *Sociology of Health & Illness*, 30 (1), 131–144.

Sauter, T. (2014) 'What's on your mind?' Writing on Facebook as a tool for self-formation. *New Media & Society*, 16 (5), 823–839.

Savage, M., Dumas, A. and Stuart, S.A. (2013) Fatalism and short-termism as cultural barriers to cardiac rehabilitation among underprivileged men. *Sociology of Health & Illness*, 35 (8), 1211–1226.

Sax, M. (2016) Big data: finders keepers, losers weepers? *Ethics and Information Technology*, 18 (1), 25–31.

Schubert, C. (2011) Making sure. A comparative micro-analysis of diagnostic instruments in medical practice. *Social Science & Medicine*, 73 (6), 851–857.

Semigran, H.L., Linder, J.A., Gidengil, C. and Mehrotra, A. (2015) Evaluation of symptom checkers for self diagnosis and triage: audit study. *British Medical Journal.* Accessed 28 January 2016. Available from www.bmj.com/content/351/bmj.h3480.

Sharon, T. and Zandbergen, D. (2017) From data fetishism to quantifying selves: self-tracking practices and the other values of data. *New Media & Society*, online ahead of print.

Shaw, R. (2015) Being-in-dialysis: the experience of the machine–body for home dialysis users. *Health:*, 19 (3), 229–244.

Sher, D. (2014) Two hospitals in Cambridge implementing 3D printing for augmented patient care. *3D Printing Industry.* Accessed 24 October 2014. Available from http://3dprintingindustry.com/2014/09/24/two-hospitals-cambridge-implementing-3d-printing-augmented-patient-care.

Sims, C. (2014) From differentiated use to differentiating practices: negotiating legitimate participation and the production of privileged identities. *Information, Communication & Society*, 17 (6), 670–682.

Skea, Z.C., Entwistle, V.A., Watt, I. and Russell, E. (2008) 'Avoiding harm to others' considerations in relation to parental measles, mumps and rubella (MMR) vaccination discussions – an analysis of an online chat forum. *Social Science & Medicine*, 67 (9), 1382–1390.

Slezak, M. (2011) The Facebook treatment for MS. *Sydney Morning Herald.* Accessed 9 July 2011. Available from www.smh.com.au/world/science/the-facebook-treatment-for-ms-20110330-1cgfi.html.

Smith, G.J.D. and Vonthethoff, B. (2017) Health by numbers? Exploring the practice and experience of datafied health. *Health Sociology Review*, 26 (1), 6–21.

Smith, M., Morita, H., Mateo, K.F., Nye, A., Hutchinson, C. and Cohall, A.T. (2015) Development of a culturally relevant consumer health information website for Harlem, New York. *Health Promotion Practice*, 15 (5), 664–674.

Smith, N., Wickes, R. and Underwood, M. (2015) Managing a marginalised identity in pro-anorexia and fat acceptance cybercommunities. *Journal of Sociology*, 51 (4), 950–967.

Sparling, K. (2014) CGM in the cloud: personal preferences. *Six Until Me*. Accessed 8 July 2016. Available from http://sixuntilme.com/wp/2014/07/16/cgm-cloud-personal-preferences.

Spector, R.E. (2002) Cultural diversity in health and illness. *Journal of Transcultural Nursing*, 13 (3), 197–199.

Stafford, B.M. (1993) *Body Criticism: Imaging the Unseen in Enlightenment Art and Medicine*. Boston, MA: The MIT Press.

Starcevic, V. and Berle, D. (2013) Cyberchondria: towards a better understanding of excessive health-related internet use. *Expert Review of Neurotherapeutics*, 13 (2), 205–213.

Starr, P. (1982) *The Social Transformation of American Medicine*. New York: Basic Books.

Statista. (2015a) Cumulative number of apps downloaded from the Apple App Store from July 2008 to June 2015 (in billions). Accessed 26 June 2015. Available from www.statista.com/statistics/263794/number-of-downloads-from-the-apple-app-store.

Statista. (2015b) Number of apps available in leading app stores as of May 2015. Accessed 26 June 2015. Available from www.statista.com/statistics/276623/number-of-apps-available-in-leading-app-stores.

Steinhubl, S., Muse, E. and Topol, E. (2013) Can mobile health technologies transform health care? *Journal of the American Medical Association*, 310 (22), 2395–2396.

Stragier, J., Evens, T. and Mechant, P. (2015) Broadcast yourself: an exploratory study of sharing physical activity on social networking sites. *Media International Australia*, 155 (1), 120–129.

Striphas, T. (2015) Algorithmic culture. *European Journal of Cultural Studies*, 18 (4–5), 395–412.

Stusak, S., Tabard, A., Sauka, F., Khot, R.A. and Butz, A. (2014) Activity sculptures: exploring the impact of physical visualizations on running activity. *IEEE Transactions on Visualization and Computer Graphics*, 20 (12), 2201–2210.

Sugawara, Y., Narimatsu, H., Tsuya, A., Tanaka, A. and Fukao, A. (2016) Medical institutions and Twitter: a novel tool for public communication in Japan. *JMIR Public Health Surveillance* (1). Accessed 23 June 2016. Available from http://publichealth.jmir.org/2016/1/e19/.

Sumartojo, S., Pink, S., Lupton, D. and LaBond, C.H. (2016) The affective intensities of datafied space. *Emotion, Space and Society*, 21, 33–40.

Swan, M. (2009) Emerging patient-driven health care models: an examination of health social networks, consumer personalized medicine and quantified self-tracking. *International Journal of Environmental Research and Public Health*, 6 (2), 492–525.

Swan, M. (2012) Health 2050: the realization of personalized medicine through crowdsourcing, the quantified self, and the participatory biocitizen. *Journal of Personalized Medicine*, 2 (3), 93–118.

Swan, M. (2013) The quantified self: fundamental disruption in big data science and biological discovery. *Big Data* (2). Accessed 2 March 2014. Available from http://online.liebertpub.com/doi/abs/10.1089/big.2012.0002.

Symons, X. (2015) Privacy 1: security flaws. *BioEdge*. Accessed 8 February 2015. Available from www.bioedge.org/index.php/bioethics/bioethics_article/11318.

Tang, P.C., Ash, J.S., Bates, D.W., Overhage, J.M. and Sands, D.Z. (2006) Personal health records: definitions, benefits, and strategies for overcoming barriers to adoption. *Journal of the American Medical Informatics Association*, 13 (2), 121–126.

Taylor, N.P. (2013) Genentech asks iPad gamers to save San Fran from mutant cheese. *FierceBiotechIT*. Accessed 4 May 2014. Available from www.fiercebiotechit.com/story/genentech-asks-ipad-gamers-save-san-fran-mutant-cheese/2013-05-27.

Tembeck, T. (2016) Selfies of ill health: online autopathographic photography and the dramaturgy of the everyday. *Social Media + Society* (1). Accessed 27 April 2016. Available from http://sms.sagepub.com/content/2/1/2056305116641343.abstract.

The Wellcome Trust. (2013) Summary Report of Qualitative Research into Public Attitudes to Personal Data and Linking Personal Data. No place of publication provided: The Wellcome Trust.

The White House. (2015) Precision Medicine Initiative: Privacy and Trust Principles. Accessed 8 April 2016. Available from www.whitehouse.gov/sites/default/files/microsites/finalpmiprivacyandtrustprinciples.pdf.

The White House Press Office. (2015) Fact sheet: President Obama's Precision Medicine Initiative. Accessed 8 April 2016. Available from www.whitehouse.gov/the-press-office/2015/01/30/fact-sheet-president-obama-s-precision-medicine-initiative.

Thilakanathan, D., Chen, S., Nepal, S., Calvo, R. and Alem, L. (2014) A platform for secure monitoring and sharing of generic health data in the Cloud. *Future Generation Computer Systems*, 35, 102–113.

Thomas, G.M. and Lupton, D. (2015) Threats and thrills: pregnancy apps, risk and consumption. *Health, Risk & Society*, 17 (7–8), 495–509.

Thrift, N. (2004) Intensities of feeling: towards a spatial politics of affect. *Geografiska Annaler*, 86 B (1), 57–78.

Thrift, N. (2005) *Knowing Capitalism*. London: Sage.

Tighe, J.P., Goldsmith, C.R., Gravenstein, M., Bernard, R.H. and Fillingim, B.R. (2015) The painful tweet: text, sentiment, and community structure analyses of tweets pertaining to pain. *Journal of Medical Internet Research* (4). Accessed 17 June 2016. Available from www.jmir.org/2015/4/e84/.

Tiidenberg, K. (2015) Odes to heteronormativity: presentations of femininity in Russian-speaking pregnant women's Instagram accounts. *International Journal of Communication*, 9 (13), 1746–1758.

Tilki, M. (2006) The social contexts of drinking among Irish men in London. *Drugs: Education, Prevention and Policy*, 13 (3), 247–261.

Tilson, J.K., Loeb, K., Barbosa, S., Jiang, F. and Lee, K.T. (2016) Use of tablet computers to promote physical therapy students' engagement in knowledge translation during clinical experiences. *Journal of Neurologic Physical Therapy*, 40 (2), 81–89.

Topol, E. (2012) *The Creative Destruction of Medicine: How the Digital Revolution Will Create Better Health Care*. New York: Basic Books.

Topol, E. (2015) *The Patient Will See You Now: The Future of Medicine is in Your Hands*. New York: Basic Books.

Totaro, P. and Ninno, D. (2014) The concept of algorithm as an interpretative key of modern rationality. *Theory, Culture & Society*, 31 (4), 29–49.

Treato. (2016) Accessed 14 March 2016. Available from http://treato.com.

Tucker, I. and Goodings, L. (2015) Managing stress through the Stress Free app: practices of self-care in digitally mediated spaces. *Digital Health*, 1. Accessed 13 February 2017. Available at http://dhj.sagepub.com/content/1/2055207615580741.abstract.

Tucker, I. and Goodings, L. (2017) Medicated bodies: mental distress, social media and affect. *New Media & Society*, online ahead of print.

Tulloch, J. and Lupton, D. (1997) *Television, AIDS and Risk: A Cultural Studies Approach to Health Communication*. Sydney: Allen & Unwin.

Tulloch, J. and Lupton, D. (2003) *Risk and Everyday Life*. London: Sage.

Turner, B. (1995) *Medical Power and Social Knowledge*. 2nd ed. London: Sage.

Understanding Your Data. (2014) Accessed 13 June 2014. Available from www.wellocracy. com/understanding-your-activity-tracker-data/.

Underworlds. (2016) Accessed 8 April 2016. Available from http://underworlds.mit.edu/.

Unidentified Dead Bodies. (2016) Accessed 30 June 2016. Available from http://unidenti-fieddeadbodies.com/DeadBody_AboutUs.aspx.

US National Library of Medicine. (2016) Videos of surgical procedures. Accessed 18 June 2016. Available from www.nlm.nih.gov/medlineplus/surgeryvideos.html.

Van Der Velden, M. and El Emam, K. (2013) "Not all my friends need to know": a qualitative study of teenage patients, privacy, and social media. *Journal of the American Medical Informatics Association*, 20 (1), 16–24.

van Deursen, A. and van Dijk, J. (2014) The digital divide shifts to differences in usage. *New Media & Society*, 16 (3), 507–526.

van Dijck, J. (2011) *The Transparent Body: A Cultural Analysis of Medical Imaging*. Seattle, WA: University of Washington Press.

van Dijck, J. (2013a) *The Culture of Connectivity: A Critical History of Social Media*. Oxford: Oxford University Press.

van Dijck, J. (2013b) 'You have one identity': performing the self on Facebook and LinkedIn. *Media, Culture & Society*, 35 (2), 199–215.

van Dijck, J. (2014) Datafication, dataism and dataveillance: Big Data between scientific paradigm and ideology. *Surveillance & Society*, 12 (2), 197–208.

van Dijk, J. and Hacker, K. (2003) The digital divide as a complex and dynamic phenomenon. *The Information Society*, 19 (4), 315–326.

van Hout, A., Pols, J. and Willems, D. (2015) Shining trinkets and unkempt gardens: on the materiality of care. *Sociology of Health & Illness*, 37 (8), 1206–1217.

Veitch, K. (2010) The government of health care and the politics of patient empowerment: New Labour and the NHS reform agenda in England. *Law & Policy*, 32 (3), 313–331.

Ventura, P. (2012) *Neoliberal Culture: Living with American Neoliberalism*. Farnham: Ashgate.

Verily. (2016) Accessed 7 July 2016. Available from https://verily.com.

Vertesi, J., Kaye, J., Jarosewski, S.N., Khovanskaya, V.D. and Song, J. (2016). Data narratives: uncovering tensions in personal data management. *Proceedings of the 19th ACM Conference on Computer-Supported Cooperative Work & Social Computing* (CSCW '16). San Francisco: ACM Press, 478–490.

Vogel, L. (2011) Dr. YouTube will see you now. *Canadian Medical Association Journal*, 183 (6), 647–648.

Waitzkin, H. (2000) *The Second Sickness: Contradictions of Capitalist Health Care*. Oxford: Rowman & Littlefield.

Wald, H., Dube, C. and Anthony, D. (2007) Untangling the web – the impact of internet use on health care and the physician-patient relationship. *Patient Education and Counselling*, 68 (3), 218–24.

Waldby, C. (2000) *The Visible Human Project: Informatic Bodies and Posthuman Medicine*. London: Routledge.

Waldby, C. (2002) Stem cells, tissue cultures and the production of biovalue. *Health*, 6 (3), 305–323.

Wan, J.K., Selvanathan, S., Vivekananda, C., Lee, G.Y. and Ng, C.T. (2014) Medical students' perceptions regarding the impact of mobile medical applications on their clinical practice. *Journal of Mobile Technology in Medicine*, 3 (1), 46–53.

Warin, M., Turner, K., Moore, V. and Davies, M. (2008) Bodies, mothers and identities: rethinking obesity and the BMI. *Sociology of Health & Illness*, 30 (1), 97–111.

Weber, G., Mandl, K. and Kohane, I. (2015) Finding the missing link for big biomedical data. *Journal of the American Medical Association*, 311 (24), 2479–2480.

Webster, A. (2012) Introduction: Bio-objects: exploring the boundaries of life. In N. Vermeulen, S. Tamminen and A. Webster (eds) *Bio-Objects: Life in the 21st Century*. Farnham: Ashgate, 1–10.

Weeg, C., Schwartz, A.H., Hill, S., Merchant, M.R., Arango, C. and Ungar, L. (2015) Using Twitter to measure public discussion of diseases: a case study. *Journal of Medical Internet Research Public Health Surveillance* (1). Accessed 17 June 2016. Available from http://publichealth.jmir.org/2015/1/e6/.

Welltok – Solutions – CafeWell. (2014) Accessed 25 June 2014. Available from http://welltok.com/solutions.html.

Welltok – Solutions – CafeWell Rewards. (2014) Accessed 25 June 2014. Available from http://welltok.com/cwrewards.html.

West, K. (2014) Melbourne-made 3D-printed body parts could replace cadavers for medical training. *ABC News*. Accessed 23 October 2014. Available from www.abc.net.au/news/2014-07-22/an-3d-body-parts-could-replace-cadavers-for-medical-training/5615210.

Whitsitt, J., Mattis, D., Hernandez, M., Kollipara, R. and Dellavalle, R.P. (2015) Dermatology on Pinterest. *Dermatology Online Journal* (1). Accessed 1 July 2016. Available from https://escholarship.org/uc/item/7dj4267p.

Wicklund, E. (2016a) Doctors still don't trust mHealth apps. *MHealth Intelligence*. Accessed 28 February 2016. Available from http://mhealthintelligence.com/news/doctors-still-dont-trust-mhealth-apps#.

Wicklund, E. (2016b) Giving wearables a place in the patient record. *MHealth Intelligence*. Accessed 28 February 2016. Available from http://mhealthintelligence.com/news/giving-wearables-a-place-in-the-patient-record.

Wicklund, E. (2016c) Hospital's mHealth project finds value in Fitbit data. *mHealth Intelligence*. Accessed 28 February 2016. Available from http://mhealthintelligence.com/news/hospitals-diabetes-mhealth-project-finds-value-in-fitbit-data.

Wicks, P. and Chiauzzi, E. (2015) 'Trust but verify' – five approaches to ensure safe medical apps. *BMC Medicine* (1). Accessed 8 October 2015. Available from www.biomedcentral.com/1741–7015/13/205.

Wike, K. (2013) Patient generated data analysis is the next HIT step. *Health IT Outcomes*. Accessed 28 May 2016. Available from www.healthitoutcomes.com/doc/patient-generated-data-analysis-is-the-next-hit-step-0001.

Willis, K., Collyer, F., Lewis, S., Gabe, J., Flaherty, I. and Calnan, M. (2016) Knowledge matters: producing and using knowledge to navigate healthcare systems. *Health Sociology Review*, 25 (2), 202–216.

Winkelman, W.J., Leonard, K.J. and Rossos, P.G. (2005) Patient-perceived usefulness of online electronic medical records: employing grounded theory in the development of information and communication technologies for use by patients living with chronic illness. *Journal of the American Medical Informatics Association*, 12 (3), 306–314.

Wischhover, C. (2016) The Dr Miami effect: how plastic surgeons are grappling with Snapchat. *Racked*. Accessed 9 July 2016. Available from www.racked.com/2016/5/23/11723482/dr-miami-plastic-surgeons-snapchat.

World Privacy Forum. (2013) *Testimony of Pam Dixon before the Senate Committee on Commerce, Science, and Transportation: What Information Do Data Brokers Have on Consumers, and How Do They Use It?* No place of publication provided: World Privacy Forum.

Wyatt, S., Harris, A., Adams, S. and Kelly, S.E. (2013) Illness online: self-reported data and questions of trust in medical and social research. *Theory, Culture & Society*, 30 (4), 131–150.

Wyatt, S., Harris, A. and Kelly, S.E. (2016) Controversy goes online: schizophrenia genetics on Wikipedia. *Science & Technology Studies*, 29 (1), 13–29.

Yetisen, A.K., Martinez-Hurtado, J., da Cruz Vasconcellos, F., Simsekler, M.C.E., Akram, M.S. and Lowe, C. (2014) The regulation of mobile medical applications. *Lab on a Chip*, 14 (5), 833–840.

Yin, Z., Fabbri, D., Rosenbloom, T.S. and Malin, B. (2015) A scalable framework to detect personal health mentions on Twitter. *Journal of Medical Internet Research* (6). Accessed 17 June 2016. Available from www.jmir.org/2015/6/e138/.

Zamosky, L. (2014) Digital health tools are a growing part of workplace wellness programs. *iHealthBeat*. Accessed 2 August 2014. Available from www.ihealthbeat.org/insight/2014/digital-health-tools-are-a-growing-part-of-workplace-wellness-programs.

Zhang, Y., He, D. and Sang, Y. (2013) Facebook as a platform for health information and communication: a case study of a diabetes group. *Journal of Medical Systems*, 37 (3), 1–12.

Zickuhr, K. (2013) Who's not online and why. *Pew Research Center*. Accessed 26 September 2013. Available from www.pewinternet.org/files/old-media//Files/Reports/2013/PIP_Offline%20adults_092513_PDF.pdf.

Ziebland, S. and Wyke, S. (2012) Health and illness in a connected world: how might sharing experiences on the internet affect people's health? *Milbank Quarterly*, 90 (2), 219–249.

Zola, I.K. (1972) Medicine as an institution of social control. *The Sociological Review*, 20 (4), 487–504.

Zuboff, S. (2015) Big other: surveillance capitalism and the prospects of an information civilization. *Journal of Information Technology*, 30 (1), 75–89.

INDEX

Aboriginal communities 85
abuse online 97
activism 49, 68, 123
actor-network theory 12
'affective atmospheres' 19
affective attachment to digital
    technology 131
affordances of digital devices 13
agitation for social change 132
Alere MobileLink 31
algorithmic manipulation of data 17–18, 25,
    52, 131
Alliance Health networks 70
Amazon (company) 34
Amoore, L. 45, 47
anatomical replicas 55–7
Andrejevic, M. 76
Anthem Inc. 75
Apple (company) 33, 52, 63, 78, 82
apps related to health and medical issues
    32–8, 89–91, 105, 108–10, 114
Article 29 Data Protection Working
    Party 79
'assemblage' concept 12–13, 17, 21–4,
    53, 56–60
Australia 32, 61, 76, 85–7, 90, 97,
    109–10, 125–6
avatars 38

Beer, D. 69
behaviour change 36, 42
'being-in-the-world' 18
Bell, S.L. 12
benefits offered by digital health 130

Bentham, Jeremy 16
'big data' 4–5, 17, 60, 120; for
    health promotion and public
    health 64–8
biomarkers 63–4
biomedicalisation 9–10, 121–2, 129
biometric data 47
biopolitics 17–18
biovalue and biocapital 72–3
blogs 95
body modification practices 51
Brainform 55
British Medical Journal 116
broadband access 81
Burrows, R. 69

cancer sufferers 96–7
care.data program 71
caregiving 131
CarePredict device 31
Carmel, S. 119
Carolinas Healthcare 61
Castlight Health (company) 30
Centers for Disease Control and
    Prevention 29
Chicago Department of Public
    Health 115–16
Christie, M. 85
chronic conditions 88, 96, 99, 105
civil rights 92
Clarke, A. 9
clinical trials 62–3
cloud computing 4–5, 74
commercial motivations 70–1, 75

commodification of personal data
11, 68–73
'communities of hope' 124
community, sense of 94
confession 16–17, 25
confidentiality 110–11, 116–17
conflict theory 8
Consumer eHealth Program 62
Consumer Electronics Association 78
consumerism 40
content analysis 65–6
Cook, Tim 78
Copleton, D. 101
criminality 24, 75
critical approach to research 2–3, 19,
118–19, 130–3
crowdsourcing 62–3, 66
cultural beliefs and practices 84–5
cultural norms 82, 85, 97
cultural studies 19
cultural trends 85
'cyberchondria' 115
'cyborg' concept 57–9
cycling 102

data brokers 71–4, 91–2
data mining 70–3, 77, 91–2
data protection 74, 79
'data sculptures' 56
datafication 44, 52, 54, 59–60, 128, 132
dataveillance 22–5, 43, 58–9, 74, 79, 93,
128, 132
Davidson, J. 19
death and dying, images of 49–50
Deleuze, F. 12
de-medicalisation 10
Dentzer, S. 40
de-professionalisation 122–6
Deterding, S. 37
diabetes 96–9, 104–5
'digital divide' 76, 80–1
Digital Exclusion Heatmap (website) 81
digital health technologies 1, 5, 26;
current availability of 3–4; further
research on 130–3; key features of
127–30; socioeconomic status related
to 10–11; theory under-lying 8; users
participating in 5–6
digitisation: of the concepts of home,
community, bodies and behaviour 132;
of humans 58
disabilities, people with 49–50, 83, 88
disability activism 49
disadvantaged groups 10–11, 18, 93, 130
Disney (company) 34

dissection 45
distribution of content across different
platforms 6
DNA data 71
Dobransky, K. 88
Doctor on Demand app 30
doctor–patient relationship 10, 18, 20,
131
doctors' views on digital health 113–17
Dodge, M. 21
domestic domain of healthcare 102
DrEd platform 30
Duncan, D. 91

Ebeling, Mary 72, 76
Eli Lilly (company) 34
Ellis, K. 83
Elmer, G. 58
emotions: expression of 95; importance of
19–20; and self-care 97–100
empowerment of patients 117, 126
encryption of data 74
ethical issues 25, 36, 73, 117
European Union (EU) 79
European Wheelmap platform 66–7
exchange of data 69
exclusion from digital technology 93
'exergames' 37
exploitation of personal data for
profit 11, 24

face-to-face communication 105–6,
119
Facebook 6, 28, 48–51, 65, 78, 81–2
fatalism about health and illness 84
fatness 50–1
Federal Bureau of Investigation (FBI) 78
Fitbit (company) 35, 63, 77–8, 100
Fogg, B.J. 35, 38
Forlano, Laura 98, 104–5
Foucault, Michel (and Foucauldian theory)
14–18, 23–4, 41–2, 103, 121
Franko, O.I. 109
Freidson, Eliot 9
French, M. 120–1

gamification 37–41
Gardner, J. 118
gaze, medical 15, 17, 45, 102–5, 118
Gehl, R. 70
Gehrig, Karolyn 50
gendered differences 82–3, 87, 91
Genentech (company) 37
genetic testing 73
Gigaom (blog) 60

global positioning systems (GPS) 21
Google (company) 13, 28, 33, 63–4, 78, 86, 124–5
governmentality 17
Greene, J. 39
Greenhalgh, T. 106, 120
Griffis, M.H. 111
Gruman, Jessie 105
Guattari, F. 12

hacking 73–5
Hall, S. 45, 47
Hargittai, E. 88
Harris, A. 69
'harvesting' of data 70–2, 75
Hawn, C. 54
health promotion 41–3, 51, 64–5, 68
health psychology 36
Health Tap (website) 69
healthcare providers 111–12, 115–16, 125, 129
HealthGrades (platform) 69
healthism 84, 127
HealthMap (platform) 66
HealthUnlocked 68–9
'healthy city' concept 67, 132
healthy eating 38
Heywood, Jamie 68
Hibbard, J.H. 39
Hudson Yards, New York 67
Hughes, L.S. 65
Human Genome Project 47–8, 73
Hunt, Jeremy 32
Husain, I. 40

IBM (company) 64
images, medical 44–7
imaging technologies 55
implants 98–9
India 85
inequality, social 80–7, 91, 127, 130
'infodemiology' 66
information ethics 25
Instagram 28, 46–50, 81–2
intellectual property 73
internet-based health and medical information 27–8
Internet of Things 4, 131
internet use 4, 81–5, 88
intersections of corporate, state and personal interests 128–9
intimate surveillance 24, 54
'invisible work' 120
iPhone Wello 31
iTriage (app) 34

J'accede (platform) 66–7
Japan 111
Jawbone (company) 39, 64
Journal of the American Medical Association 1
Jurel, Annemarie 34

Kent, M. 83
Kish, L. 53
Kitchin, R. 21
Krebs, P. 91

Labond, Christine Heyes 102
Law, J. 104
leaks 74
Lee, Sandra 46
Li, I. 35
LinkedIn 6
lived experience of digital health 93–4, 99, 103
locative media 21
Lupton, Deborah (author) 2, 34, 76, 95, 102, 126
Lyon, D. 23

McNaughton, Brendon 55
marginalised groups 95–7, 130, 132
'materialities of care' 14
materiality in relation to digital health technologies 129
Mayo Clinic 111
medical authority 114–17, 121–6, 129
medical education 109
Medical Realities (company) 46
'medical tourism' 124
medicalisation 9; *see also* bio-medicalisation; de-medicalisation
Medicare 111
medication, digital 31
Merck (company) 29
Merleau-Ponty, M. 18
Michael, Mike 76, 112
Microsoft (company) 62, 78
Milligan, C. 19
Mol, A. 104
'mommy blogs' 48
moral opprobrium 97
Mort, M. 106, 120
multiple sclerosis 123–4
multisensory ways in which doctors know their patients' bodies 118
Mumsnet 95

National Cancer Institute, US 87
National Health Service (NHS), UK 29, 32, 64, 71

National Library of Medicine, US 46
natural language processing 71
neoliberalism 10, 22, 41
'networked privacy' 25
New York City 67, 77, 99
NHS Choices (website) 29
norms, failure to conform to 97;
    see also cultural norms
'nudge' approach 41–3
nurses' use of digital technology 109

Obama, Barack 62
'Obamacare' 32
older people 106
online forums 95–7, 123
Open Effect organisation 74
Oudshoorn, N. 98, 103, 106

Pager (app) 30
Panopticon concept 16, 23
parenting forums 97
paternalism 42, 117, 125, 129
patient engagement 70, 39–43,
    97–9, 113–14
patient-generated data 61
Patient Opinion (websites) 29, 69
patient support websites 68–70, 75
patients' assessment of healthcare
    providers 111
PatientsLikeMe (website) 29, 63, 68–70
Patterson, H. 77
Pedersen, Sarah 95
pedometers, use of 101
'personalised medicine' 61–2
pharmaceutical companies 29, 70–1
phenomenology of the body 18–22
Pink, Sarah 21, 102
Pinterest 28, 47–9
political economy perspective 8–11, 121
power relations 14–15, 22, 26, 121, 128
'precision medicine' 61–2
pregnancy 37–8, 48, 91, 95, 126
Prentice, R. 119
preventive medicine 41
privacy issues 7, 25, 73–4, 78, 92,
    116–17, 121
professional uses for digital technology 108
professionalisation; *see also*
    de-professionalisation
professionalism 122–6; and professional
    standards 117
profiles of people 23, 25, 72
'prosumption' and 'prosumers' 4, 70
pseudonyms, use of 94
public attitudes 77

Public Health England 35
public health initiatives 64–5

Quantified Self movement 54

radical possibilities in digital health
    technologies 132
RateMDs (platform) 69
reactions of patients to the work of
    healthcare professionals 107
records, medical 89, 96–7
Reddit (discussion forum) 81
Reddy, E. 65
reward programmes 92
robots 31, 106, 118
Rolls, K. 110

Salzhauer, Michael 46
Samsung (company) 33
San Bernardino shootings (2015) 78
San Francisco Bay Area 77
schizophrenia 124
'scraping' the web 70–1
search engines 13, 86, 122, 125
Second Life 38
security agencies 23, 74
self, sense of 50, 102–4
self-care 85, 97–105
self-diagnosis 34, 114
self representation 48–51
self-surveillance 100–4
self-tracking devices 32–5, 38–42, 52–4, 61,
    76, 90, 99–102, 110, 112, 116, 119
'selfies' 16, 50
sensory studies 19, 44
sentiment analysis 66
sewerage systems 67
sharing of information and experience
    69–70, 94, 96
Shaw, R. 103
Sickweather (platform) 66
simulators 119
'smart city' concept 67
'smart' devices 31, 33, 91
SmartPatients 63
smartphones, ownership and use of 81, 85,
    109, 122
smell, sense of 19
Smith, A. 120
Snapchat 46, 116
Snowden, Edward 23, 74
sociability 101
social determinants of ill health 10
social media 1, 6, 17, 22–5, 28–9, 32–3, 42,
    48–54, 61, 65–6, 71, 74, 81–4, 87–8, 95,

115–17, 122–3; and self-representation
48–51; use by health professionals 110–13
social relationships 106
social structuring of digital health 80–2
social surveillance 23–4, 54
social web, the 4
sociomaterialism 12–14, 18
'sousveillance' 23
Sparling, Kerry 98–9
Starr, P. 9
stem cell therapies 124
stethoscopes, use of 20
Strava platform 52
Stusak, S. 56
Sumartojo, Shanti 102
support groups 88
surgery 47, 119
surveillance 17, 22–3, 47, 53–4, 58, 104,
119–21; *public* and *private* 128
Swan, M. 39, 53, 112
Sweden 111
Symplur (company) 111–12
synoptic veillance 34

'technologies of the self' 16–17, 50
technology use, patterns of 86–91
telemedicine 5, 29–32, 47, 88–9, 98,
102–5, 118
'therapeutic landscapes' 12
3D Babies (company) 55
3D printing 54–7, 122
Thrift, N. 19
Tilson, J.K. 109
Tirell, T.F. 109
Topol, Eric 48, 53, 113
touch, sense of 56
tracking *see* self-tracking devices
transformation in health and medical care
through digital technologies 129
Treato (platform) 71
TripAdvisor 67
trust in medical expertise 105, 126
Tumblr 50, 81
23andMe (company) 69, 71
Twitter 6, 28, 49, 65–6, 71, 82–3, 111

Underworlds project 67
Unidentified Dead Bodies
(website) 49
UnitedHealth (company) 38
unlocking of iPhones 78
user-generated content 87

van Hout, A. 118
Verily initiative 63
Verran, H. 85
victim-blaming 10
virtual bodies 47
virtual reality 21, 58
Visible Embryo (website) 46
Visible Human Project 46
Vitals 30

walking, monitoring of 101
Walmart (retail chain) 30
wearable devices 32–3, 91, 100
Web 2.0 technology 4
Weber, G. 65
WebMi (website) 28
websites related to health and medical
issues 5, 27–8
weight loss 96
Wellcome Trust 76–7
Wellocracy (website) 52–3
Welltok Cafe 39
Wikipedia 6, 28, 124
Williams, C. 118
workplace wellness programmes 34–5,
39, 122
World Health Organisation 29, 67
World Wide Web 4–5

Xbox devices 37

Yelp (website) 67, 69
YouTube 6, 28, 46–9, 115

ZocDoc (platform) 30, 69
Zola, Irving 9
Zombies, Run! (app) 37
Zuboff, S. 24